The Films of the Seventies

Also by Robert Bookbinder
The Films of Bing Crosby

The Films of the
Seventies

ROBERT BOOKBINDER

CITADEL PRESS • Secaucus, New Jersey

First edition
Copyright © 1982 by Robert Bookbinder
All rights reserved
Published by Citadel Press
A division of Lyle Stuart Inc.
120 Enterprise Ave., Secaucus, N.J. 07094

In Canada: Musson Book Company
A division of General Publishing Co. Limited
Don Mills, Ontario

Manufactured in the United States of America by
Halliday Lithograph, West Hanover, Mass.

Designed by Angelica Design Group

Library of Congress Cataloging in Publication Data

Bookbinder, Robert.
    The films of the seventies.

    1. Moving-pictures—United States—Plots,
themes, etc.   I. Title.
PN1993.5.U6B65   791.43′75   82-1285
ISBN 0-8065-0790-X   AACR2

FOR HARRY

ACKNOWLEDGMENTS:

Paramount Pictures, Metro-Goldwyn-Mayer, Columbia Pictures, 20th Century-Fox, United Artists, Universal Pictures, Warner Bros., National General Pictures, the Malpaso Company, and Buena Vista Productions. For help in gathering the many photographs, I am indebted to the Larry Edmunds Bookstore, the Hollywood Book and Poster Company, the Memory Shop West, Cinemonde, the Cinema Shop, and the Galactic Starport.

INTRODUCTION

The 1970's represents one of the truly remarkable eras in motion picture history. No other decade can claim such spectacular success at the box office, and the current list of the highest-grossing films of all time is dominated by titles from the seventies. It was a rich and fruitful period for the movie industry, and the ten-year span between *Patton* (1970) and *Star Trek* (1979) saw the production of an unusually high number of first-rate entertainments, many of which have achieved "classic" status in a remarkably short time. Films such as *The Godfather, The Exorcist, Jaws, Star Wars,* and *Superman* are superb examples of creative moviemaking, and their impact on audiences was astounding, evidenced by the fact that each came close to or exceeded $100 million in box-office receipts.

These and many similar films were responsible for rekindling the public's interest in moviegoing, something that had seen a marked decline during the fifties and sixties. Once thought to be slipping as a major form of popular entertainment, the movies experienced a "rebirth" during the seventies, and audience attendance once again reached impressive levels, despite the fact that ticket prices were now in the four- to five-dollar range.

Aside from the many mammoth successes it produced, the seventies was also memorable as the period in which filmmaking reached its technical apex, and the decade saw major innovations in the areas of photography, sound, makeup, and special effects. Most seventies films were shot in a breath-taking wide-screen process known as 70mm Panavision, and the era's newer, better film stocks and color processes gave its movies a richness not seen since the great Technicolor heyday of the thirties and forties. Many films also featured six-track Dolby stereo, a sound system which totally engulfed an audience and was especially effective when used in the decade's many fine fantasy and science fiction films. No screen effect, however incredible or complex, proved too difficult for the decade's special effects and makeup wizards such as Doug Trumbull, L. B. Abbott, Dick Smith, and Rick Baker; and their dazzling camera magic in films such as *The Towering Inferno, King Kong, Close Encounters of the Third Kind,* and *The Fury* has few equals in the cinema.

Motion picture censorship virtually ceased to be a problem during the seventies, and, for the first time, filmmakers had almost unlimited freedom. Subjects once regarded as taboo were explored openly, and the candid examinations of such areas as homosexuality (*The Boys in the Band*) and child prostitution (*Taxi Driver* and *Pretty Baby*) would have been unthinkable in previous decades. Nudity, adult language, and strong violence also became commonplace in seventies cinema, as did some surprisingly graphic depictions of sexual activity in movies such as *Last Tango in Paris* and *Shampoo.*

The only echo of censorship was the rather lenient Motion Picture Rating System, which replaced the old Production Code in 1968 and is still in use today. The old Code, which had been dictating with an iron hand what could and couldn't be shown on screen for over thirty years, seemed ridiculous in the "let it all hang out" atmosphere of the late sixties, and was wisely abolished in favor of the new system, which simply labels films with a "G," "GP," "R," or "X" according to how adult they are in theme. Not surprisingly, the end of the Production Code set the stage for an increasing frankness in movies, and many films produced during the 1967–1970 period—*Who's Afraid of Virginia Woolf, The Wild Bunch, Rosemary's Baby, Bonnie and Clyde, Midnight Cowboy,* and *M.A.S.H.,* to name but a few—helped establish a new level of maturity in the commercial cinema.

Generally speaking, the seventies was a time in which audiences were more informed and sophisticated than they had been in past decades. Various polls conducted revealed that the average moviegoer was young, college-educated, earning a respectable income, and surviving in an especially troubled era seeing more than its share of political scandal, crime, inflation, and unemployment. Audiences of the seventies were less vulnerable to the romantic illusions that played an important part in films produced during the forties, fifties, and sixties, and needed a cinema that came to realistic terms with contemporary problems and at the same time provided a spectacular escape from them. The general output of films during the seventies seemed to reflect this, and though many examined topical areas such as urban alienation (*Taxi Driver*), the power of the media (*Network*), violent crime (*The French Connection* and *Dirty Harry*), the Watergate affair (*All the President's Men*), organized crime (the *Godfather* films), Vietnam (*Coming Home, The Deer Hunter,* and *Apocalypse Now*), international terrorism (*Black Sunday*), divorce (*An Unmarried Woman* and *Kramer vs. Kramer*), and political assassination (*The Day of the Jackal*), an equal number were magnificent "escapist" entertainments, providing audiences with much needed diversion from the frustrations of modern living.

While the seventies saw changes in the areas of film technique, censorship, and audience needs, many of the most profound changes took place within the industry itself, and the "business" aspect of film also underwent great transition. The major studios were now owned by mammoth conglomerates like Gulf and Western, MCA and the Transamerica Company, and were being headed by slick executives with an eye toward profit and very little else.

Unlike previous decades, when a studio might back a project that had questionable salability but that had certain "artistic merits," a film's commercial potential was the *only* consideration during the seventies. Producing and distributing the average film now meant spending upwards of $10 million, and, with that kind of money at stake, a studio could ill afford the luxury of a box-office failure. Every possible precaution was taken to insure a film's success, like aggressive media advertising months before its release, endless "air spots" on radio and television, and "talk show" appearances by major cast members and the director. Studios realized that a successful film meant not only making millions at the box office, but also an additional fortune from the hawking of consumer products ranging from T-shirts and bedspreads to stereo soundtracks and paperback novelizations.

The decade's really "hot" films such as *Star Wars, Close Encounters, Rocky,* and *Star Trek* were ingeniously merchandised in this manner, and virtually any product bearing the trademark of a hit movie could be sold to the public. During the seventies, the selling of a film became as much of an "art" as making it, and there were, indeed, several instances (1978's *Animal House,* for example) in which a film's advertising budget actually *exceeded* its production cost by several million dollars.

Movie stars of the seventies were a very different breed from those of past decades. Many were also brilliant actors and actresses—Jack Nicholson, George C. Scott, Robert De Niro, Al Pacino, Jane Fonda, Dustin Hoffman, Donald Sutherland, Robert Duvall, Laurence Olivier, Michael Caine, Bruce Dern, Faye Dunaway, Meryl Streep, Jon Voight—able to play a wide variety of characters and not merely "larger-than-life" personalities. Several were skilled business people—Clint Eastwood, Barbra Streisand, Robert Redford, Burt Reynolds, Warren Beatty, Paul Newman—who took full charge of their careers, often serving as their own producers and directors and having almost complete control over any film in which they appeared.

Stars working in the seventies were responsible for sustaining their own careers, as the studio "contract" system was a thing of the past. Film projects were no longer assigned by studios to actors and directors, but were sold to the studio from "outside" as individual deals. A group of actors and writers would, for example, come up with what they thought was a salable idea, get hold of a top director, sell him on the idea, and then approach the studio who, they hoped, would be impressed enough to finance the enterprise. With production costs so high, studios were seldom interested in backing any projects except those involving the right combination of what the industry termed "bankable" talent—those actors, writers and directors with a proven track record at the box office.

With studios no longer nurturing careers, actors and directors realized they could only be as successful as their last film, and even the decade's superstars had to choose their vehicles carefully. Also, the industry's output was considerably lower than it had been in the past, and choice roles were few and far between. Earlier stars like Bogart, Gable, Tracy, and Cooper played something like five or six roles a year—even toward the end of their careers—but a seventies superstar usually averaged only one a year. This scarcity of vehicles led to the widespread practice of stars demanding (and usually getting) a hefty percentage of a film's profits in addition to a straight salary, and major performers such as Eastwood, Streisand, Redford, Newman, Brando, and McQueen garnered tremendous fortunes from their box-office hits. This not only enabled them to be extremely choosy about in what films they appeared, but also to wait out in comfort any "dry spells" during which a role that suited them might not come along.

This book is a profile of nearly a hundred motion pictures produced during this remarkable period, certainly one of the most successful in film history. The emphasis in this work has been on the decade's major commercial films, the box-office "blockbusters" that had an almost unprecedented impact on audiences, as well as on the movies which best represent the decade's trend toward cinematic realism.

In an effort to assemble as well-rounded a list as possible, I have also endeavored to include several of the seventies' unsung masterpieces—such as Brian De Palma's *Phantom of the Paradise* and Hal Ashby's *Bound for Glory,* which were unsuccessful despite their quality—in addition to pure "escapist" fare such as *The Black Hole, 1941,* and *Star Trek,* all of which were successful despite their weaknesses.

While the limitations of space prevent a lengthy assessment of the decade's foreign offerings, the most compelling works of such fine European directors as Ken Russell, Federico Fellini, Franco Zeffirelli, Ingmar Bergman, and Werner Herzog have also been examined.

1970

George C. Scott

PATTON

A 20th Century-Fox Picture; Directed by Franklin J. Schaffner; Produced by Frank McCarthy; Screenplay by Francis Ford Coppola and Edmund H. North; Based on factual material by Ladislas Farago and Omar N. Bradley; Photography by Fred Koenekamp; Associate producer: Frank Caffey: Assistant directors: Eli Dunn and José Lopez Rodero; Music by Jerry Goldsmith; Filmed in DeLuxe Color and Dimension 150; Running time: 171 minutes

CAST:
Gen. George S. Patton, Jr. (GEORGE C. SCOTT), *Gen. Omar N. Bradley* (Karl MALDEN), *Field Marshal Erwin Rommel* (Karl Michael Vogler), *Capt. Chester B. Hansen* (Stephen Young), *Brig. Gen. Hobart Carver* (Michael Strong), *Lt. Col. Henry Davenport* (Frank Latimore), *Capt. Richard N. Jenson* (Morgan Paull), *Gen. Patton's driver* (Bill Hickman), *Gen. Bradley's driver* (Cary Loftin), *Moroccan minister* (Albert Dumortier), *Sgt. William G. Meeks* (James Edwards), *Lt. Gen. Harry Buford* (David Bauer), *Col. John Welkin* (Peter Barkworth), *Tank captain* (Clint Ritchie), *Gen. Bernard Mont-*

gomery (Michael Bates), *Soldier who gets slapped* (Tim Considine), *Lt. Col. Charles R. Codman* (Paul Stevens), *Third Army Chaplain* (Lionel Murton), *Clergyman* (David Healy), *Correspondent* (Sandy Kevin), *Capt. Oskar Steiger* (Siegfried Rauch), *Col. Gen. Alfred Jodl* (Richard Muench), *1st Lt. Alexander Stiller* (Patrick J. Zurica), *Col. Gaston Bell* (Lawrence Dobkin)

At the height of World War II, a U.S. tank division is wiped out by Rommel's Afrika Korps at the Kasserine Pass in Tunis. Surveying the battlefield after the skirmish, General Omar N. Bradley (Karl Malden) reasons that a strong retaliation against the Germans is the only way to even up the loss, and he subsequently appoints one of the fiercest officers in the U.S. Army, General George S. Patton (George C. Scott), commander of the American tank corps.

Assuming his command, Patton orders the division into the most rigid training imaginable, and turns a sloppy, second-rate battalion into the sharpest in the Army. Over the succeeding months, Patton and his troops launch a series of devastating counterattacks against Rommel. Well-known for his outspokenness, fanatic approach to battle, and rather eccentric nature, Patton is absolutely fearless, and this has earned him the nickname "Blood and Guts."

George C. Scott

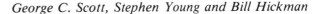

George C. Scott, Stephen Young and Bill Hickman

15

George C. Scott

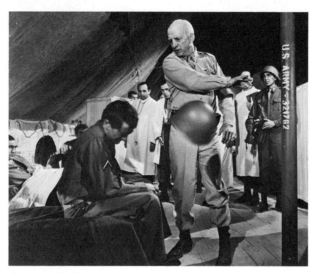

George C. Scott

After his victory over Rommel, Patton confesses to Bradley that he loves war more than anything in the world. An intelligent, quick-witted man who does not pull punches either in battle or in private life, Patton begins a running feud with British commander Montgomery (Michael Bates), whom Patton considers overly glorified and inefficient. Averse to anything even resembling cowardice, Patton later slaps a young soldier (Tim Considine) suffering from battle fatigue at a medical outpost near the war zone. When this incident makes headlines, Patton is ordered to make a public apology.

As the war draws to a close, Patton is placed in command of the Third Army, and despite a spectacular showing at the Battle of the Bulge he is forbidden from taking Prague by Eisenhower, who allows the Russian forces to do so instead. Angered by this and suspicious of the Russians, Patton openly criticizes them, which costs him his command.

Ordered into retirement, Patton bids a final, emotional farewell to his loyal aides and reluctantly leaves his post, realizing that "all glory is fleeting."

This film, which made a superstar of George C. Scott and which became the first "blockbuster" of the seventies, is one of the true "classics" of the decade. It is both a fascinating historical chronicle and a top-notch entertainment, and it won the Academy Award as the Best Picture of 1970. It was produced by 20th Century-Fox in the hope that it would duplicate the success of its earlier war epic, *The Longest Day,* which was one of the studio's biggest money-makers of the sixties.

Patton more than fulfilled the studio's wishes, and it managed to completely surpass the earlier film in almost every respect. It was far better scripted, acted, and directed, and it had the advantage of being photographed both in color and in a wide-screen process known as Dimension 150, which gave audiences an especially gigantic on-screen image. This lent itself particularly well to the many epic battle scenes in which the tank divisions of Patton and Rommel square off on the vast desert landscapes of North Africa, and to the unforgettable opening shot of Patton addressing his troops against the backdrop of an enormous American flag.

WOMEN IN LOVE

A United Artists Picture; Directed by Ken Russell; Produced and written by Larry Kramer; From the novel by D. H. Lawrence; Photography by Billy Williams; Assistant director: Jonathan Benson; Co-producer: Martin Rosen; Music by Georges Delerue; Associate producer: Roy Baird; Choreography by Terry Gilbert; Costumes by Shirley Russell; Photographed in DeLuxe Color; Running time: 132 minutes

CAST:
Rupert Birkin (ALAN BATES), *Gerald Crich* (OLIVER REED), *Gudrun Brangwen* (GLENDA JACKSON), *Ursula Brangwen* (JENNIE LINDEN), *Hermione Roddice* (Eleanor BRON), *Mrs. Crich* (Catherine Willmer), *Laura Crich* (Sharon Gurney), *Thomas Crich* (Alan Webb), *Lupton* (Christopher Gable), *Loerke* (Vladek Sheybal), *Tom Brangwen* (Michael Gough), *Anna Brangwen* (Norma Shebbeare), *Minister* (James Laurenson), *Contessa* (Nike Arrighi), *Barber* (Leslie Anderson), *Palmer* (Michael Cox), *Winifred* (Sarah Nicholls)

England. Rupert Birkin (Alan Bates) and Gerald Crich (Oliver Reed), two aristocrats in their early

Jennie Linden, Glenda Jackson

thirties, have been close friends for most of their lives. At an outdoor party given by their wealthy, eccentric friend Hermione Roddice (Eleanor Bron), they meet Gudrun (Glenda Jackson) and Ursula (Jennie Linden) Brangwen, two attractive schoolteachers from a lower rung of society. Though the girls are sisters, they are complete opposites in character—Ursula is a relatively simple woman seeking to marry a man from the upper class, while Gudrun is a complex neurotic who secretly despises the rich.

Soon, Rupert and Gerald begin courting the sisters (Gerald with Gudrun and Rupert with Ursula) and, over the next few months, become deeply involved with them. The relationship that develops between Rupert and Ursula is a healthy one, based primarily on sexual attraction and emotional rapport, and hampered only by Ursula's possessiveness and constant need to justify lust by calling it "love."

The ensuing romance between Gerald and Gudrun is another matter entirely—Gerald, a serious, sensitive man with a need for a meaningful relationship, and Gudrun, whose emotional problems have rendered her incapable of really feeling anything, are a dreadful error in matchmaking. Though she enjoys sleeping with Gerald, her contempt for his money and position often manifests itself in rather cruel "game playing," in which she tortures Gerald by insisting the relationship has played itself out, then passionately, teasingly seduces him five minutes later.

Rupert and Ursula eventually marry, but sometime afterward Rupert confesses to his wife that he also needs the "love" of a man. When Ursula protests, Rupert visits Gerald, and, getting drunk, the two men engage in a nude wrestling match, during which their latent homosexuality slowly manifests itself.

Later, Rupert and Ursula join Gerald and Gudrun on a skiing holiday in the Alps. At this stage of their increasingly destructive affair, Gudrun has begun to openly abuse Gerald, at one point telling him "you are primitive, vulgar and you brutalize me" in reference to their lovemaking. During the holiday, she torments him further by becoming involved with a bisexual painter (Vladek Sheybal), whose flighty nature closely parallels her own. He persuades her to return to Berlin with him, and, utterly shattered by this, Gerald walks into the snowy wilderness. The next day, Gerald is discovered frozen to death, his destruction by Gudrun complete.

Ken Russell, who directed *Women in Love* from a script by Larry Kramer, the film's producer, was one

Eleanor Bron, Alan Bates

Oliver Reed, Glenda Jackson

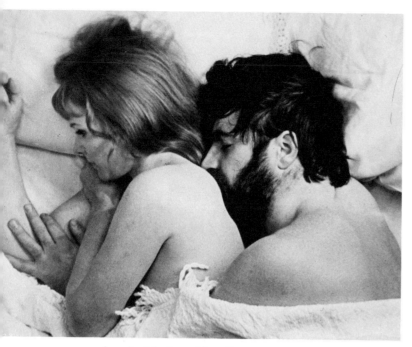

Jennie Linden, Alan Bates

Alan Bates, Oliver Reed

of the decade's most gifted and controversial film-makers. His major seventies films—*Women in Love* (1970), *The Devils* (1971), *The Music Lovers* (1971), *Tommy* (1975), *Lisztomania* (1975) and *Mahler* (1976)—are as flamboyant and undisciplined as they are brilliant, and they exhibit a complete disregard for the conventional forms of moviemaking. While he is a superb director of actors, never failing to

wring excellent performances from his casts, it is Russell's talent as a visual stylist that makes him unique. The images he creates for his films are a stunning combination of the beautiful, the sensual, and the grotesque; the outlandish, cartoon-like sequences of *Lisztomania,* the soft, glowing ambers bathing Oliver Reed and Alan Bates throughout their nude wrestling match in *Women in Love,* and Elton John's fabulous ''Pinball Wizard'' number in *Tommy* are but a few examples of Russell's ability.

Women in Love, Russell's much-heralded version of D. H. Lawrence's novel, is perhaps his best all-around film, containing flawless performances by Alan Bates, Oliver Reed, Glenda Jackson, and Jennie Linden as well as some of the most resourceful use of lighting and color in seventies cinema. Released in early 1970, the film was Russell's first major success, and most critics were quick to point out how closely it followed the novel. In bringing Lawrence's complex study of human love and passion to the screen, Russell made a film of both emotional impact and visual power. The way he handled the intimate encounters of the four principles was especially good, and the lovemaking in the film has all the grace and beauty of ballet, the characters caressing and embracing in fluid slow motion.

Vladek Sheybal, Oliver Reed, Glenda Jackson

Oliver Reed, Glenda Jackson

18

LOVE STORY

A Paramount Picture; Directed by Arthur Hiller; Produced by Howard G. Minsky; Executive producer: David Golden; Screenplay by Erich Segal; Photography by Dick Kratina; Music by Francis Lai; Costumes by Pearl Somner and Alice Martin; Assistant director: Peter Scoppa; Photographed in Technicolor; Running time: 100 minutes

CAST:
Jenny Cavilleri (ALI MacGRAW), *Oliver Barrett IV* (RYAN O'NEAL), *Oliver Barrett III* (Ray MILLAND), *Phil Cavilleri* (John MARLEY), *Dean Thompson* (Russell Nype), *Oliver's Mother* (Katherine Balfour), *Dr. Shapely* (Sydney Walker), *Dr. Addison* (Robert Modica), *Hank* (Tommy Lee Jones), *Steve* (John Merensky), *Ray* (Walker Daniels)

During his senior year as a pre-law student at Harvard, Oliver Barrett IV (Ryan O'Neal) falls in love with Jenny Cavilleri (Ali MacGraw), a music major at Radcliffe. Though Oliver wants to marry Jenny, his wealthy, influential father (Ray Milland) opposes the idea, chiefly because Jenny comes from a lower level of society. He threatens to cut Oliver off financially if he goes through with the marriage, but despite this Oliver and Jenny marry after graduation.

Realizing he'll now have to get along without his father's aid, Oliver applies for a law scholarship at Harvard. The dean (Russell Nype), however, finds the idea of granting a scholarship to a millionaire's son ridiculous, and tells Oliver he'll have to pay tuition. Deciding to work his way through, Oliver takes a series of odd jobs and tells Jenny they'll have to struggle along on whatever he can bring in. To supplement their income, Jenny forsakes her music studies and takes a job as vocal coach for a boys' choir. With Jenny's help, Oliver finishes law school, graduating with the third highest marks in his class.

Later, Oliver is hired by a prominent New York law firm and starts drawing a good salary, allowing him and Jenny to move into an expensive apartment. At last realizing the fruits of their lean four-year struggle, Oliver and Jenny try conceiving a child, without success. Both undergo physical examinations, and some time later their doctor (Sydney Walker) calls Oliver in to discuss the diagnosis.

Devastated by the news that Jenny is dying of a rare disease, Oliver buys two plane tickets to Paris, the one place that Jenny always wanted to visit. Jenny, however, tells Oliver that she wants only to spend

Ali MacGraw, Ryan O'Neal

Ali MacGraw

Ryan O'Neal, Ali MacGraw

Ryan O'Neal, Ali MacGraw

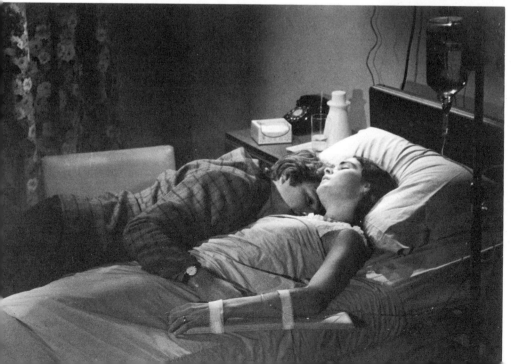

her remaining time at home with him. Admitted to a hospital some time later, Jenny dies with Oliver at her bedside.

Afterward, Oliver encounters his father, who has just learned of Jenny's illness and has come to apologize for his prior attitude. Before he is able to, Oliver hushes him with the famous line, "Love means never having to say you're sorry."

Love Story, the most popular romantic film of the decade, was also the biggest money-maker of the year for its studio, Paramount. The picture's phenomenal box-office receipts surprised nearly everyone in the industry, especially those who, for a number of reasons, felt that the project was doomed to fail from the start. Interestingly, when Paramount production chief Robert Evans first announced his intention to make *Love Story*, he was warned by colleagues that it would not succeed as a film, and that its old-fashioned romanticism would not be marketable in 1970.

Adding to the general lack of faith was *Love Story*'s comparatively modest budget and the fact that neither of its stars, Ryan O'Neal or Ali MacGraw, was considered a "heavyweight" at the box office. Also, many felt that its story line was far too "formula," as the theme of ideal love cut tragically short by death had already been explored in countless films throughout the thirties, forties, and fifties. The film did, however, manage to become an enormous success with audiences the world over, and it became one of the few films in history to introduce a new saying ("Love means never having to say you're sorry") into the language.

Aside from the fact that *Love Story* was very well made, the reason for its triumph is simple to understand—audiences have *always* loved a good tearjerker, and since *Love Story* was one of the most perfectly packaged "weepers" in Hollywood history, it could hardly miss success. Literally everything about the movie is expertly geared to arouse feelings of poignant sentimentality in its audience, including the acting, direction, and the gentle musical scoring of Francis Lai. Even audience members who might have ordinarily found the movie silly could not escape being touched by Erich Segal's irresistibly schmaltzy dialogue for Oliver and Jenny's final exchange when, lying on the hospital bed, she says, "Dying is like falling off a cliff. You've never fallen off a cliff in your life, have you, Ollie?" To which Oliver replies, "Yes I did. When I met you."

Not surprisingly, *Love Story* has often been compared with the great soap operas of the thirties and forties, and it has been said that the film, though well made, fails to pack the emotional wallop of an old "classic" like *Dark Victory*. This is a moot point, however, and after several viewings *Love Story* proves itself quite the equal of the older film in terms of dramatic impact. While *Dark Victory* relied on the dynamic and powerful acting of Bette Davis to bring a touching reality to the scene in which she finds out about her terminal illness, *Love Story* handled the matter more subtly, but just as effectively. When the doctor informs Oliver that Jenny is dying, Ryan O'Neal reacts in a rather understated manner, simply saying, "It can't be true. There must be some mistake." The camera then cuts to a shot of Oliver walking back to the apartment in a kind of emotional vacuum, unable to relate to the world around him. This scene is a triumph of Arthur Hiller's direction, as he photographs O'Neal from odd, distorted angles, while on the soundtrack the first five notes of the theme song are repeated over and over by an isolated piano.

FELLINI SATYRICON

A United Artists Release; Directed by Federico Fellini; Produced by Alberto Grimaldi; Screenplay by Federico Fellini and Bernardino Zapponi; Assistant director: Maurizio Mein; Costumes by Danilo Donati; Music by Nino Rota; Filmed in Panavision and DeLuxe Color; Running time: 120 minutes

Magali Noel (right)

Martin Potter, Max Born (extreme right)

Hiram Keller, Capucine

CAST:
Encolpio (Martin Potter), *Ascylto* (Hiram Keller), *Giton* (Max Born), *Tryphaena* (Capucine), *Eumolpus* (Salvo Randone), *Lichas* (Alain Cuny), *Vernacchio* (Fanfulla), *Robber* (Gordon Mitchell), *Fortunata* (Magali Noel), *Trimalchio* (Mario Romagnoli), *The minotaur* (Luigi Montefiori), *Habinnas* (Giuseppe Sanvitale), *Oenothea* (Donyale Luna), *Caesar* (Tanya Lopert), *Husband* (Joseph Wheeler), *Wife* (Lucia Bose), *Handsome soldier* (Wolfgang Hillinger), *Nymphomaniac* (Sibilla Sedat)

Rome, circa A.D. 56. Encolpio (Martin Potter), a young student, is distressed when his male lover

Giton (Max Born) runs away with his best friend Ascylto (Hiram Keller). Deciding to soothe his bruised vanity by "seeing the world," Encolpio visits his artist friend Eumolpus, who takes him to an orgy. Getting their fill of food, drink, and sex, Encolpio and Eumolpus later relax under the calm dark blues of the night sky, and Eumolpus tells his young friend his greatest dream is to be rich some day.

Falling asleep and dreaming of his "cruel love" Giton, Encolpio awakens to find himself a prisoner of Lichas (Alain Cuny), a corrupt official who scours the countryside collecting beautiful sex partners (male and female) for the decadent young Caesar. Taken aboard a transport ship, Encolpio is reunited with Giton and Ascylto, who've also been captured by Lichas. Later, Encolpio is amused to find himself the heart's desire of the ugly, middle-aged Lichas, and in a grotesquely comic ceremony the two are joined in unholy marriage.

Arriving at the Emperor's retreat some time later, Lichas and his crew learn the young Caesar has been murdered by subversives, and in the excitement Encolpio and Ascylto escape.

Searching for adventure, they find more than their share, and over the next few days make love to a slave girl in a deserted temple; become involved with a nymphomaniac whose desire is so strong that she must be tied to a wagon; loot the sacred oracle of Hermaphrodite (an asexual albino infant with healing powers); and engage in a life-and-death struggle with a vicious robber.

Separated from Ascylto, Encolpio wanders into a hostile mountain village on a remote coastline. The village overseer, a corrupt senator, arrests Encolpio for trespassing, but offers him freedom if he fights a

Max Born, Hiram Keller

large minotaur (Luigi Montefiori) in the gladiatorial arena. Anxious to be free, Encolpio fights valiantly, but he is no match for the hulking man-beast. He pleads with the minotaur for mercy, and vows to love the monster if it spares him. He is relieved when his adversary turns out to be nothing more than a smiling, robust man wearing the overhead mask of a bull. Laughing heartily and embracing Encolpio, the "minotaur" shouts: "I will fight no more. I have made a friend this day."

Impressed, the senator grants Encolpio freedom for winning the minotaur over through humility, and as a bonus he is invited to make love to a beautiful maiden. Suddenly impotent, Encolpio leaves the village for the "Garden of Delights," where he hopes to be cured. He is reunited with Ascylto and Eumolpus, who has fulfilled his dream by becoming wealthy.

Despite the efforts of the Garden's seductive handmaidens, Encolpio remains impotent, and taking Eumolpus's advice he visits Oenothea (Donyale Luna), a witch who finally cures him. Saddened when Ascylto is killed in a fight, Encolpio departs for Africa aboard Eumolpus's ship, continuing his search for adventure.

Satyricon, Federico Fellini's surreal, epic tale of ancient Rome, is one of his least appreciated films. Many find its lack of a tangible plot distressing, while others are offended by its preoccupation with sex and its depiction of man as a wholly corrupt being for whom there is little hope of salvation. It is truly unfortunate that *Satyricon* never gained the acceptance it should have, for it is among Fellini's finest works, and is certainly his most unique and fascinating contribution to seventies cinema.

The screenplay, exceptional in its pacing, character development, and dialogue, was the work of Fellini and Bernardino Zapponi, who took much of their material from an ancient satirical novel written by Petronius Arbiter in first century A.D. The book recounted in graphic detail the perverse sexual exploits of three young Romans—Encolpio, a student; Giton, his male lover; and Ascylto, his best friend. The moment he read Arbiter's book, Fellini realized that the three young men would make exceptional screen "heroes" for the liberal new decade, as they were attractive, fearless, sexually uninhibited, and apparently searching for any kind of adventure they could find—the more bizarre the better.

To play the characters in the film, Fellini cast three unknown actors solely on the basis of their looks. He chose Martin Potter, an attractive, ethereal-looking Englishman to play the sensitive Encolpio; and he selected a lean, ruggedly handsome American, Hiram Keller, to portray the lusty, boisterous Ascylto. For

Giton, Fellini cast Max Born, a young actor possessing a decidedly feminine beauty. The three young players turned in superb performances, compelling the audience to follow them on their strange, dreamlike odyssey through a Rome utterly saturated with decadence.

While it appears on the surface to be little more than an erotic, offbeat adventure story set in ancient times, *Satyricon* is also profound and thought-provoking, and like Fellini's earlier study of human decadence, *La Dolce Vita, Satyricon* emerged as a highly moral film despite all the kinky goings-on. In addition to a stunning visual entertainment, the director created in *Satyricon* a kind of brilliant, disturbing caricature of the society without morals, values, or conscience that modern man seems forever in danger of becoming.

Jack Nicholson

FIVE EASY PIECES

A Columbia Picture; Directed by Bob Rafelson; Produced by Bob Rafelson and Richard Wechsler; Screenplay by Adrien Joyce; Story by Bob Rafelson and Adrien Joyce; Photography by Laszlo Kovaks; Film editors: Christopher Holmes and Gerald Sheppard; Sound recording by Charles Knight; Executive producer: Bert Schneider; Assistant director: Sheldon Schrager; Associate producer: Harold

Schneider; Filmed in Technicolor; Running time: 98 minutes

CAST:
Bobby Eroica Dupea (JACK NICHOLSON), *Rayette Dipesto* (Karen Black), *Catherine Van Ost* (Susan Anspach), *Partita Dupea* (Lois Smith), *Elton* (Billy "Green" Bush), *Palm Apodaca* (Helena Kallianiotes), *Terry Grouse* (Toni Basil), *Stoney* (Fannie Flagg), *Carl Dupea* (Ralph Waite), *Betty* (Sally Ann Struthers), *Twinky* (Marlena Macguire),

Spicer (John Ryan), *Samia Glavia* (Irene Dailey), *Waitress* (Lorna Thayer), *Nicholas Dupea* (William Challee)

Bobby Eroica Dupea (Jack Nicholson) comes from a high-bred family of musicians, and once showed great promise as a concert pianist. By nature a restless, angry individual, Bobby left his family and his music when he could no longer stomach the dull, cloistered routine of daily practice. He took to the road, wanting to "see the world," and perhaps find something or someone to quell his inner turmoil.

Now, however, at 33, he has settled in a small town as an oil rigger, where his life consists of going to work, arguing with his dimwitted but loving girlfriend Rayette (Karen Black), and bowling every Thursday night with his friend Elton (Billy "Green" Bush). Not surprisingly, this routine also begins to disgust Bobby and, fed up, he decides to pay his family a visit.

He calls on his sister Partita (Lois Smith), who tells him their father (William Challee) has had a stroke. Leaving Rayette at a nearby motel, Bobby goes home and is reunited with his brother Carl (Ralph Waite), who's engaged to a beautiful, sensitive musician, Catherine Van Ost (Susan Anspach). Drawn to Catherine, Bobby seduces her while Carl is away. The possibility of a deeper relationship disturbs Catherine, whose gentleness clashes with Bobby's intensely rebellious, fiercely honest spirit. Later, Rayette shows up at the Dupea home unannounced. The family welcomes her out of courtesy, but her addle-brained innocence quickly seems out of place in a house full of somber musicians. (At one point, she asks: "Excuse me, is there a *television* in this house?")

Sometime afterward, Bobby asks Catherine to run away with him but she refuses, explaining his restlessness frightens her. Before leaving with Rayette, Bobby tells his father (who can't respond because of the stroke) about his unstable life, and apologizes for never pursuing his music. Ashamed, Bobby breaks into tears. On their way home, Bobby and Rayette stop at a gas station and, while Rayette orders coffee at a neighboring cafe, Bobby hitches a ride on a logging truck bound for Alaska, leaving her stranded.

Jack Nicholson's brilliant portrayal of Bobby Eroica Dupea in *Five Easy Pieces* completely captivated the moviegoing public, and he went on to establish himself as one of the most important screen actors of the era. His list of credits includes some of the seventies' most memorable films—*Five Easy Pieces, Carnal Knowledge, The Last Detail, Chinatown,* and *One Flew Over the Cuckoo's Nest*—and it could be argued that no other movie star of the period was allowed to play so many plum roles. Though Nicholson enjoyed the rare privilege of being both a top box-office attraction and a highly respected actor, stardom had not come easily, and it was the end result of eleven lean, hard-working years as an obscure actor in "grade-B" melodramas.

Nicholson's career began in 1958 when, at the age of twenty-one, he made his debut in the largely forgotten *Cry Baby Killer*, a fast-moving "youth" drama shot by Roger Corman in ten days on a budget of around $7,000. Though, at the time of its release, Nicholson was confident the film would make him a star, he served, over the next eleven years, a seemingly interminable apprenticeship in "B" picture after "B" picture, never seeming to find a role strong enough to lift him from obscurity to front-ranking stardom.

All this changed, however, when in 1969, Nicholson was asked to play a major supporting role in Peter Fonda's ode to the sixties' youth culture, *Easy*

Sally Struthers, Jack Nicholson, and Marlena Macguire

Jack Nicholson, Karen Black

THE BOYS IN THE BAND

A National General Picture; Directed by William Friedkin; Produced by Mart Crowley; Screenplay by Mart Crowley; From his play; Photography by Arthur J. Ornitz; Costumes by Robert LaVine; Production design by John Robert Lloyd; Executive producers: Dominick Dunne and Robert Jiras; Assistant director: William C. Gerrity; Associate producer: Kent Utt; Filmed in DeLuxe Color; A Cinema Center Films Presentation; Running time: 118 minutes

CAST:
Michael (Kenneth Nelson), *Harold* (Leonard Frey), *Hank* (Laurence Luckinbill), *Emory* (Cliff Gorman), *Alan* (Peter White), *Donald* (Frederick Combs), *Larry* (Keith Prentice), *Cowboy* (Robert LaTourneaux), *Bernard* (Reuben Greene)

New York City, where a group of homosexual friends anxiously prepare for a birthday celebration. Shortly before the party, Michael (Kenneth Nelson), who's giving the affair, gets an unexpected phone call from Alan (Peter White), his old roommate from college. A conservative "straight" who is unaware of Michael's homosexuality, Alan implores Michael to let him drop over, explaining, almost in tears, his need to discuss a personal problem that's been nagging at him for some time. Realizing Alan would be shocked to learn Michael and his friends are gay, Michael refuses.

Later on, all the celebrants arrive except the "guest of honor," Harold (Leonard Frey). Hank (Laurence Luckinbill), Emory (Cliff Gorman), Donald (Fred-

Susan Anspach, Jack Nicholson

Rider. In the film, Nicholson appeared as George Hanson, a cynical yet poetic young lawyer who befriends Fonda and Dennis Hopper during their cross-country odyssey, and who is eventually murdered by small-town bigots. Nicholson's portrait of the alcoholic, disillusioned lawyer was electrifying, and critics began referring to him as one of the most dynamic young actors to come along in years. Bob Rafelson's offbeat *Five Easy Pieces* followed one year later, and it provided the actor with yet another splendid showcase for his talents. Nicholson's intense, fiery rendition of the discontented young drifter was a powerful tour de force, and it laid the foundation for Nicholson's popular image as the great "rebel-hero" of seventies cinema. Though he would later essay similar portraits of fierce individualists battling "the system" in films such as *The Last Detail* and *One Flew Over the Cuckoo's Nest,* the impact of his work in *Five Easy Pieces* was extraordinary.

Released in 1970, *Five Easy Pieces* was a formidable hit despite its unorthodox nature, and aside from Nicholson the film also featured excellent performances by Karen Black, Susan Anspach, and especially Helena Kallianiotes as the eccentric hitchhiker Nicholson picks up during his travels.

26

Cliff Gorman

Kenneth Nelson, Frederick Combs

Kenneth Nelson

Kenneth Nelson, Cliff Gorman and Robert LaTourneaux

Leonard Frey

erick Combs), Larry (Keith Prentice), and Bernard (Reuben Greene) have all brought gifts for Harold, but Emory's is the most unique—a genuine "midnight cowboy" (Robert LaTourneaux) hired to cater to Harold's every whim. Suddenly, Alan shows up and learns the truth about Michael and his chums. Oddly, however, he isn't the least disturbed, and later tells Michael he's been battling his own homosexual urges. Harold finally arrives and the celebration gets under way.

The group represents a small cross-section of the homosexual world. Both Michael and Harold are approaching middle age, and have frequent bouts of self-loathing. Whereas Harold has come to accept his homosexuality with wry humor, Michael has become deeply religious, continually praying for release from the homosexual "curse." Hank and Larry, who live together, have no qualms about their relationship, and it is revealed that Hank actually left his wife and children to move in with Larry. Emory is blatantly effeminate, and he delights in flaunting his sexual preference. He has a sardonic sense of humor, and during the party he taunts the confused Alan until the latter gets angry and hits him.

As the evening wears on, the embittered Michael instigates an unusual parlor game. He orders his guests to call the one person they have loved all their lives, and to confess their feelings over the phone. Not surprisingly, the game becomes cruelly embarrassing, and the celebrants realize that Michael has intentionally hurt them. They all leave except Harold, who tells Michael he must sooner or later face his homosexuality, and that all the praying in the world won't change him. Realizing he has alienated his friends, Michael begins sobbing hysterically. Regaining his composure, Michael attends midnight mass at a nearby church.

Mart Crowley's *The Boys in the Band* is one of the minor masterpieces of modern drama. It was the first major American play to deal at length with the subject of homosexuality, a topic that was, for many years, considered taboo on both stage and screen. The vehicle was a powerful, riveting drama in the tradition of *Long Day's Journey Into Night* and *Who's Afraid of Virginia Woolf?*, and it had a long and successful run on the New York stage in the late sixties. Its nine characters—a group of gay friends interacting over the course of a birthday "celebration"—were roles of solid dimension, providing the cast with an actor's field day.

Shortly after the play opened, Crowley produced this splendid film version through National General Pictures, featuring all nine actors from the original stage company under the direction of William Friedkin. Shot quickly and economically, the film was beautifully done, and ranks as one of the best screen versions of a stage work ever produced. The actors were uniformly excellent in their roles, although Kenneth Nelson as the tortured, embittered Michael, and Leonard Frey as the cynical, dryly humorous Harold, tended to dominate the picture. Director Freidkin managed to turn the vehicle into an outstanding piece of cinema, even though he remained faithful to the play by confining the action to Michael's apartment.

Cliff Gorman

Frederick Combs, Kenneth Nelson, Reuben Greene, Cliff Gorman and Keith Prentice

1971

Sonny Grosso, Eddie Egan

THE FRENCH CONNECTION

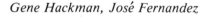

Gene Hackman, José Fernandez

A 20th Century-Fox Picture; Directed by William Friedkin; A Philip D'Antoni/Schine-Moore Production; Screenplay by Ernest Tidyman; Based on the novel by Robin Moore; Executive producer: G. David Schine; Director of photography: Owen Roizman; Assistant directors: Terry Donnelly and William C. Gerrity; Music score by Don Ellis; Photographed in Technicolor; Running time: 104 minutes

CAST:
Jimmy Doyle (GENE HACKMAN), *Buddy Russo* (Roy SCHEIDER), *Alain Charnier* (Fernando Rey), *Sal Boca* (Tony LoBianco), *Angie Boca* (Arlene Farber), *Pierre Nicoli* (Marcel Bozzuffi), *Devereaux* (Frederic De Pasquale), *Marie Charnier* (Ann Rebbot), *Simonson* (Eddie Egan), *Klein* (Sonny Grosso), *Weinstock* (Harold Gary), *Mulderig* (Bill Hickman), *La Valle* (Andre Ernotte), *Drug pusher* (Alan Weeks)

New York. Detectives Jimmy Doyle (Gene Hackman) and Buddy Russo (Roy Scheider) have a strong hatred of drug pushers. They will go to extraordinary lengths to make a drug bust, and they are not above harassing someone they suspect is a dealer.

Marcel Bozzuffi, Fernando Rey

Gene Hackman

Following a wild hunch, Doyle and Russo investigate Sal Boca (Tony LoBianco), a handsome playboy who lives like a king despite the fact that his cafe business yields only $7,000 per year. Their investigation reveals the business is only a "front," and that Boca is really chief negotiator for a drug syndicate importing heroin from foreign markets. The detectives learn the syndicate is managed by Weinstock (Harold Gary), a wealthy underworld figure, and that he and Boca are awaiting the arrival of a large heroin shipment from France. Not wanting to blow their chance for a multiple arrest, Doyle and Russo decide to take no action until Boca and Weinstock are contacted by their "French connection."

Meanwhile, in Marseilles, preparations for the shipment have begun, as a wealthy businessman (also head of France's illegal drug traffic), Alain Charnier (Fernando Rey), ingeniously hires popular television star Devereaux (Frederic De Pasquale) to assist him in making the delivery to Boca and Weinstock. Figuring American police won't suspect Devereaux of any wrongdoing, the crafty Charnier hides the heroin inside the actor's Lincoln Continental, then arranges to have the car transported to America.

In New York, Doyle learns of Charnier through

the underworld grapevine, and doggedly shadows the Frenchman when he arrives in town. Charnier, however, is use to this sort of thing, and, spying Doyle in the background on three separate occasions, he realizes he's being tailed. Fearing Doyle is onto him, Charnier orders his murderous accomplice Pierre (Marcel Bozzuffi) to eliminate the detective, but the ensuing assassination attempt fails. Doyle chases Pierre, who eludes him by hijacking a commuter train. Doyle flags down the first car he sees, explaining to the driver he's a police officer in urgent need of an automobile. Securing the car, Doyle drives at high speeds to keep up with Pierre. Meanwhile, Pierre murders the train's conductor and engineer for refusing to comply with his demands. Without an engineer, the train loses its ability to stop, resulting in a severe crash. Escaping the wreckage and unaware that Doyle has been following him, Pierre rushes down the train depot stairs, only to be confronted by Doyle drawing a bead on him with a .38 Special. Ignoring the detective's command to "hold it," Pierre tries to run away, and Doyle kills him.

Later on, Doyle, Russo, and a squad of armed patrolmen witness the heroin deal involving Boca, Weinstock, and Charnier. The police engage the criminals in a furious gunfight, during which Boca is killed and Weinstock taken into custody. The elusive Charnier, however, disappears into an old warehouse with Doyle in pursuit, but it is later revealed that the Frenchman was never caught.

In 1961, a major narcotics case involving foreign shipments of heroin to a New York drug syndicate

Gene Hackman, Marcel Bozzuffi

was solved by detective Eddie "Popeye" Egan and his partner Sonny Grosso. Long known for their dogged, relentless efforts to put an end to the city's illegal drug traffic, the pair were, for many years, the most respected and feared law officers in Manhattan, and their solving of the spectacular "French Connection" case involved endless stakeouts, interrogations, and dealings with underworld informants. As a result of their cracking the case, Egan and Grosso became celebrities of sorts, and were the subjects of numerous magazine articles recounting their ingenious, often flamboyant methods and total dedication to their work. The exploits of Egan and Grosso later served as the basis for a novel by Robin Moore titled, appropriately, *The French Connection*, which featured as its main characters a couple of hard-hitting street sleuths named Jimmy "Popeye" Doyle and Buddy Russo.

The book was filmed by 20th Century-Fox in 1971, featuring Gene Hackman as Doyle and Roy Scheider as Russo under the direction of William Friedkin. One of the toughest, most realistic crime films ever made, *The French Connection* was a critical and financial success, and it won five Academy Awards—including the year's Best Picture. Directed by Friedkin in a straightforward, businesslike manner, the film remains one of the decade's "classic" thrillers.

The French Connection succeeds brilliantly in capturing the harsh realism of Moore's book, and has an almost documentary-like flavor, enhanced by the director's use of some especially dingy New York locations. Particularly effective are the sleazy bar that Doyle and Russo raid early in the story, and the ancient subterranean warehouse on Wards Island through which Doyle pursues Charnier at the conclusion.

Comparing it with some of the seventies' later crime dramas, *The French Connection* lacks the stylish dramatics of *Dirty Harry*, and the harshness with which Doyle and Russo treat even petty criminals makes it a far cry from a compassionate, human-interest drama like *Serpico*. Also, the scenes of violence in *The French Connection* have an unusually stark, brutal quality, especially the one in which an innocent woman is suddenly gunned down on the streets by a sniper who was aiming at Hackman. The performances of Hackman (who won an Oscar), Scheider, Fernando Rey, and Tony Lo-Bianco are exceptional, and their scenes together have such a spontaneous quality that one gets the impression most of them were improvised.

CARNAL KNOWLEDGE

An Avco Embassy Picture; Directed and produced by Mike Nichols; Screenplay by Jules Feiffer; Photography by Giuseppe Rotunno; Film editor: Sam O'Steen; Assistant director: Tim Zinnemann; Set decorations: George R. Nelson; Sound recording by Lawrence O. Jost; Executive producer: Joseph E. Levine; Production manager: Joe L. Cramer; Associate producer: Clive Reed; Filmed in Technicolor and Panavision; Running time: 97 minutes

CAST:
Jonathan (JACK NICHOLSON), *Bobbie* (ANN-MARGRET), *Susan* (CANDICE BERGEN), *Sandy* (ART GARFUNKEL), *Louise* (Rita Moreno), *Jennifer* (Carol Kane), *Cindy* (Cynthia O'Neal)

Unbeknown to each other, college roommates Jonathan (Jack Nicholson) and Sandy (Art Garfunkel) begin simultaneous relationships with the same girl, Susan (Candice Bergen). While they are close friends, the two boys are complete opposites. Jonathan is a handsome, swaggering "stud" who re-

Jack Nicholson, Art Garfunkel

Candice Bergen, Art Garfunkel

gards women primarily as conquests, while Sandy is shy, sensitive, and a virgin. Apparently, both fill a different need in Susan—she sleeps with Jonathan but never confides in him, while she tells all to Sandy but denies him sex. Resenting her relationship with his friend, Jonathan breaks with Susan, and after graduation she marries Sandy.

Years later, the marriage crumbles, and Sandy visits Jonathan, now a successful executive in New York. Following Jonathan's advice, Sandy starts "playing the field," and he later enters an "open" relationship with Cindy (Cynthia O'Neal), a feminist. Still the roving bachelor, Jonathan strikes up with Bobbie (Ann-Margret), a voluptuous model who becomes his mistress. As the novelty of her body wears off, however, Jonathan tires of her, and mockingly suggests to Sandy that they swap sex partners for a while. However, Bobbie wants to marry Jonathan, and gets her wish after attempting suicide.

Art Garfunkel, Jack Nicholson

Years later, Bobbie sues Jonathan for divorce, draining his finances. Fed up, Jonathan shows Sandy (now a middle-aged "hippie") slides of all his sexual conquests, saying bitterly that he now regards all women as "ballbusters" who only want to drag him down. Consumed by his contempt for the opposite sex, Jonathan is reduced to visiting a prostitute (Rita Moreno) twice a week, having her recite a speech about his superiority over women, which is now the only way he can attain sexual satisfaction.

Few American films have approached the subject of sex with more frankness and candor than *Carnal Knowledge.* Released in 1971, the film was a serious exploration of human relationships, and of the emotional damage that results when men and women treat sex as a "game." The story examined the sexual lives of two men—Jonathan and Sandy—over a

Jack Nicholson

twenty-year period, following them from their college days to their middle years, when both become confused and embittered over their inability to form satisfying alliances with women.

Directed by Mike Nichols from an original screenplay by Jules Feiffer, *Carnal Knowledge* emerged as a thoughtful, compelling, if somewhat depressing film, and it contained a truly unique and offbeat cast. It featured two stars primarily known for their musical talents—Ann-Margret and Art Garfunkel—in serious dramatic roles, and it cast the

Jack Nicholson, Art Garfunkel and Carol Kane

Jack Nicholson, Rita Moreno

usually likable Jack Nicholson as a thoroughly despicable male chauvinist. Though Garfunkel as Nicholson's sensitive friend and Ann-Margret as the beautiful mistress Nicholson almost destroys were both excellent, it is Nicholson's all-out performance that makes *Carnal Knowledge* an unforgettable film.

The role of Jonathan was a complete departure for the actor, and ranks as, perhaps, the first instance in his career when the audience comes to dislike the character he's playing. Nicholson's Jonathan is a masterly piece of acting, a disturbing portrait of a man who, throughout his life, never matures in his attitude toward women, and who even in middle age continues the pose of a cocky seducer out to "score," even though it is no longer appropriate.

Ann-Margret, Jack Nicholson

PLAY MISTY FOR ME

A Universal Presentation of a Malpaso Company Film; Directed by Clint Eastwood; Produced by Robert Daley; Screenplay by Jo Heims and Dean Riesner; Story by Jo Heims; Photography by Bruce Surtees; Associate producer: Bob Larson; Art direction by Alexander Golitzen; Costumes by Helen Colvig; Music by Dee Barton; Assistant director: Bob Larson; Songs: "Misty," composed and performed by Errol Garner; "The First Time Ever I Saw Your Face," sung by Roberta Flack; Filmed in Technicolor; Running time: 102 minutes

CAST:

Dave Garland (CLINT EASTWOOD), *Evelyn Draper* (Jessica Walter), *Tobie* (Donna Mills), *Frank* (Jack Ging), *Al Monte* (James McEachin), *Sgt. McCallum* (John Larch), *Madge* (Irene Hervey), *Murphy* (Donald Siegel), *Birdie* (Clarice Taylor), *Jay Jay* (Juke Everts), *Man* (George Fargo), *Deputy sheriff* (Tim Frawley), *Anjelica* (Brit Lind), *Locksmith* (Mervin W. Frates), *Madalyn* (Ginna Patterson)

Dave Garland (Clint Eastwood) is the star disc jockey at a radio station in Monterey, California. He is the host of an evening show featuring mood music "for lonely lovers on a cool, cool night," and his listeners often phone in requests. His most ardent fan is a mysterious woman who calls almost nightly, always requesting Errol Garner's "Misty." After work one evening, Dave relaxes in his favorite cock-

Clint Eastwood, Jessica Walter

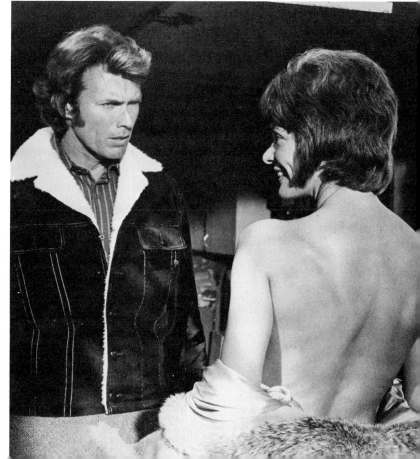

Jessica Walter, Clint Eastwood

tail lounge, where he is "picked up" by Evelyn Draper (Jessica Walter), who turns out to be the "Misty" girl. Although Dave takes her to bed, he views the incident as a "one-night stand" and is thus surprised when Evelyn comes over the next night unannounced.

Meanwhile, Dave resumes the relationship with his estranged girlfriend Tobie (Donna Mills), an artist whose finest work is a portrait of Dave. Though Dave begins spending almost all his spare time with Tobie, Evelyn continues hounding him, and, tired of inventing excuses for not seeing her, Dave has her over for a drink. When he tells her about Tobie, Evelyn behaves irrationally, becoming almost psychotic in her profession of love for Dave, and slashing her wrists when he orders her to leave. Treated by a doctor, Evelyn spends several days recovering at Dave's.

Later, Dave's home is vandalized, and his cleaning lady is ravaged with a carving knife. The police arrest Evelyn for the crime, and she is committed to a mental hospital. Believing himself free of Evelyn, Dave is alarmed when, weeks later, he receives a phone call and the familiar voice says, "Play 'Misty' for me." Dave is relieved when Evelyn assures him she's been cured and apologizes for causing so much trouble. Playing "Misty" for the first time in weeks, Dave again dedicates it to "lonely lovers on a cool, cool night . . . and, especially, for Evelyn."

Clint Eastwood, Donna Mills

Irene Hervey, Clint Eastwood

Still dangerously psychotic, however, Evelyn answers Tobie's ad for a roommate, intending to murder Tobie at the first opportunity. Moving into Tobie's cliff-top home, Evelyn slashes Dave's portrait with a knife before trying to do the same to Tobie. Luckily, Dave arrives in time to prevent this, and in the struggle Evelyn falls to her death in the Monterey coast waters.

Clint Eastwood remained one of the biggest box-office draws throughout the seventies. Certainly, no other actor of the decade could guarantee a film's success by simply putting his name on it, and the fact remains that even the weakest of his films were listed among the biggest money-makers of the year.

Though he frequently finds himself under attack by critics who object to the violence in his pictures, Eastwood is one of those rare stars who can seemingly do no wrong in the eyes of the filmgoing public. He is also one of the few actors in history to take *complete* control of his career. The formation of his own production unit, the Malpaso Company, allowed Eastwood the freedom to make his movies the way he wanted them to be made. In addition, Eastwood is one of the only superstars who has managed to establish himself as a fine director. While all his vehicles of the seventies were major successes, many of the most interesting are those in which Eastwood directed himself, and perhaps the finest to date remains his first—*Play Misty for Me*.

The film was produced in early 1971, when Eastwood was still primarily identified with epic westerns like *A Fistful of Dollars* (1966), *For a Few Dollars More* (1967), *The Good, the Bad, and the Ugly* (1968), *Hang 'Em High* (1968), and *Two Mules for Sister Sara* (1970).

Considering his experience with the genre, one speculates that it would have been natural for Eastwood to select a western saga for his directorial

debut, but perhaps his familiarity with this type of film offered the actor no real challenge. Going completely against "type" and obviously seeking a difficult story property, Eastwood chose this complex psychological thriller (written by his friend Jo Heims) because he knew it would require exceptional direction if it were to be effective.

The critics who dislike Eastwood were, no doubt, skeptical about his ability to direct as well as star in a film, but when *Play Misty for Me* finally made its debut, most of them were awed by the superb style with which Eastwood had made it. The story of a sexy disc jockey who becomes involved with a beautiful psychopath, *Play Misty for Me* emerged as a major triumph for Eastwood, both as a director and an actor. His portrayal of Dave Garland was far more di-

Clarice Taylor, Jessica Walter

mensional than any of his western heroes had been, and it showed that there was considerably more to Eastwood's talent than mere presence. His Dave Garland was handsome, super-cool, and in love with the "good life," but he was also vulnerable and compassionate with women.

Eastwood's direction of the film cannot be faulted, and he wisely injected it with all the tried and true elements of the great suspense films of old. Similar to such forties efforts as *Laura, The Uninvited* and *Portrait of Jennie, Play Misty for Me* featured as its main theme a "classic" love song that is both sensual and mysterious, and the film's heroine was an attractive, enigmatic, and very obviously disturbed young woman. Also, *Play Misty for Me* is permeated with a romantic aura not unlike the "classic" Alfred Hitchcock mysteries. Eastwood's breathy delivery of the "Misty" dedication—"for lonely lovers on a cool, cool night"—the opening shots of the beautiful Monterey coast, and the erotic interludes between Dave and Evelyn helped to set an appropriately sexy mood.

THE LAST PICTURE SHOW

A Columbia Picture; Directed by Peter Bogdanovich; Produced by Stephen J. Friedman; Executive producer: Bert Schneider; Screenplay by Peter Bogdanovich and Larry McMurty; Based on the novel by Larry McMurty; Photography by Robert Surtees; Production designed by Polly Platt; Assistant director: Robert Rubin; Associate producer: Harold Schneider; Running time: 118 minutes

Jeff Bridges, Timothy Bottoms

CAST:
Sonny Crawford (Timothy Bottoms), *Duane Jackson* (Jeff Bridges), *Sam the Lion* (Ben Johnson), *Jacy Farrow* (Cybill Shepherd), *Lois Farrow* (Ellen Burstyn), *Ruth Popper* (Cloris Leachman), *Billy* (Sam Bottoms), *Abilene* (Clu Gulager), *Genevieve* (Eileen Brennan), *Lester* (Randy Quaid), *Coach Popper* (Bill Thurman), *Charlene* (Sharon Taggart), *Gene Farrow* (Robert Glenn), *Jimmie Sue* (Helena Humann), *Miss Mosey* (Jessie Lee Fulton), *Bobby Sheen* (Gary Brockette), *Teacher* (John Hillerman), *Chester* (Noble Willingham), *Mrs. Jackson* (Joye Hash), *Johnny* (Mike Hosford)

A small Texas town in the early fifties. Sonny Crawford (Timothy Bottoms) and Duane Jackson (Jeff Bridges) spend their time going to high school, hanging around the pool hall, and "making out" with their girlfriends. Having almost no parental guidance in their lives, Sonny and Duane idolize Sam the Lion (Ben Johnson), a crusty old cowpoke who owns the pool hall as well as a small café and a run-down movie house.

While Sonny's girlfriend is rather placid and frumpy, continually refusing to go "all the way," Duane's is the prettiest in the senior class—Jacy Farrow (Cybill Shepherd). Unlike Sonny's girl, Jacy believes sexual experimentation is normal, and she's eager to lose her virginity. Deciding their first sexual encounter should be a "public event," Jacy and Duane rent a motel room, while outside their envious friends await the results. Inside, Duane and Jacy undress and get into bed, but to his dismay Duane is unable to perform. Not wanting to disappoint their friends, however, they stride out of the room smug and dreamy-eyed, as if they had experienced ecstasy.

Discontented with this girlfriend, Sonny enters into an affair with Ruth Popper (Cloris Leachman), the love-starved wife of his football coach. Unlike Duane and Jacy, Sonny and Ruth complete a sex act, but it is rather perfunctory. However, proud of their recent sexual experiences, Sonny and Duane decide to introduce Sam's retarded ward Billy (Sam Bottoms) to the "joys of sex," and they hire a fat prostitute to initiate him. Billy's encounter with the woman is cruelly embarrassing, and when Sam learns what Duane and Sonny have done, he orders them to stay away from the cafe, pool hall, and movie house. This leaves the boys with almost nothing to do; bored senseless, Sonny apologizes to Sam and Billy.

After graduation, Duane and Sonny celebrate by driving to Tijuana for a little hell-raising. Days later, they return severely hung over and are shocked to learn that Sam died of a stroke while they were away. When Duane takes a job as an Oklahoma oil rigger sometime afterward, Sonny starts going with Jacy, which leaves Ruth out in the cold. Later, Sonny and Jacy marry, but her mother (Ellen Burstyn) has the marriage annulled before it is consummated.

Lonely once again, Sonny goes to see Ruth and finds that his neglect has made her an emotional shambles. Awakening to the realization that he has caused her great agony, Sonny weeps over his

Cybill Shepherd, Ellen Burstyn

thoughtlessness. Later, Sonny is horrified when Billy is hit by a truck and killed while sweeping the streets. He is sickened by the callous attitude of the driver and several townspeople, who gather around Billy's corpse, coldly commenting that the "idiot" had no business in the street in the first place. Angered by their inhumanity, Sonny picks up Billy and screams: "He was sweeping! That's what he was doing in the street, you heartless bastards!" He then carries Billy into the pool hall.

The Last Picture Show—based on the novel by Larry McMurty, who collaborated on the screenplay with the film's director, Peter Bogdanovich—became one of the most widely acclaimed motion pictures of the decade. It also launched the careers of Bogdanovich, Timothy Bottoms, Jeff Bridges, Cybill Shepherd, Ellen Burstyn, Cloris Leachman, Eileen Brennan, and Randy Quaid.

The story told of a young man's coming of age in a small Texas town during the early fifties, when the nation was still suffering from the post-war doldrums, and Bogdanovich used this simple premise to fashion one of the most powerful and touching explorations of small-town American life the cinema has ever seen. Upon its release, the film so impressed critics that many of them called it the most impressive debut by a young director since *Citizen Kane* (although it was technically Bogdanovich's second film, for he had already proven his talents in an excellent modern-day horror thriller, *Targets*, released in 1969).

Before becoming a director, Bogdanovich had been a film student and scholar (he was writing monographs on film for the Museum of Modern Art in his early twenties) who spent countless hours studying the works of Hollywood's master directors. When he began his own career, Bogdanovich often incorporated the techniques of the great filmmakers into his movies to make them more effective. Bod-

Timothy Bottoms, Eileen Brennan

Jeff Bridges, Timothy Bottoms

ganovich's love for the Hollywood of old is apparent in all his films, and cinema students continue to marvel at the way Bogdanovich and his veteran photographer, Robert Surtees, gave *The Last Picture Show* the look and feel of a thirties "classic" by filming it in high-contrast black-and-white.

Bogdanovich has often admitted that, visually, a great deal of the film was inspired by the works of

Ben Johnson, Timothy Bottoms, Sam Bottoms

John Ford and Orson Welles, and this is evident throughout. Many of *The Last Picture Show*'s key scenes were obviously modelled after Ford's *The Grapes of Wrath* (1940), featuring lighting and texture very similar to that of the earlier classic. Also, Bogdanovich depicts the small Texas town as a dreary, desolate place completely cut off from the outside world, and this intense feeling of isolation is precisely the effect Orson Welles achieved with the sleazy Mexican border town in *Touch of Evil* (1958).

Ben Johnson won an Academy Award for his portrayal of Sam the Lion, the gruffly paternal cowboy whose wisdom helps mold Sonny into a sensitive, responsible adult. His brilliant monologue about his days as a restless young buck is a classic of its kind, and is a textbook example of how a screen soliloquy should be delivered. Cloris Leachman also won an Oscar for her emotionally draining performance as the older woman who tries to escape her life's hollow boredom by having an affair with a younger man, only to find herself heartbroken.

Timothy Bottoms, Cybill Shepherd

Jeff Bridges, Randy Quaid

Clint Eastwood

THE BEGUILED

A Universal Production of a Malpaso Company Film; Produced and directed by Don Siegel; Screenplay by John B. Sherry and Grimes Grice; Photography by Bruce Surtees; Based on a novel by Thomas Cullinan; Associate producer: Claude Traverse; Music by Lalo Schifrin; Assistant director: Burt Astor; Costumes by Helen Colvig; Production designed by Ted Haworth; A Jennings Lang Production; Photographed in Technicolor; Running time: 109 minutes

CAST:
John McBurney (CLINT EASTWOOD), *Martha* (Geraldine Page), *Edwina* (Elizabeth Hartman), *Amy* (Pamelyn Ferdin), *Hallie* (Mae Mercer), *Carol* (Jo Ann Harris), *Doris* (Darleen Carr), *Lizzie* (Peggy Drier), *Janie* (Pattye Mattick), *Abigail* (Melody Thomas)

During the Civil War, John McBurney (Clint Eastwood), a Union soldier, is wounded in the leg attempting to ambush Confederate scouts. In great pain, McBurney spies a young girl, Amy (Pamelyn Ferdin), gathering mushrooms in an open field, and

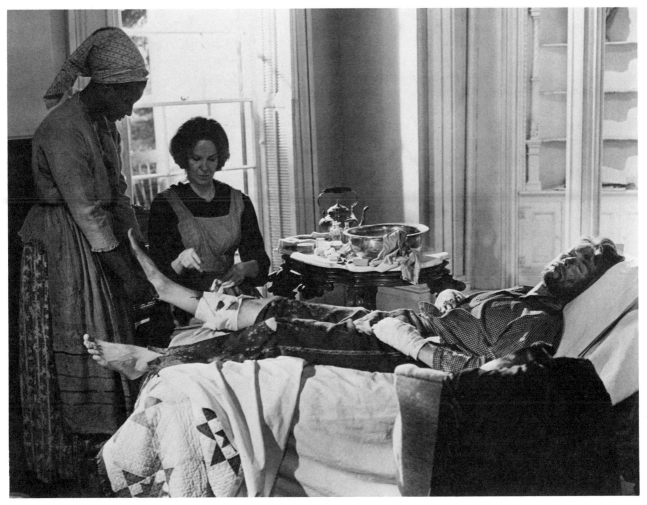

Mae Mercer, Geraldine Page, Clint Eastwood

persuades her to take him to the all-girl boarding school where she is a student. Since the school is run by the puritanical Miss Martha (Geraldine Page), McBurney's intrusion is resented; but soon, the handsome soldier becomes an object of desire for the cloistered students, and even Miss Martha develops an attraction for him.

Trying to hide this, Miss Martha tells McBurney he will be turned over to the Confederates as soon as he's well. Sensing her lust, however, McBurney sweet-talks her into letting him stay on, and later Carol (Jo Ann Harris), one of the more seductive students, tells McBurney she's available to him whenever he wishes. This pleases McBurney very much, as he realizes the women are slowly falling under his power.

Aside from Carol, McBurney begins wooing the sensitive Edwina (Elizabeth Hartman), the school's teacher, who is unaware McBurney is nothing more than a sexual opportunist. McBurney soon realizes Edwina loves him and, hoping she'll yield sexually, vows to marry her after the war, insisting girls like Carol mean nothing to him. When Edwina refuses to

sleep with him because she's "saving herself for marriage," McBurney makes a pass at the middle-aged Martha, awakening her long-dormant sexuality. She gives him the key to her room in the hope that he'll come to her bed later that night. However, McBurney is unable to resist a similar invitation from the sensuous Carol.

Awakened by the naughty giggles coming from Carol's room, Edwina is horrified to find McBurney and Carol in bed together. Enraged, Edwina pushes McBurney down the long staircase, which awakens the entire household—including Martha, who realizes John has also forsaken her for the young nymphet. After examining the unconscious McBurney, Martha finds that, in her estimation, the fall has made his wounded leg potentially gangrenous. With the help of her maid Hallie (Mae Mercer), Martha amputates it, and later McBurney awakens to the gruesome fact that he is now a one-legged man.

Shattered, McBurney curses Martha, insisting she removed the leg because he went to Carol's bed instead of hers. "I'm going to have to watch you from now on," he says with bitter sarcasm. "You might just decide to cut off my (pause) other leg." In a drunken rage, McBurney kills Amy's pet turtle, which causes the child also to hate him.

Regaining his senses some time afterward, McBurney apologizes to Martha and Amy, and renews his proposal to Edwina. Although appearing to accept his apologies, the women's hatred of McBurney has become quite fiendish. During a dinner "celebrating" John's proposal to Edwina, they serve him poisonous mushrooms, handpicked by Amy. McBurney dies horribly, and the women conduct a grotesque funeral service.

Geraldine Page, Peggy Drier, Elizabeth Hartman

Geraldine Page, Clint Eastwood, Elizabeth Hartman

By the early seventies, Clint Eastwood had become one of the major screen stars of the decade, as evidenced by the enormous popularity of his films. Despite his success, however, the actor was understandably concerned about being forever "type-cast" as an action-adventure hero. His portrayals of the enigmatic gunman in the Sergio Leone westerns of the late sixties were what first brought him to prominence, and his first few starring vehicles in America had all been of a western or adventure type.

In an effort to escape, at least temporarily, from the "action-hero" mold, Eastwood directed and starred in the excellent *Play Misty for Me*, a decidedly different kind of vehicle, and then starred in the even more atypical *The Beguiled*, a brooding psychological horror story set during the Civil War. The chilling tale of an amorous Union soldier who inspires jealousy, revenge, and ultimately murder at an all-girl boarding school, *The Beguiled* was as far removed from a rough-hewn action drama as Eastwood could get, and remains his most unusual film.

Released in 1971, *The Beguiled* was a critical success, although the audience response was somewhat less than usual for an Eastwood picture. However, *The Beguiled* has always been of particular interest to the actor's fans because it contains one of his few truly villainous portrayals. The ignoble John McBurney, a cunning and deceitful man, is a far cry from the larger-than-life heroes the actor usually plays. Eastwood's McBurney is a selfish, hedonistic lout who regards women as no more than conquests and who perhaps even takes cruel pleasure in toying with the emotions of sensitive women like Martha and Edwina.

KLUTE

A Warner Bros. Picture; Produced and directed by Alan J. Pakula; Screenplay by Andy and Dave Lewis; Photography by Gordon Willis; Co-producer:

Rita Gam, Roy Scheider, Jane Fonda

Jane Fonda, Donald Sutherland

David Lange; Film editor: Carl Lerner; Music by Michael Small; Set decorations by John Mortensen; Art direction by George Jenkins; Costumes by Ann Roth; Makeup by Irving Buchman; Sound by Chris Newman; Assistant director: William Gerrity; Filmed in Technicolor and Panavision; Running time: 114 minutes

CAST:
Bree Daniels (JANE FONDA), *John Klute* (DONALD SUTHERLAND), *Peter Cable* (Charles Cioffi), *Frank Ligourin* (Roy Scheider), *Trina* (Rita Gam), *Lt. Trask* (Nathan George), *Arlyn Page* (Dorothy Tristan), *Psychiatrist* (Vivian Nathan), *Mr. Goldfarb* (Morris Strassberg), *Berger* (Barry Snider), *Tom Gruneman* (Robert Milli), *Holly Gruneman* (Betty Murray), *Mama Reese* (Shirley Stoler), *Goldfarb's secretary* (Jean Stapleton)

The disappearance of research scientist Tom Gruneman leads to an investigation by his friend Detective John Klute (Donald Sutherland). Questioning Gruneman's associate Peter Cable (Charles Cioffi), Klute learns that Gruneman had recently written an obscene love letter to Bree Daniels (Jane Fonda), a Manhattan call girl.

Klute stakes out Bree's apartment, watching her every move. He follows her to the garment factory of the aged, benevolent Mr. Goldfarb (Morris Strassberg), who simply hires Bree to strip in front of him. Contacting Bree several weeks later, Klute asks her about Gruneman but she insists the name means nothing. However, she admits to receiving mysterious phone calls from a sadistic former client who once beat her up. Although she doesn't recall the man's name, she tells Klute that her friend Arlyn Page (Dorothy Tristan) once spent a brutal night with him, too. Klute visits Arlyn, who says the man who beat her up was older than Gruneman by about ten years.

Meanwhile, Klute and Bree fall in love, although Bree finds it difficult to express tender emotion in a sexual situation. Bree receives another letter from Gruneman and Klute analyzes it, discovering it wasn't written by his friend at all. A consistent typing error reveals it came from Cable, who hoped to shield himself by using Gruneman's name. Klute then realizes that Cable is the sadist, and that he no doubt killed Gruneman when the latter discovered his perversion.

Terrified by another threatening phone call, Bree seeks the comfort of the paternal Mr. Goldfarb. She finds his office deserted but, in a darkened corner, she spies Cable, who's been stalking her the whole time. Cable tries to kill Bree but he is stopped by Klute, who arrives with the police. Struggling with Klute, Cable falls out a window to his death, and later Klute persuades Bree to abandon her "corrupt" life in the city.

Donald Sutherland, director Alan J. Pakula

Donald Sutherland

The murder mystery, for many years a film genre limited to rather tame "whodunit" fare like the Sherlock Holmes pictures, finally reached maturity in the 1960's. Films such as *Experiment in Terror* (1962), *Wait Until Dark* (1966), and *No Way to Treat a Lady* (1968) featured villains that were, in addition to being homicidal, rather sexually perverse as well—which was reflected in the sordid, hideous crimes they committed.

Appropriately, the first major murder mystery of the seventies—*Klute*—epitomizes the trend toward sexual frankness initiated by the earlier pictures; but whereas *Experiment in Terror, Wait Until Dark,* and

Donald Sutherland, Jane Fonda

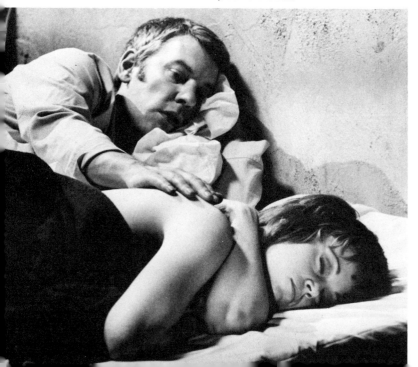

No Way to Treat a Lady merely hinted at the sexual horrors committed by their psychotic antagonists, *Klute* explored the sadistic perversions of Peter Cable with almost clinical detail. As a result, many found *Klute* a little *too* graphic to be entertaining, and the film received a somewhat mixed response from audiences and critics, though nearly everyone applauded the exceptional performance of Jane Fonda.

Also, many who saw the film felt that the title was rather misleading, since the character played by Donald Sutherland was decidedly less important to the story than Fonda's hip call girl. Fonda deservedly won her first Academy Award for her complex portrayal of Bree Daniels, and never before in her career had the actress been allowed to explore a character in such depth. Her performance as well as the fine acting of Sutherland as Klute and Charles Cioffi as the killer are the best things about the picture, and they prevent *Klute* from becoming just another sensational murder mystery.

Technically, the film leaves a great deal to be desired. It is much too slowly paced to be completely effective as a suspense drama, and the potentially thrilling climax, during which all the principles converge in the darkened garment factory for a final showdown, falls strangely flat.

In its favor, however, is the overall "look" of the film, and the story's stark and raw nature is heightened by photographer Gordon Willis's coldly harsh Technicolor tones, which have a lurid quality reminiscent of the Herman Cohen horror films of the late fifties.

A CLOCKWORK ORANGE

A Warner Bros. Picture; Produced, directed and written by Stanley Kubrick; Based on the novel by Anthony Burgess; Photography by John Alcott; Production design by John Barry; Art direction: Russell Hagg and Peter Shields; Film editor: Bill Butler; Costumes by Milena Canonero; Makeup by Fred Williamson, George Parleton, and Barbara Daly; Assistant directors: Derek Cracknell and Dusty Symonds; Location manager: Terence Clegg; Executive producers: Max L. Raab and Si Litvinoff; Stunt arranger: Roy Scammel; Sound: John Jordan, Bill Rowe, Eddie Haben, and Brian Blamely; Production coordinator: Mike Kaplan; Filmed in color; Running time: 137 minutes

Adrienne Corri, Malcolm McDowell

CAST:

Alex (MALCOLM McDOWELL), *Mr. Alexander* (Patrick Magee), *Dr. Brodsky* (Carl Duering), *Dad* (Philip Stone), *Mum* (Sheila Raynor), *Dim* (Warren Clarke), *Georgie* (James Marcus), *Pete* (Michael Tarn), *Cat Lady* (Miriam Karlin), *Mrs. Alexander* (Adrienne Corri), *Old tramp* (Paul Farrell), *Lodger* (Clive Davis), *Minister of the Interior* (Anthony Sharp), *Prison governor* (Michael Gover), *Deltoid* (Aubrey Morris)

The story takes place in a bizarre society of the future, when law-abiding citizens are continually terrorized by marauding street gangs whose members are violent, psychopathic young men who plunder through the night in search of new "kicks." On one particular evening, young Alex (Malcolm McDowell) and his "droogs"—Dim (Warren Clarke), Georgie (James Marcus), and Pete (Michael Tarn)—sit in the Korova Milkbar drinking "Molocko-plus," a mind-altering combination of milk and psychedelic drugs. Looking forward to yet another evening of what Alex calls "the old ultraviolence," he and his pals leave the bar and ravage a drunken tramp (Paul Farrell) before challenging a rival gang to a street fight.

Afterward, they drive to the home of Mr. Alexander (Patrick Magee), a respected and successful novelist. After donning Halloween masks to conceal their identities, Alex and his gang barge their way in-

Malcolm McDowell

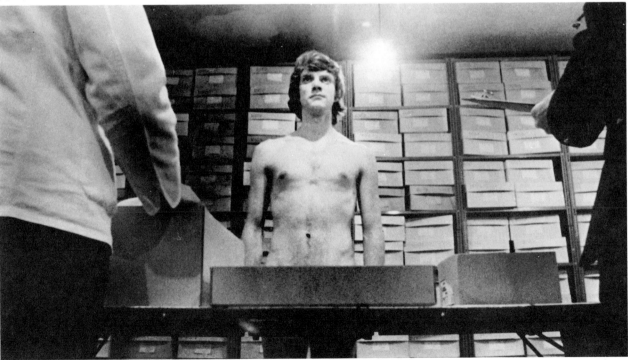

to the house. Once inside, Alex knocks Mr. Alexander to the floor and prepares to rape Mrs. Alexander (Andrienne Corri). As he cuts away her clothing with a pair of scissors, Alex croons "Singin' in the Rain," punctuating its lyrics with brutal kicks to Mr. Alexander's head and torso. Satisfied with the evening's mayhem, Alex returns home, where he relaxes by listening to a tape of Ludwig van Beethoven's Ninth Symphony, his favorite musical piece and the only thing in life he truly respects.

James Marcus, Warren Clarke, Malcolm McDowell

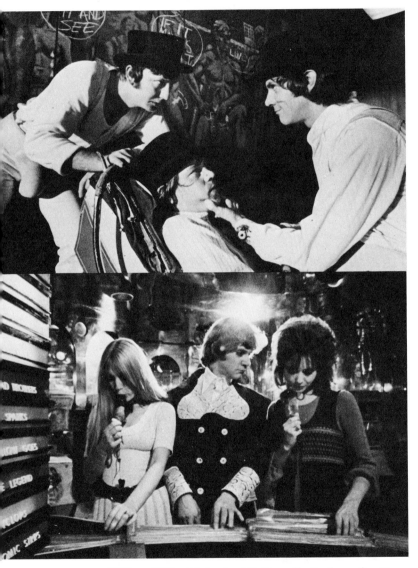

Gillian Hills, Malcolm McDowell, Barbara Scott

The next night, Alex and his droogs plot the rape of an eccentric female artist (Miriam Karlin), but after breaking into her home Alex kills her with a giant plastic phallus when she resists his advances. Suddenly hearing police sirens, the droogs abandon their leader, and Alex is arrested outside the artist's house. Later convicted of first-degree murder, Alex is sentenced to fourteen years in prison.

Finding that prison life doesn't agree with him, Alex becomes eager to get out. Through the prison grapevine he hears of a new medical treatment—the "Ludovico" technique—which supposedly curbs violent behavior. Later, the Minister of the Interior (Anthony Sharp), a strong advocate of the treatment, announces that any prisoner volunteering for the Ludovico and cured by it will be paroled.

Without hesitation, Alex volunteers, and he is immediately taken to the treatment center and given injections. He is then subjected to film footage of violence and brutality, but instead of enjoying these sights as he once would have, he is repelled to the point of convulsive nausea. Since, coincidentally, the film's soundtrack music is Alex's beloved Ninth Symphony, he is conditioned to feel sick whenever he hears it as well. Pronounced cured, Alex returns home, but finds that his parents have adopted another son (Clive Davis), who orders Alex out of the house.

Unable to protest because he feels horribly sick when he gets a violent impulse, Alex leaves. On the street, Alex bumps into the old tramp he had beaten up earlier, and with the help of his fellow derelicts the tramp exacts revenge on the helpless, dry-wretching Alex. Seriously hurt, Alex makes for the nearest home and rings the doorbell.

By chance, it is the house of Mr. Alexander, now a helpless cripple as a result of Alex's attack. Since his wife's injuries from the rape proved fatal, Alexander's sole companion is now a brawny muscleman who caters to his every need. Not recognizing Alex (who is also unaware of where he is), the good-hearted Mr. Alexander orders his servant to take the unfortunate young man upstairs for a bath. Once in the tub, Alex is revitalized by the hot, soothing water and begins to warble "Singin' in the Rain." Suddenly realizing who his guest is, Mr. Alexander drugs Alex, then locks him in an upstairs room while the Ninth Symphony is piped in through large speakers. Consumed by the awful sickness again, Alex decides to "snuff it" by jumping out a window.

Suffering only a leg fracture, however, Alex is taken to the hospital and given a series of psychiatric tests, which show that he's returning to a violent state of mind. He is then visited by the Minister of the Interior, who offers Alex a high-paying job and a respected position in society if he continues acting "cured."

The films of Stanley Kubrick are among the most brilliant and memorable in the cinema. Besides being superbly made from a technical standpoint, they are unusual, entertaining, and socially significant—rarely receiving anything less than a glowing response from audiences and critics. Their perfection reflects Kubrick's slow, meticulous method of filmmaking, and he is well known as a director who retakes scenes time after time until they are flawless.

His pre-seventies films—*The Killing* (1956), *Paths of Glory* (1958), *Spartacus* (1960), *Lolita* (1962), *Dr. Strangelove* (1963), and *2001: A Space Odyssey* (1968)—continue to be objects of serious study by film students and scholars, and most have developed a devoted "cult" following over the years.

Following the phenomenally successful *2001* (it was MGM's biggest money-maker to that time), Kubrick began work on a film version of Anthony Burgess's darkly satirical novel, *A Clockwork Orange*, a frightening yet amusing look at what life in the not-too-distant future could easily be like. The story took place in a bizarre society apparently stripped of all art, religion, entertainment, and moral values, in which most of the young were forced to form violent street gangs simply because they had no other outlet for their energies. The protagonist was Alex, a psychopathic young bully who rapes and plunders for "kicks," and yet has an all-consuming love for Beethoven's Ninth Symphony.

Kubrick was utterly fascinated by the book, and the resulting film, released in 1971, emerged as a fine achievement. He and his production designer John Barry skillfully re-created the soulless, plastic environment of Burgess's novel, and he drew a truly splendid performance from Malcolm McDowell as Alex.

Malcolm McDowell, James Marcus, Warren Clarke, Michael Tarn

Clint Eastwood

DIRTY HARRY

A Warner Bros. Presentation of a Malpaso Company Film; Produced and directed by Don Siegel; Executive producer: Robert Daley; Screenplay by Harry Julian Fink, R. M. Fink, and Dean Riesner; Photography by Bruce Surtees; Associate producer: Carl Pingitore; Assistant director: Robert Rubin; Art direction by Dale Hennesy; Music by Lalo Schifrin; Set decorations by Robert De Vestel; Sound by William Randall; Makeup by Gordon Bau; Assistant to the producer: George Fargo; Filmed in Panavision and Technicolor; Running time: 101 minutes

CAST:
Harry Callahan (CLINT EASTWOOD), *Chico* (Reni Santoni), *The mayor* (John Vernon), *Scorpio* (Andy Robinson), *Bressler* (Harry Guardino), *The chief* (John Larch), *DiGeorgio* (John Mitchum), *Norma* (Lyn Edgington), *Mrs. Russell* (Mae Mercer), *Bus driver* (Ruth Kobart), *Mr. Jaffe* (Woodrow Parfrey), *Bannerman* (William Paterson), *Sgt. Reineke* (Craig G. Kelly), *Girl swimmer* (Diana Davidson), *Liquor proprietor* (James Nolan), *Bank robber* (Albert Popwell)

San Francisco is plagued by a series of brutal murders committed by Scorpio (Andy Robinson), a psychotic sniper. In a letter addressed to the mayor, Scorpio threatens to continue killing unless the city pays him $100,000. Going along with Scorpio's demand that a lone police officer deliver the money, the mayor (John Vernon) chooses Homicide Inspector Harry Callahan (Clint Eastwood) for the job.

Nicknamed "Dirty Harry" because he always draws the "dirtiest" assignments, Harry is tough and

47

Clint Eastwood

Clint Eastwood

Andy Robinson

Harry Guardino, Reni Santoni, Clint Eastwood

uncompromising with criminals, and he has a particular hatred of killers. Prepared for any situation which may arise on the streets, Harry carries a .44 Magnum revolver, the most powerful handgun in the world. Although he'd much rather confront Scorpio at gunpoint, Harry goes along with the plan to give the killer $100,000 in marked bills. Stuffing the money into a small travel bag, Harry receives telephoned instructions from Scorpio, who intends "bouncing" Harry all over town to make sure he's alone. The masked killer eventually confronts Harry at the Mount Davidson monument, where he instructs Harry to throw away his weapon. After being kicked repeatedly about the head and torso by the laughing killer, Harry produces a long stiletto and stabs Scorpio in the leg. The killer limps off into the darkness and Harry returns to headquarters after retrieving the money.

The next day, Harry checks local emergency hospitals for word of anyone being admitted the previous night with a leg wound. Luckily, Harry learns that such a man was treated and claimed to be the groundskeeper at Kezar Stadium. That night, Harry visits Kezar and suddenly encounters Scorpio in a darkened hallway. In an effort to escape, Scorpio hobbles onto the playing field, but Harry fells

Reni Santoni, Clint Eastwood

Clint Eastwood

him with one quick shot to the leg. Harry then arrests the killer, but the case never makes it to trial due to lack of evidence, and Scorpio is released.

Angered, Harry begins tailing Scorpio on his own time. Later, the killer steals a gun and hijacks a school bus. Hearing of this, Harry follows the bus to Marin County, jumping on board at the first opportunity. This unnerves Scorpio, and he grabs the wheel away from the driver (Ruth Kobart) and runs the bus off the road.

Leaving the bus, Scorpio runs to an old gravel quarry with Harry in hot pursuit, and during the chase they exchange gunfire several times. Scorpio grabs a helpless youngster and, holding his gun to the boy's head, orders Harry to drop his piece. A superb marksman, however, Harry gets off a quick shot to the killer's shoulder, allowing the child to get away. Wounded, Scorpio attempts to retrieve his gun, but Harry draws a bead on him and warns, "I know what you're thinkin'. 'Did he fire six shots or only five?' Well, to tell the truth, I kinda' forgot myself in all this *excitement*. But bein' this is a .44 Magnum, the most powerful handgun in the world, and will blow your head *clean* off, there's only one question you should ask yourself. . . 'Do I feel lucky?' Well, do ya, punk?'' Laughing wildly, Scorpio makes a play for his gun but Harry shoots him dead.

Dirty Harry is one of Clint Eastwood's best all-around films, and is perhaps the actor's most famous and well-remembered vehicle to date. The film was released by Warner Bros. in 1971 and became an instant success with audiences, though critics, for the most part, objected to the picture's graphic violence. *Dirty Harry* reigned as Eastwood's highest-grossing

49

film until the release of its sequel *Magnum Force* (1973), which did even bigger business.

The story property, written by Harry Julian Fink and R. M. Fink, was originally owned by Universal, who sold it to Warners for a substantial sum. Interestingly, when Warners first decided to film the property, they assigned its direction to Irvin Kershner and the title role to Frank Sinatra, but this idea fell through when Sinatra bowed out at the last minute due to discomfort following hand surgery. Still interested in producing the vehicle, Warners subsequently gave the project to Don Siegel and Clint Eastwood who, with films like *Coogan's Bluff* (1968), *Two Mules for Sister Sara* (1970), and *The Beguiled* (1971) to their credit, were fast becoming one of the most successful star-director combinations in Hollywood.

Besides being good friends in private life, Eastwood and Siegel work splendidly together, and their many collaborations are exceedingly stylish and entertaining films. Eastwood is one of the seventies' few "traditional" screen stars, and Siegel is a veteran craftsman with close to forty years of filmmaking to his credit. Though his films of the forties, fifties, and early sixties established him as a slick and skilled director of action dramas, Siegel's talents were never used as effectively as in his collaborations with Eastwood. Despite mixed reviews, *Coogan's Bluff, Two Mules for Sister Sara,* and *The Beguiled* are superbly made, and each contains an especially strong performance by Eastwood who, with Siegel's help, was rapidly broadening his range as an actor.

In *Dirty Harry,* the two found their most rewarding vehicle—it was the story of an honest rogue cop in San Francisco, a complex, brooding, cynical, yet heroic idealist at constant odds with his inept superiors over his maverick approach to crime fighting. Here was a character Eastwood could play to the hilt, and the story contained many grim encounters between Harry and the insane murderer he was pursuing, which would be a field day for Siegel.

Containing the ideal Eastwood balance between heroism and menace, Harry Callahan could, when the situation called for it, be just as vicious, taunting, and sadistic as the deadly criminals he was opposing, and to make this point more emphatic, Harry's duty sidearm was the awesomely powerful .44 Magnum, a weapon capable, in Harry's own words, of blowing the head of a wrongdoer "clean off." The gun itself, photographed from strategic angles by Bruce Surtees to emphasize its great size, became as important to the story as Harry, and, in several famous scenes, the appearance of the huge gun actually deters a shootout.

Eastwood's controlled performance and Siegel's knowing direction made *Dirty Harry* their most satisfying and profitable film. However, the film's effectiveness was also enhanced by the virtuoso acting of Andy Robinson in the role of Scorpio, the psychotic killer who terrorizes San Francisco until Harry intervenes.

Clint Eastwood

1972

PLAY IT AGAIN, SAM

A Paramount Picture; Directed by Herbert Ross; Produced by Arthur P. Jacobs; Executive producer: Charles Joffe; Screenplay by Woody Allen; Based on his play; Associate producer: Frank Capra, Jr.; Photography by Owen Roizman; Assistant director: William Gerrity; Production designed by Ed Wittstein; Costumes by Anna Hill Johnstone; Music by Billy Goldenberg; Additional music composed and performed by Oscar Peterson; An APJAC Picture; Filmed in Technicolor; Running time: 87 minutes

CAST:
Allan (WOODY ALLEN), *Linda* (Diane KEATON), *Dick* (Tony ROBERTS), *Bogart* (Jerry LACY), *Nancy* (Susan ANSPACH), *Sharon* (Jennifer Salt), *Julie* (Joy Bang), *Jennifer* (Viva), *Dream Sharon* (Mari Fletcher), *Girl in museum* (Diana Davila), *Girl in disco* (Suzanne Zenor), *Tough* (Michael Greene), *Tough* (Ted Markland)

San Francisco. Allan Felix (Woody Allen), a neurotic film journalist whose column appears monthly in a high-brow movie magazine, becomes depressed

Woody Allen

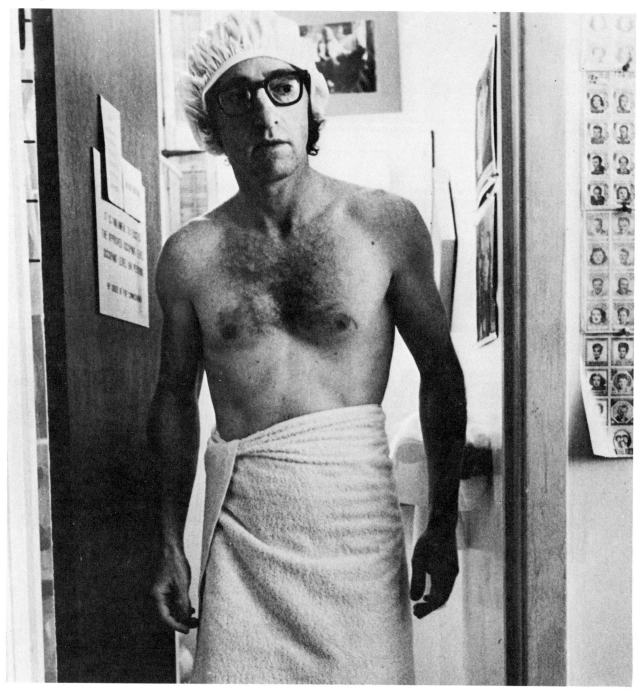

52

Diane Keaton, Woody Allen

The show business careers of Woody Allen have been many, and he has made his mark in virtually every medium of the industry. He has been a successful comedy writer, television writer, stand-up comic, screenwriter, social satirist, film actor, composer, and playwright, and he has lately established himself, with films such as *Annie Hall* (1977), as a major force in American moviemaking.

His first brush with cinema occurred in 1965, when he wrote the screenplay for and played a major supporting role in *What's New, Pussycat?*, a slick but uneven comedy featuring a hilarious performance by Peter Sellers in the role of a wacky psychiatrist. Allen followed this with the uproariously funny *What's Up, Tiger Lily?* (1966), a lavish Japanese spy film completely re-dubbed by Allen to great comedic effect. In 1969, Allen directed his first full-length feature, *Take the Money and Run*, and then wrote

Woody Allen

when his wife Nancy (Susan Anspach) takes a powder with another man. A true film fanatic, Allan finds watching "classic" movies a kind of catharsis, and whenever he's feeling low he goes to see *Casablanca*, his all-time favorite.

After seeing the picture for the umpteenth time, he is visited by his faithful friends Dick (Tony Roberts) and Linda (Diane Keaton) Christie who, in an effort to lift Allan's spirits, arrange several blind dates for him. All turn out disastrous, however, and Allan concludes he's hopelessly inept with women. In Allan's imagination, the spectre of his idol, Humphrey Bogart (Jerry Lacy), often visits him, offering helpful advice ("I never met a dame who didn't understand a slap in the mouth or a slug from a .45.")

Meanwhile, Linda drops in on Allan while Dick is away on business, and, goaded by Bogie, Allan makes a pass at her. To Allan's astonishment, Linda confesses that she's been secretly in love with him for some time. The two begin an ongoing affair, but Allan is disturbed when Dick later tells him he suspects Linda of infidelity and intends to beat the homewrecker's brains out.

Finding out that Dick is suddenly being transferred to Cleveland, Linda calls Allan and, in tears, tells him she can't decide what to do and wants him to make the decision for her. Realizing he can't betray his best friend, Allan rushes to the airport and, in a re-creation of his favorite scene from *Casablanca*, tells Linda that she must "get on that plane with Dick." Following Linda's tearful departure, Allan is confronted by Bogie, who naturally approves of his gallant gesture.

and starred in the stage comedy, *Play It Again, Sam.*

The play, which featured Allen as a neurotic film journalist with an active fantasy life, had its Broadway opening on February 12, 1969, and enjoyed a healthy run of 453 performances. This excellent screen adaptation, for which Allen recruited Diane Keaton, Tony Roberts, and Jerry Lacy to re-create their stage roles, appeared in 1972 and was an instant smash.

Interestingly, *Play It Again, Sam* emerged as a decidedly more restrained film than either of Allen's previous screen comedies, *Take the Money and Run* (1969) and *Bananas* (1971), both of which were noted for rather outrageous humor. *Play It Again, Sam* also ranks as one of the unique items in Allen's career because it is one of the few films he did not direct. The vehicle was entrusted to Herbert Ross, a fine craftsman more than equal to the task, who took full advantage of the beautiful San Francisco locations to enhance the romantic aura of the story. Allen's portrayal of the troubled film buff was a splendidly comic tour de force, and *Play It Again, Sam* marked the beginning of his long association with Diane Keaton, his number one leading lady throughout the decade.

With its many references to *Casablanca* and Jerry Lacy's flawless impersonation of Humphrey Bogart, *Play It Again, Sam* is one of the seventies' most delightful exercises in nostalgia, and its tongue-in-cheek re-creation of *Casablanca*'s climax is one of the cleverest scenes in a Woody Allen picture. Incidentally, after his appearance in the stage and screen versions of *Play It Again, Sam,* Jerry Lacy played the Bogart character on a number of television commercials.

Jerry Lacy

Diane Keaton, Woody Allen

Ernest Borgnine, Stella Stevens, Gene Hackman

THE POSEIDON ADVENTURE

A 20th Century-Fox Picture; Directed by Ronald Neame; Produced by Irwin Allen; Screenplay by Stirling Silliphant and Wendell Mayes; Based on the novel by Paul Gallico; Photography by Harold E. Stine; Production designer: William Creber; Film editor: Harold F. Kress; Set decorations: Raphael Bretton; Special photographic effects: L. B. Abbott; Sound by Theodore Soderberg and Herman Lewis; Makeup by Ed Butterworth, Del Acevedo, and Allan Snyder; Costumes by Paul Zastupnevich; Assistant directors: Norman Cook, Les Warner, and Don White; Associate producer: Sidney Marshall; Production manager: Hal Herman; Music by John Williams; Filmed in DeLuxe Color; Running time: 117 minutes

CAST:
Reverend Frank Scott (GENE HACKMAN), *Mike Rogo* (ERNEST BORGNINE), *James Martin* (RED BUTTONS), *Belle Rosen* (SHELLEY WINTERS), *Linda Rogo* (STELLA STEVENS), *Nonnie Parry* (CAROL LYNLEY), *Manny Rosen* (JACK ALBERTSON), *Acres* (RODDY McDOWALL), *The captain* (LESLIE NIELSEN), *The chaplain* (ARTHUR O'CONNELL), *Susan Shelby* (Pamela Sue Martin), *Robin* (Eric Shea), *Doctor* (Jan Arvan), *Purser* (Byron Webster), *Linarcos* (Fred Sadoff), *Nurse* (Sheila Mathews), *M.C.* (Bob Hastings), *Chief engineer* (John Crawford)

On New Year's Eve, the *S.S. Poseidon*, a luxury liner, is capsized by a ninety-foot tidal wave. As the huge ship floats upside down in the water, the surviving passengers band together to escape. They include Reverend Frank Scott (Gene Hackman), a chaplain who believes that action is more important than prayer; Mike and Linda Rogo (Ernest Borgnine and Stella Stevens), a gruff cop and his beautiful ex-prostitute wife; Belle and Manny Rosen (Shelley Winters and Jack Albertson), an older Jewish couple; Susan and Robin Shelby (Pamela Sue Martin and Eric Shea), a teenaged girl and her younger brother; James Martin (Red Buttons), a mild-mannered health enthusiast; Nonnie Parry (Carol Lynley), a young singer whose brother was killed

Stella Stevens, Ernest Borgnine, Jack Albertson, Shelley Winters, Red Buttons, Eric Shea, Carol Lynley, Pamela Sue Martin

when the ship overturned; and Acres (Roddy McDowall), a steward.

Realizing the only escape route is upwards toward the hull, Scott leads the group on a long and treacherous journey through the destroyed vessel. Although Scott, Mrs. Rosen, and Linda Rogo lose their lives along the way, the rest are eventually rescued.

Producer Irwin Allen has long been one of the great purveyors of adventure-fantasy in both film and television. His films include *The Animal World* (1956), *The Story of Mankind* (1957), *The Big Circus* (1959), *The Lost World* (1961), *Voyage to the Bot-*

Gene Hackman, Ernest Borgnine

tom of the Sea (1962), and *Five Weeks in a Balloon* (1963); and he was responsible for such successful television series as *Voyage to the Bottom of the Sea, Lost in Space, The Time Tunnel,* and *Land of the Giants.*

In the early seventies, Allen bought the film rights to a novel called *The Poseidon Adventure* for $100,000. The book, written by Paul Gallico, dealt with the capsizing of a luxury liner and the efforts of the surviving passengers to escape. It was a good, solid adventure story, and Allen believed that if properly filmed it could be a sure-fire winner at the box office.

Initially, however, Allen had trouble finding a studio willing to back the venture, as bringing the epic saga to the screen might prove rather expensive. Allen realized the budget would have to be a minimum of $5,000,000, and when 20th Century-Fox eventually agreed to invest $2,500,000 in the project, Allen secured the rest of the money elsewhere.

Interestingly, author Gallico got the idea for *The Poseidon Adventure* in 1937—he had been a passenger on the *Queen Mary* during a rough storm that nearly capsized the ship. Enormously successful, the film grossed over twenty times its budget, and started a cycle of "disaster" movies—the only film genre truly "born" in the seventies.

THE GODFATHER

A Paramount Picture; Directed by Francis Ford Coppola; Produced by Albert S. Ruddy; Associate producer: Gary Frederickson; Photography by Gordon Willis; Film editors: William Reynolds and Peter Zinner; Art direction by Warren Clymer; Screenplay by Mario Puzo and Francis Ford Coppola; Based on the novel by Mario Puzo; Musical score by Nino Rota; Makeup by Dick Smith; Filmed in Technicolor; Running time: 176 minutes

CAST:
Don Vito Corleone (MARLON BRANDO), *Michael Corleone* (AL PACINO), *Sonny Corleone* (JAMES CAAN), *Tom Hagen* (ROBERT DUVALL), *Kay Adams* (Diane Keaton), *Barzini* (Richard Conte), *Jack Woltz* (John Marley), *McCluskey* (Sterling Hayden), *Connie Rizzi* (Talia Shire), *Carlo Rizzi* (Gianni Russo), *Johnny Fontane* (Al Martino), *Fredo Corleone* (John Cazale), *Mama Corleone* (Morgana King), *Bonasera* (Salvatore Corsitto), *Apollonia* (Simonetta Stefanelli), *Phillip Tattaglia* (Victor Rendina), *Clemenza* (Richard Castellano), *Tessio* (Abe Vigoda), *Cuneo* (Rudy Bond), *Luca Brasi* (Lenny Montana), *Paulie Gatto* (John Martino), *Sollozzo* (Al Lettieri), *Sandra Corleone* (Julie Gregg), *Nazorine* (Vito Scotti)

1945. At his New York estate, aging Mafia chieftain Vito Corleone (Marlon Brando) celebrates the marriage of his daughter Connie (Talia Shire) to a young bookmaker, Carlo Rizzi (Gianni Russo). Also in attendance are Corleone's sons Michael (Al Pacino), Sonny (James Caan), and Fredo (John Cazale), as well as his right-hand man and legal advisor, Tom Hagen (Robert Duvall).

Michael has just returned from the war a celebrated hero, and the elder Corleone has great hopes for him in the world of legitimate business. Sonny, older than Michael by several years and a violent, hot-tempered young man, is his father's second-in-command and will become the new "godfather" of the Mafia when Don Vito passes away.

Sometime after the wedding reception, the Corleones hold a conference with their archrivals the Tattaglias, another powerful Mafia family. During the meeting, the Tattaglias encourage Don Vito to join them in a new business venture—the sale of narcotics in America—but the Don, a highly moral man despite his criminal connections, refuses to become

Al Pacino, Marlon Brando, James Caan, John Cazale

part of such a vile undertaking. Because of his opposition to the Tattaglia drug scheme, Don Vito is later shot by a pair of phantom gunmen, but manages to survive the incident.

Soon afterward, Michael learns the assassination attempt was the work of the Tattaglia hit man Sollozzo (Al Lettieri) and Captain McCluskey (Sterling Hayden), a corrupt cop anxious to profit from the Sollozzo and McCluskey at point-blank range in a small neighborhood restaurant.

To protect Michael from any reprisal, Clemenza sends him to Italy, where he meets and marries the beautiful Apollonia (Simonetta Stefanelli). The marriage is rather short-lived, however, and she is tragically killed when a bomb planted in Michael's car by one of his own men explodes.

Robert Duvall, Tere Livrano, John Cazale, Gianni Russo, Talia Shire, Morgana King, James Caan, Julia Gregg

narcotics trade. Michael tells his father's lieutenant, Clemenza (Richard Castellano), that he is willing to kill both men in cold blood, despite his father's wish that he stay out of mob affairs. Although Clemenza protests, Michael soon persuades him to go along, and in a daring act of vengeance Michael shoots

Michael returns to New York, where he attends a "peace conference" between the recovered Don and the rival Mafia families. After supposedly striking a "truce" with the other family heads, the Don returns home, but the pact is later betrayed when Sonny is shot to death by rival gangs. Not long afterward,

Robert Duvall, Marlon Brando

Al Pacino

Richard Conte, Marlon Brando

Don Vito suffers a fatal heart attack while playing with his grandson, leaving Michael to assume the leadership of his criminal empire.

Few films of the seventies had the impact of Francis Ford Coppola's *The Godfather*. Within weeks of its release, the rather modestly budgeted ($6 million) film became a record-breaking "blockbuster," and by the end of 1972 it had grossed over $100 million—making it the decade's most profitable film to that time.

The film, which Paramount had been reluctant to make due to the failure of an earlier Mafia picture, *The Brotherhood*, did much to advance the careers of those who worked on it, and it made front-ranking stars of Al Pacino, James Caan, Robert Duvall, Diane Keaton, and Talia Shire. In addition, *The Godfather* revived the flagging screen career of Marlon Brando, who won and refused the year's Best Actor Oscar.

Brando's brilliant portrait of Vito Corleone made him, once again, one of the hottest actors in the industry—a position he had not enjoyed since the early sixties. This was a wonderful piece of acting—every gesture, movement, vocal inflection, and expression perfectly conveying the essence of the aging Mafia patriarch. It was one of the most challenging roles of Brando's career as, at 47, he was required to play a man in his late sixties. For the role, Brando affected a raspy character voice (that has since become a favorite of impersonators), and was physically transformed into Don Vito by Dick Smith, one of Hollywood's most accomplished makeup artists. Though his credits include such makeups as Linda Blair's for *The Exorcist*, Hal Holbrook's for *Mark Twain Tonight*, and Dustin Hoffman's for *Little Big Man*, Smith's subtle work on Brando for *The Godfather* is one of his finest achievements.

Though it is now difficult to imagine anyone else in the part, Brando had to fight for the coveted role. He had always been the favorite choice of the picture's producer, Al Ruddy, and its director, Francis Coppola, but Paramount was initially dead set against casting him. The studio felt that his days as a box-office draw were over, and they knew full well that the actor had the reputation of being a difficult man to work with. Paramount preferred Laurence Olivier, who was closer to the character's actual age, but he refused the part for reasons of ill health.

Determined to get Brando for the role, Coppola and Ruddy came up with a unique idea. They first sent the actor a copy of Mario Puzo's book, which by this time had become a best-seller. Brando read it in three days and informed Ruddy and Coppola that he wanted the part badly. Ruddy then went to the actor's home in the Hollywood hills, where he videotaped a screen test of Brando affecting the voice

59

and mannerisms of the Don. The result was so impressive that Paramount immediately agreed on Brando after seeing the test.

A superb piece of screen entertainment, *The Godfather* established its director Francis Ford Coppola as a major cinematic talent, and because the young filmmaker had a generous "piece of the action," his returns from the film enabled him to become one of the biggest powers in the movie business.

Al Pacino, Robert Duvall

Marlon Brando

Laurence Olivier

SLEUTH

A Palomar Picture released by 20th Century-Fox; Directed by Joseph L. Mankiewicz; Produced by Morton Gottlieb; Screenplay by Anthony Shaffer; Based on his play; Photography by Oswald Morris; Production designer: Ken Adam; Art direction by Peter Lamont; Sound by John Mitchell; Costumes by John Furniss; Executive producer: Edgar J. Scherick; Film editor: Richard Marden; Makeup by Tom Smith; Music by John Addison; Set decorations by John Jarvis; Filmed in DeLuxe Color; Running time: 139 minutes

CAST:
Andrew Wyke (LAURENCE OLIVIER), *Milo Tindle* (MICHAEL CAINE), *Inspector Doppler* (Alec Cawthorne), *Marguerite* (Margo Channing), *Detective Tarrant* (John Matthews), *Constable Higgs* (Teddy Martin)

Andrew Wyke (Laurence Olivier) is a celebrated, wealthy mystery writer obsessed with game-playing. His books—all recounting the adventures of a brilliant, fictional detective, St. John Lord Merridew—have been greatly successful. However, Wyke is disturbed by his wife Marguerite's affair with Milo Tindle (Michael Caine), a suave hairdresser.

Inviting Tindle for cocktails, Wyke tells him he knows of the affair, and actually relishes the idea of divorcing Marguerite so Tindle can marry her. To Tindle's further astonishment, Wyke invites him to take part in an ingenious scheme that will benefit both of them financially. Acting the part of a cat burglar, Tindle will enter the house, steal Marguerite's jewels, and sell them to a "fence" while Wyke collects the insurance money. Intrigued, Tindle decides to go along, and like overgrown children he and Wyke prepare the elaborate "heist."

First, they vandalize several rooms to give the house a ransacked appearance, then they retire downstairs to select Tindle's "disguise."

Laurence Olivier

Michael Caine

Insisting Tindle wear an awkward and grotesque "Joey the Clown" costume, Wyke instructs him to enter the house through an upstairs window. Doing this, Tindle tiptoes to the wall safe and extracts the jewels after blowing it open. What he doesn't know is Wyke staged the whole thing to provide himself an excuse for killing Tindle, who'd appear nothing more than a thief caught in the act. Producing a loaded gun, Wyke says he's now going to shoot Tindle for stealing Marguerite, and terrified, Tindle pleads for mercy. Refusing to be moved, Wyke fires point-blank at Tindle's head.

Sometime later, Wyke is visited by Inspector Doppler, who is investigating Tindle's disappearance. Shocked to learn he's the prime suspect in Tindle's "murder," Wyke nervously confesses he played a cruel joke on Tindle by firing a blank cartridge at him, but assures Doppler Tindle simply fainted after the shot, then regained consciousness and went

Michael Caine, Laurence Olivier

home. However, the Inspector unearths several incriminating clues on the premises—such as dried blood on the staircase where Tindle fell and Tindle's clothes hidden in Wyke's bedroom.

Satisfied with the evidence, Doppler arrests Wyke, who gets hysterical. Tearfully assuring the inspector it was "only a game," Wyke is dumbfounded as Doppler peels off heavy layers of makeup, revealing himself to be Tindle in disguise. Amazed by the younger man's game-playing skill, Wyke suggests they now play a "real" game, at which point Tindle reveals he killed Wyke's mistress a few hours earlier, and has planted clues around the house pointing the finger at Wyke. Tindle tells him he has fifteen minutes before the police arrive, and hearing this Wyke frantically searches the house from top to bottom, finally unearthing the clues. When Tindle confesses it was "just another game," Wyke's mind snaps, and the older man loads his gun with real bullets and shoots Tindle in the back. Horrified by the sound of a real police car pulling up in front of the house, Wyke looks helplessly at the dying Tindle, who says, "Tell them it was only a game."

Sleuth, Anthony Shaffer's mind-teasing gem of a play, ranks as one of the few stageworks transferred to the screen with all its original punch completely intact. Following a triumphant premiere in London, the play had its broadway opening on November 12, 1970, and ran a total of 1,222 performances with Anthony Quayle and Keith Baxter in the roles of Wyke and Tindle. Critics and audiences adored this clever, innovative mystery, and it was hailed as one of the most entertaining stage dramas to come along in years. Shortly after the play finished its American run, Joseph L. Mankiewicz directed this splendid film version starring Laurence Olivier and Michael Caine.

Mankiewicz has long been known as a specialist with witty, sophisticated material (*A Letter to Three Wives, All About Eve,* etc.) and he was certainly in his element with *Sleuth.* Interestingly, when the film was first planned, it was announced that Albert Finney would be cast as Milo Tindle, but this never worked out and the part was given to Michael Caine. Like the play, the film listed fictitious names such as "Alec Cawthorne" and "Margot Channing" in the credits to enhance the overall charade and to conceal the fact that the two lead actors played all the parts themselves.

The performances of Olivier and Caine were no less than perfect, and to add to the fun Mankiewicz cleverly incorporated the marvelous set decorations of John Jarvis into a good deal of the action. Most of *Sleuth* takes place in Wyke's sitting room, an atmospheric menagerie of arcade games, amusement park robots, and mechanical dolls—all reflecting Wyke's pronounced taste for the unusual. Whenever there's a crisis or turning point in the story, Mankiewicz photographs the dolls and robots so they appear to "react" to the charades played by Wyke and Tindle. As such, these humanoid gadgets assume a bizarre life of their own over the course of the story—particularly the life-sized carnival robots Jolly Jack Tar (a crusty old sailor who laughs and applauds on command) and a mysterious Hindu (whose expression becomes increasingly grave as Wyke and Tindle's games grow deadlier).

LAST TANGO IN PARIS

A United Artists Release; Directed by Bernardo Bertolucci; Produced by Alberto Grimaldi; Screenplay by Bernardo Bertolucci and Franco Arcalli; Photography by Vittorio Storaro; Set design supervision: Ferdinando Scarfiotti; Set decorations: Phillipe Turlure and Maria Paola Maino; Costumes by Gitt Magrini; Hairstyles by Jole Cecchini; Film editor: Franco Arcalli; Music by Gato Barbieri; Music arranged and conducted by Oliver Nelson; French dialogue adapted by Agnes Varda; Filmed in color on location in France; Running time: 129 minutes

CAST:
Paul (MARLON BRANDO), *Jeanne* (MARIA SCHNEIDER), *Marcel* (Massimo Girotti), *Catherine* (Catherine Allegret), *Tom* (Jean-Pierre Leaud), *Concierge* (Darling Legitimus), *Olympia* (Luce Marquand), *Rosa's mother* (Maria Michi), *Jeanne's mother* (Gitt Magrini)

Paris. Paul (Marlon Brando), a 45-year-old American, agonizes over his life, which has been little more than a series of failed attempts to find himself. His despair has been intensified by the recent suicide of his wife Rosa, and he now seeks to shut himself off from the world.

Hiding away in a vacant apartment, Paul meets Jeanne (Maria Schneider), a pretty Parisienne interested in renting the place. Suddenly consumed by lust, they engage in a brutally passionate sex act, then calmly return to their individual lives afterward. Jeanne meets with her fiance Tom (Jean-Pierre Leaud), a documentary filmmaker who wants to do an impromptu movie about her. Paul has a bitter encounter with his mother-in-law over the way he was treated by Rosa who, at the time of her death, was having an affair with his friend, Marcel (Massimo Girotti).

The next day, Paul and Jeanne again meet at the apartment and strike an unusual pact—they will meet periodically at the place for the sole purpose of lovemaking. Furthermore, they agree to remain anonymous, and Paul tells Jeanne he doesn't even want to know her name. Over the next few days, the two engage in every sexual act imaginable, and on several occasions Paul's torment causes him to abuse the girl. Meanwhile, Paul visits a mortuary to pay final respects to Rosa, who is "lying in state" amid a stunning arrangement of violets. Trying to understand her suicide, Paul curses her for being unfaithful, then sobs when he realizes she's lost to him forever. The experience is emotionally trying, but it relieves Paul's depression and renews his enthusiasm for life.

Marlon Brando

Maria Schneider

Maria Schneider and Marlon Brando

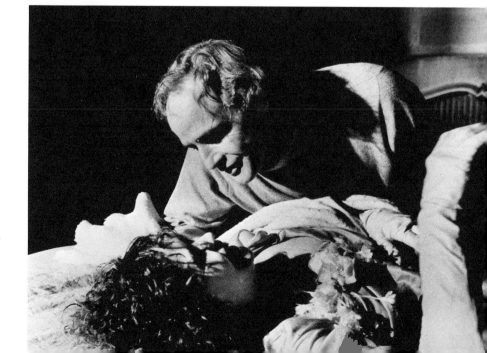

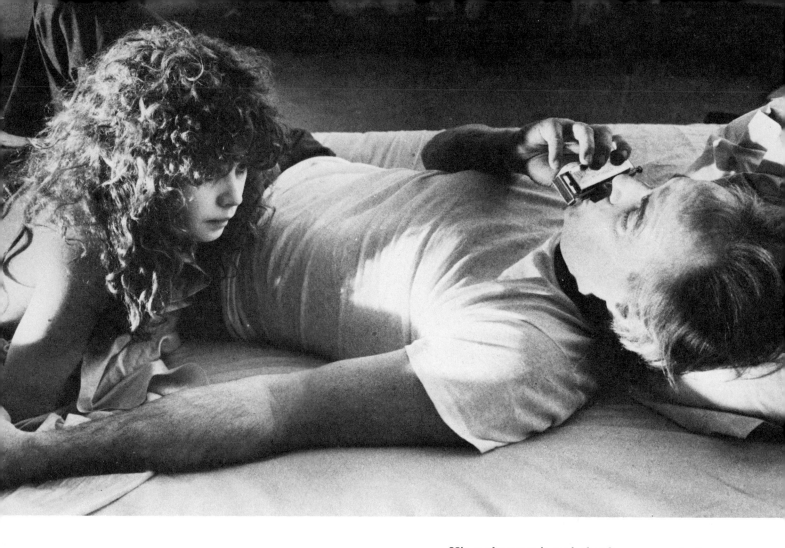

Maria Schneider and Marlon Brando

His exuberance is such that he proposes to Jeanne. She refuses, however, explaining that she and Tom are to be wed the following week. Paul, however, is so forceful and persistent in his declaration of love that Jeanne becomes alarmed. She runs from him, repeating "It's over, it's all over." However, Paul refuses to accept this and follows her home, even though she threatens to call the police. On the verge of panic, Jeanne shoots Paul with her father's pistol, then rehearses what she'll say to the police when they arrive.

Perhaps the decade's most spectacular comeback was that of Marlon Brando. Long regarded as the most complex and gifted of American film actors, Brando's career took a disastrous downward plunge in the late sixties. From 1968 on, virtually all of the actor's vehicles had failed at the box office. *Candy, The Night of the Following Day, Burn!,* and *The Nightcomers* were all fairly interesting movies, but none of them made money, and with four flops in a row to his credit rumor began spreading that Brando had lost his drawing power.

Then, in 1972, Brando once again took the world by storm with his portrayal of Vito Corleone in the hugely successful *The Godfather,* and soon found himself, for the first time in almost a decade, one of the most sought-after stars in the business. Rather typical of Brando, however, he next appeared in a rather experimental, unorthodox film that, by nature of its subject matter, was destined to be controversial. It was *Last Tango in Paris,* written and directed by the brilliant 31-year-old filmmaker Bernardo Bertolucci, who had made quite a name for himself at major film festivals with fascinating, offbeat items such as *The Grim Reaper, Before the Revolution, The Spider's Strategy,* and *The Conformist.*

Last Tango in Paris dealt with the bizarre sexual odyssey of an embittered middle-aged man and a modish young woman. The sexual aspects of the picture were handled in such a raw and candid manner that Brando was actually gambling with his renewed popularity by appearing in it, as the audience's reaction could easily have been negative.

However, when *Last Tango in Paris* made its debut at the 1972 New York Film Festival, it proved a smashing success with audiences and critics alike. The film featured a great deal of obscene language, and the sexual encounters between Paul and Jeanne were certainly the most graphic to have ever appeared in a major motion picture. However, it was all done with such style and taste by Bertolucci and his cast that audiences, for the most part, were enthralled rather than offended. Brando's portrayal of the tortured Paul was hailed as one of his all-time best, and its intensity reminded many critics of Brando's earlier work in films such as *A Streetcar Named Desire* and *On the Waterfront.*

Last Tango in Paris will probably be remembered as the film in which Brando essayed one of his last great performances. His appearances since then have either been tongue-in-cheek romps such as *The Missouri Breaks* or expensive guest shots such as his brief but impressive cameos in *Superman* and *Apocalypse Now.*

DELIVERANCE

A Columbia-Warner Picture; Directed and produced by John Boorman; Screenplay by James Dickey; Based on his novel; Photography by Vilmos Zsigmond; Film editor: Tom Priestly; Assistant directors: Al Jennings and Miles Middough; Art direction: Fred Harpman; Special effects: Marcel Vercoutere; Sound recording: Walter Goss; Creative associate: Rospo Pallenberg; Filmed in Technicolor and Panavision; Running time: 109 minutes

CAST:
Ed (JON VOIGHT), *Lewis* (BURT REYNOLDS),

Bobby (Ned Beatty), *Drew* (Ronny Cox), *Mountain man* (Billy McKinney), *Toothless man* (Herbert "Cowboy" Coward), *Sheriff Bullard* (James Dickey), *Old man* (Ed Ramey), *Lonny* (Billy Redden)

During a weekend holiday, four upper-middle-class businessmen—Ed Gentry (Jon Voight), Lewis Medlock (Burt Reynolds), Bobby Trippe (Ned Beatty), and Drew Ballinger (Ronny Cox)—drive to a small village in the Appalachian mountains. Lewis, a fanatical outdoorsman, has persuaded his friends to join him on a possibly hazardous canoe trip down an uncharted river to Aintry County, located several miles from the village. The inhabitants of the mountain community are filthy, impoverished rustics who warn Ed, Lewis, Bobby, and Drew of the dangers of such a trip, but the four are determined to spend their holiday on the river.

Burt Reynolds, Ned Beatty, Ronny Cox

Lewis and his friends embark on their adventure in two small canoes, and, as they travel farther downriver, they become intoxicated by the thrill of shooting their first rapids. Later, however, Bobby and Ed are separated from Lewis and Drew, and decide to rest in a deserted forest near the river. Suddenly, two sadistic and degenerate mountain men (Billy McKinney and Herbert "Cowboy" Coward) appear and begin harassing them. Holding Ed and Bobby at the point of a shotgun, one of the men ties Ed to a tree before sexually molesting Bobby,

Ned Beatty, Jon Voight, Ronny Cox, Billy McKinney, Burt Reynolds

rocky, jagged shoreline, the men elect Ed the new leader.

Hoping to find someone who will come to their aid, Ed explores the mountainous region high above the shore. There, he sees a mysterious figure lurking in the distance, and, assuming that it is the toothless man coming to seek revenge, Ed shoots him with Lewis's bow and arrow. After disposing of the body, Ed joins Bobby and the injured Lewis on the last mile of the journey. Along the way, they discover Drew's drowned corpse, and, not wanting any evidence linking them with the events of the past few days, they dispose of it as well. They finally reach Aintry, where Lewis is hospitalized.

To cover up the horrible truth, Ed concocts an airtight story which the local sheriff (James Dickey) is unable to dispute. Managing to keep their gruesome odyssey a secret, Ed, Lewis, and Bobby return home

humiliating the overweight businessman by forcing him to "squeal like a pig" during the assault.

Before the mountain man has a chance to attack the helpless Ed, Lewis comes to the rescue by shooting him through the chest with a hunting arrow. The mountain man's toothless companion vanishes, and Ed, Lewis, and Bobby decide it would be best to bury the body without reporting the incident because they realize they wouldn't stand a chance if the case were tried locally. Although Drew insists they report what happened to local authorities, the others override him, and they sink the mountain man's corpse beneath the waters of a future dam site.

More out of necessity than pleasure, they resume their trip downriver and encounter a particularly vicious set of rapids. Both canoes are capsized, Drew disappears underwater without a trace, and Lewis suffers a broken leg. Forced to take refuge on a

Burt Reynolds, Ned Beatty

safely, but the nightmare of their "holiday" haunts them the rest of their lives.

John Boorman's *Deliverance,* released through Columbia and Warners in 1972, is one of the decade's most effective film adaptations of a novel. James Dickey's moody, chilling morality tale of four businessmen who get more than they bargained for during a weekend canoe trip utterly captivated the reading public, and the book became a best-seller shortly after its publication in the early seventies. The film, one of the cinema's "classic" studies in atmosphere, was an almost literal translation of the book, due in part to the fact that the screenplay was

Herbert Coward, Billy McKinney

Ned Beatty, Herbert Coward, Jon Voight, Burt Reynolds

written by Dickey, who also played a major supporting role in the picture with surprising skill.

Jon Voight, Burt Reynolds, Ned Beatty, and Ronny Cox were excellent as the businessmen, and the actors skillfully captured the confusion and horror of four ordinary citizens who were suddenly stripped of all links with the civilized world and plunged into a deadly game of survival. They were given splendid support by Billy McKinney and Herbert Coward as the vile, brutish mountain men who turn their vacation into a nightmare. The characters played by McKinney and Coward are truly terrifying, and the scene in which they accost Jon Voight and Ned Beatty is, perhaps, the most famous in the film. Its effect is enhanced by Coward's menacing voice on the soundtrack, hurling threats in a garbled, barely understandable drawl that doesn't remotely sound like anything human.

Deliverance was shot on location at the Chattooga River in the Appalachians, and in many of the scenes showing Voight, Reynolds, Beatty, and Cox battling the rapids the actors performed their own stuntwork.

James Dickey, Jon Voight

1973

BROTHER SUN, SISTER MOON

A Paramount Picture; Directed by Franco Zeffirelli; Produced by Luciano Perugia; Screenplay by Franco Zeffirelli, Lina Wertmüller, Kenneth Ross, and Suso Cecchi d'Amico; Photography by Ennio Guarniere; Music by Donovan; Art director: Gianni Quaranta; Assistant director: Carlo Cotti; Production designer: Lorenzo Mongiardino; Film editors: John Rushton and Reginald Hills; A Euro-International Production; Filmed in Technicolor; Running time: 121 minutes

CAST:
Francesco (Graham Faulkner), *Clare* (Judi Bowker), *Pope Innocent III* (Alec Guinness), *Bernardo* (Leigh Lawson), *Silvestro* (Michael Feast), *Giocondo* (Nicholas Willatt), *Paolo* (Kenneth Cranham), *Pica* (Valentina Cortese), *Pietro* (Lee Montague), *Deodato* (Francesco Guerrieri), *Consul* (Adolfo Celi), *Bishop* (John Sharp)

Kenneth Cranham, Graham Faulkner

Judi Bowker

Francesco (Graham Faulkner), a young soldier who fought valiantly in the Crusades, returns to his home in Assisi with a high fever. Delirious, Francesco has continual nightmares about the war for several weeks, and his wealthy parents begin fearing for his sanity.

Coming out of his delirium, Francesco becomes strangely "enchanted," and begins spending almost all his time singing to birds and communing with nature. He tells his merchant father to cast away all earthly goods because the real treasures are "not of this world." Seeing the toil of the poor who work in his father's factory, Francesco awakens to life's unfairness, and he gives away many of his father's expensive possessions in protest.

Learning of this, his father beats Francesco within an inch of his life, then takes him to be chastised by the village magistrate. The magistrate scolds Francesco for his "lunatic" behavior, and he orders the boy to apologize to his father. Unable to do so, however, Francesco says he no longer believes in his father's principles, and that "there must be more to life than the loveless toil we fill our days with." Stripping off his clothes, Francesco returns them to his parents and vows to live in poverty from that moment on.

Later, his friends from the Crusades join him in his new life, and they rebuild a broken-down church on the village outskirts, so the poor will have a place to worship. Francesco and his comrades become dedicated monks, travelling the countryside spreading their message of love and goodwill. Having no money, they depend on charity and transient work for survival, and their filthy, unkempt appearance often causes them to be scorned.

In an effort to make themselves more acceptable to the masses, they travel to St. Petersburg, hoping to gain the approval of Pope Innocent III (Alec Guinness). To their surprise, the monks are granted an audience with the Pope, but since His Holiness lives in splendor, Francesco is warned not to preach against material goods. During his audience with the Pope, however, Francesco remains true to himself, explaining his unorthodox philosophy and hoping His Holiness will understand.

Graham Faulkner

Moved by what he hears, the Pope descends from his golden throne to meet the young monk face to face. The old man explains that he, too, was once young and idealistic, but the corrupt ways of politics and the world gradually changed him into the wealthy figurehead he has become. He then wishes Francesco good fortune, and as a gesture of faith stuns the congregation by kneeling down to kiss Francesco's feet.

Few filmmakers can tell a tale of ancient times with the style and flair of Franco Zeffirelli. His superb version of *Romeo and Juliet* (1968) is perhaps the finest screen adaptation of Shakespeare ever attempted, and his celebrated television film *Jesus of Nazareth* was a dazzling six-hour epic, splendid in every respect.

In the early seventies, Zeffirelli began work on a film version of the St. Francis story, which had been attempted only once before in a disastrous sixties film called *Francis of Assisi.* He decided that he would not give his version a heavy-handed religious treatment (which had proven the downfall of the earlier film), but would instead present Francis and his followers as a group of enlightened young people spreading a message of love and goodwill, not unlike the "flower children" of the sixties. By doing so, Zeffirelli hoped to attract a young audience, and, in an effort to further enhance the film's appeal to youth, Zeffirelli gave it the rather catchy title *Brother Sun, Sister Moon* and hired composer Donovan to write a gentle music score, complete with soft guitar and lute strains.

Judi Bowker

70

Graham Faulkner

However, despite its refreshing "youth-oriented" approach, *Brother Sun, Sister Moon* never caught on with audiences, young or old, and the film was a box-office failure. It should be pointed out that it contained exceptional performances by its cast, and was directed by Zeffirelli with the same skill he brought to *Romeo and Juliet* and *Jesus of Nazareth,* but these qualities did little to compensate for the uneven, plodding screenplay and the story's lack of popular appeal.

What makes the picture worthy of discussion, however, is its magnificent physical presentation, which was certainly among the richest the decade had to offer. The sumptuous Technicolor photography of Ennio Guarniere and Zeffirelli's eye for beauty made *Brother Sun, Sister Moon* a breathtaking visual experience.

SERPICO

A Paramount Picture; Directed by Sidney Lumet; Produced by Martin Bregman; Screenplay by Waldo Salt and Norman Wexler; Based on the book by Peter Maas; Production designer: Charles Bailey; Photography by Arthur J. Ornitz; Film editors: Richard Marks and Dede Allen; Assistant director: Burt Harris; Art director: Douglas Higgins; Music by Mikis Theodorakis; A Dino De Laurentiis–Artists Entertainment Complex Production; Filmed in Technicolor; Running time: 130 minutes

CAST:
Frank Serpico (AL PACINO), *Capt. McClain* (Biff McGuire), *Leslie* (Cornelia Sharpe), *Laurie* (Barbara Young), *Chief Green* (John Randolph), *Tom* (Jack Kehoe), *Bob Blair* (Tony Roberts), *Rubello* (Norman Ornellas), *Comm. Delaney* (Charles White), *Lombardo* (Ed Grover), *D.A.* (Allan Rich), *Capt. Tolkin* (Gene Gross), *Berman* (Lewis J. Stadlen), *Gilbert* (John Lehne), *Daley* (George Ede), *Pasquale* (John Medici), *Potts* (Joe Bova), *Mrs. Serpico* (Mildred Clinton), *Mr. Serpico* (Sal Carollo)

Al Pacino

Al Pacino

Tony Roberts, Al Pacino

Honest New York cop Frank Serpico (Al Pacino) is appalled at the corruption within the police department. Refusing to go "on the take" time and time again, he is warned that remaining incorrupt may cost him his life, but despite this Serpico remains true to himself, fighting both crime in the streets and the larcenous activities of his fellow officers.

Unable to keep silent about the shady goings-on any longer, Frank denounces the department in a *New York Times* cover story. Realizing this has probably made him a marked man, Frank buys a 14-shot automatic pistol for protection. In the hope of finding other honest cops who will join his crusade, Frank transfers to the narcotics squad, but during a raid on a sleazy tenement he is shot by an unknown assailant.

Although Frank survives the incident, just who pulled the trigger on him remains a mystery; not knowing whether he was shot by a criminal or a fellow policeman, Frank leaves the country. Despite this, the final victory is Frank's, and his *Times* story leads to an investigation of police corruption by the Knapp Commission.

In 1972, journalist Peter Maas followed his splendid *The Valachi Papers* (1971) with another epic piece of contemporary nonfiction, *Serpico*. It was a superb action biography, detailing the life of New York police officer Frank Serpico who, in the early

Al Pacino, Nathan George (r)

Al Pacino

seventies, risked his life to expose the vast corruption within the city's police department. Like the earlier book, *Serpico* was as exciting to readers as many of the decade's popular fiction novels, and it, too, became an enormous best-seller. The film rights to this powerful portrait of a lone spirit waging a relentless battle against corruption were quickly obtained by Paramount, who proceeded to make a film that was nearly as hard-hitting as the book.

The film, released in 1973, was a realistic, documentary-like drama directed by the veteran Sidney Lumet and starring Al Pacino, now a major star as a result of his work in *The Godfather*. *Serpico* became one of the major hits of 1973, and most critics remarked that Pacino's brilliantly mercurial portrait of Serpico was his finest screenwork to that

time (he would, of course, later top it with his magnificent reprise of Michael Corleone in *The Godfather, Part II* and with his stunning tour de force as the distraught bank robber in *Dog Day Afternoon*).

As an interesting sidelight, Pacino prepared himself for this movie by spending considerable time with the real Frank Serpico prior to filming, and the two actually became good friends. The actor was clearly fascinated with his subject, and this came through in his performance, which earned him his second Oscar nomination. This was one of the actor's longest and most difficult roles, but Pacino was successful in capturing the many different sides of a unique and complex personality. He portrayed Serpico as a dedicated, hard-driving police officer who was also a sensitive, aesthetic man in private life.

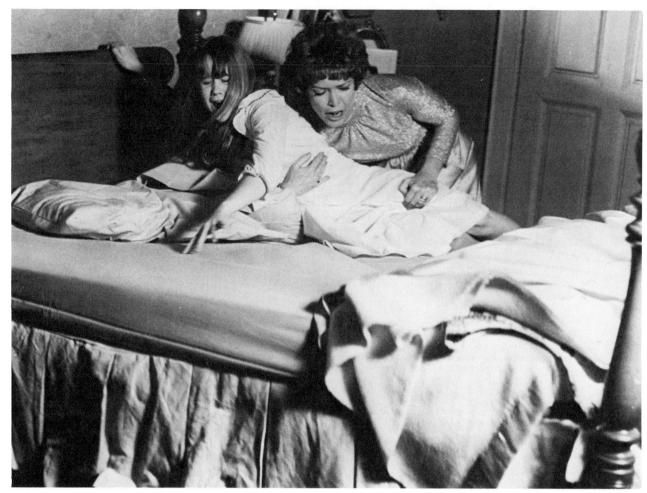

Linda Blair, Ellen Burstyn

THE EXORCIST

A Warner Bros. Picture; Directed by William Friedkin; Executive producer: Noel Marshall; Produced and written by William Peter Blatty; Based on his novel; Photography by Billy Williams and Owen Roizman; Music by Jack Nitzsche; Assistant director: Terrence A. Donnelly; Film editors: Evan Lottman, Norman Gay, Bud Smith, and Jordan Leondopoulos; Production design by Bill Malley; Photographed in Metrocolor; Running time: 121 minutes

William Friedkin, William Peter Blatty

CAST:
Mrs. MacNeil (ELLEN BURSTYN), *Father Merrin* (MAX VON SYDOW), *Father Karras* (JASON MILLER), *Lt. Kinderman* (LEE J. COBB), *Burke* (JACK MacGOWRAN), *Sharon* (KITTY WINN), *Regan* (LINDA BLAIR), *Mother Karras* (Vasiliki Maliaros), *Bishop* (Wallace Rooney), *Karras's uncle* (Titos Vandis), *Father Dyer* (Rev. William O'Malley), *The voice of the demon* (Mercedes McCambridge)

Jason Miller

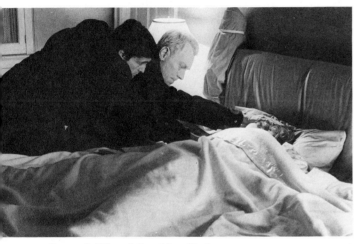

Jason Miller, Max Von Sydow

Rev. William O'Mally, Jason Miller

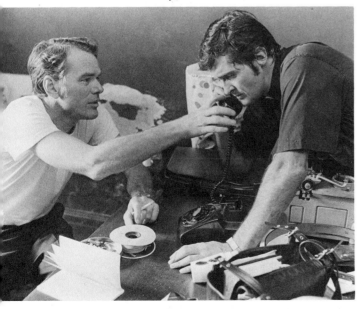

Regan MacNeil (Linda Blair), a normal, healthy twelve-year-old, suddenly falls victim to fits of bizarre behavior. Believing the problem to be medical, her mother (Ellen Burstyn), a celebrated actress, takes Regan to a team of neurologists, and the child is subjected to a series of gruelling tests. After every medical and psychiatric possibility has been exhausted, the doctors inform Mrs. MacNeil that Regan is all right physically and that the only option remaining is religious counsel. Not a very religious person, however, Mrs. MacNeil takes Regan home in the hope that the strange condition will correct itself.

Over the next few weeks, however, it grows worse and worse, and the child not only remains irrational but also becomes violent, actually attacking her mother on several occasions. When, later on, Regan transforms into a haggard, demon-like creature, speaking vile language and masturbating furiously with a crucifix, Mrs. MacNeil consults a young priest, Father Karras (Jason Miller).

Though a respected and well-loved member of the clergy, Karras's private life is in great turmoil. Lately disturbed by his own waning faith, Karras has become so despondent over the sorry state of the world that he has begun shunning its unfortunates, such as his dying mother and a battered street derelict, whose pitiful plea ("Can you help a former altar boy, Father?") sent Karras running away in disgust.

Karras does, however, sympathize with the plight of Mrs. MacNeil, and, going to see Regan, he is horrified by her monstrous appearance. Following his unpleasant encounter with the child, Karras suggests to Mrs. MacNeil that Regan may be the victim of demonic possession, and that it would be wise to summon a priest who specializes in the "exorcism" of unholy spirits. Mrs. MacNeil and Karras find such a man in Father Merrin (Max Von Sydow), an elder clergyman who has performed a number of successful exorcisms over the years.

On a dank and foggy night, Merrin arrives at the MacNeil home, and he and Karras cautiously enter Regan's room. Addressing himself to the "spirit within Regan MacNeil," Merrin asks the demon who it is and what it wants. The reply is more than he bargained for, as Regan unleashes a barrage of foul curses and spits green slime into the old priest's face. Following a terrifying exorcism ceremony, the demon induces a fatal heart attack in Father Merrin.

Angered by this, Karras attacks the demon-child, engaging it in a brutal fight, during which the demonic spirit leaves Regan's body and enters Karras. Retaining his own consciousness long enough to realize what has happened, Karras flings himself through a window, falling down a concrete stairway to his death. The demon exorcised, Regan is restored to sanity.

75

Jason Miller, William Peter Blatty, Ellen Burstyn

William Friedkin's *The Exorcist,* one of the most powerful horror films ever made, is one of the ten highest-grossing motion pictures in history. Upon its release in 1973, this nightmarish tale of a child's possession by an evil demon had an impact on audiences perhaps greater than that of any other seventies film.

Though many horror pictures produced during the seventies dealt in some way with demonic possession or invasion, *The Exorcist* was the most frightening of all, and remains the decade's definitive shocker. It is well known that the grisly spectacle of Regan's possession had an adverse affect on many viewers, who found that they, literally, could not stomach watching it. While reports of fainting and hysteria at the premiere were greatly exaggerated, many people were, indeed, profoundly disturbed by the film, so much so that they actually left the theater before it was over.

Sometime after its release, William Peter Blatty, author of the novel and screenplay, was asked why he thought the film affected people the way it did. Blatty came up with the unique theory that many audience members were, in a sense, confronted by their own subconscious "demons" while witnessing the possession on screen and were thus unable to enjoy the picture.

Asked the same question, Max Von Sydow, who played the title role, offered a slightly different view—that *The Exorcist*'s power to frighten was almost entirely due to the fact that its protagonist, Regan MacNeil, was a happy, attractive child whose gradual transformation into a hideous, psychotic demon was a little more than some people could handle.

The Exorcist grossed over $60 million during its initial run, making it the most successful horror film ever made. Aside from Linda Blair's horrifying makeup (by Dick Smith), the overall terror was intensified by Mercedes McCambridge's superb enactment of the demon's voice. Her tortured, unnaturally deep and amplified moans, coupled with her rasping curses, accounted for a good deal of *The Exorcist*'s effectiveness.

It is curious that such a fine horror movie was eventually the subject of an inept sequel. *Exorcist II: The Heretic* (1977) was a beautifully photographed (by William Fraker) but painfully embarrassing dud, filled with self-conscious performances and ridiculous plot devices, failing to convince in every respect. In this case, the producers would have been wise to leave well enough alone.

THE STING

A Universal Picture; Directed by George Roy Hill; Produced by Tony Bill and Julia and Michael Phillips; Screenplay by David S. Ward; Photography by Robert Surtees; Assistant director: Ray Gosnell; Costumes by Edith Head; Art direction: Henry Bumstead; Music adapted by Marvin Hamlisch; Piano rags by Scott Joplin; Presented by Richard A. Zanuck and David Brown; Filmed in Technicolor; Running time: 129 minutes

CAST:
Henry Gondorff (PAUL NEWMAN), *Johnny Hooker* (ROBERT REDFORD), *Doyle Lonnegan* (ROBERT SHAW), *J. J. Singleton* (Ray Walston), *Lt. William Snyder* (Charles Durning), *Loretta* (Dimitra Arliss), *Crystal* (Sally Kirkland), *Billie* (Eileen Brennan), *Luther Coleman* (Robert Earl Jones), *Kid Twist* (Harold Gould), *FBI Agent Polk* (Dana Elcar), *Erie Kid* (Jack Kehoe), *Eddie Niles* (John Heffernan)

1936. In Joliet, Illinois, aging con man Luther Coleman (Robert Earl Jones) and his young protégé Johnny Hooker (Robert Redford) successfully swindle an unsuspecting patsy out of his bankroll. The haul proves to be so rich that Luther decides to retire, but much to their dismay he and Hooker later learn that the man they swindled is a numbers runner for Doyle Lonnegan (Robert Shaw), a powerful Chicago racketeer, who is now out for their blood.

When Luther is murdered by Lonnegan's hit men, Hooker beats it for Chicago, hoping to hook up with Coleman's old friend Henry Gondorff (Paul Newman), whom Luther regarded as "the greatest con artist of them all." After locating Gondorff in one of the city's more run-down boarding houses, Hooker tells him of Luther's murder, and confides that he wants to engineer a master swindle on Lonnegan to pay him back for killing Coleman.

After thinking it over, Gondorff agrees to help Hooker carry out his plan. Knowing that Lonnegan has a weakness for playing the ponies, Gondorff and

Paul Newman

Charles Dierkop, Robert Redford, Robert Shaw

Paul Newman

Paul Newman

Robert Earl Jones, Robert Redford

Hooker, together with several of Henry's con-artist associates, set up a phony off-track betting joint in an old Chicago storefront. This naturally catches Lonnegan's eye, and he starts visiting the place on a regular basis, placing small bets to get the "feel" of the action. To insure the mobster's delight with their establishment, Gondorff and Hooker arrange for Lonnegan to win every time he places a bet.

Meanwhile, FBI Agent Polk (Dana Elcar) arrives in town looking for Hooker. Catching up with him in his hotel room, Polk offers not to arrest Hooker for the Joliet swindle if Hooker agrees to help him nail Gondorff. Although reluctant to betray Gondorff, Hooker agrees. Later, Hooker befriends Lonnegan, telling the gangster that he's tired of working for Gondorff and that he is going to help Agent Polk nail Gondorff. He tells Lonnegan that the FBI is set to raid Gondorff's place the following week, and that Lonnegan would be wise to try and win all he can before the place is shut down. Hooker tells him to put as much money as possible on a horse called Syphon.

On the day of the scheduled raid, Lonnegan, confident of Hooker's advice, places a cool million in cash on the horse, but just as the phony race gets underway Polk and his men burst into the place, arresting Gondorff, who realizes Hooker has betrayed him. Angered, Gondorff shoots Hooker and Polk blasts Gondorff. Terrified by all the gunplay, Lonnegan races out the door, leaving his million dollars behind. Moments later, Hooker and Gondorff get up, unharmed—the whole thing was an elaborate show, including Gondorff's arrest by Polk (who is not an FBI agent at all, but rather a friend of his). Hooker's revenge is complete, having "stung" Lonnegan out of a million dollars.

Butch Cassidy and the Sundance Kid (1969) was enormously successful, and certainly ranks among the most popular films of the sixties. William Goldman's screenplay, which he sold to 20th Century-Fox for a whopping $400,000, was filled with clever situations and dialogue, and the film featured superb photography, settings, and a winning musical score by Burt Bacharach. The film's overwhelming popularity was, however, primarily due to the teaming of Paul Newman and Robert Redford in the roles of Butch and Sundance. The stars worked splendidly together, and their combined acting skills, charisma, and sex appeal made *Butch Cassidy and the Sundance Kid* virtually irresistible to audiences.

It seemed inevitable that Newman and Redford would get together again, and it finally happened four years later when they were cast in the Richard Zanuck–David Brown production of *The Sting*. For the film, they were reunited with their director from

Butch Cassidy, George Roy Hill, and were once again able to generate the special screen chemistry that had made the earlier picture such a hit.

Produced with all the loving care that a major studio could muster, *The Sting* was Universal's premiere production of 1973. The studio realized that, with Newman and Redford in the leads, they would probably have a huge success on their hands, and spared no expense in giving *The Sting* a truly lavish treatment. Universal's enthusiasm paid off in spades, and *The Sting* became an even greater success than *Butch Cassidy*—eventually winning seven Academy Awards, including Best Picture.

Though the slick, breezy acting of Newman, Redford, and Robert Shaw accounts for most of the film's appeal, it should be pointed out that *The Sting* is also one of the most stylish "period" pieces ever made by Hollywood, and its settings and costumes perfectly capture the look and feel of the thirties. Adding to the overall enjoyment is the fact that *The Sting* permeates with an aura of "good old-fashioned fun"—not unlike that of a Keystone Kops picture—from the free-wheeling spirit of the cast to the ragtime music of Marvin Hamlisch and Scott Joplin.

The film's "nostalgic" flavor was further enhanced by Universal's precedent-breaking use of their classic plexiglass global trademark to herald the opening titles of *The Sting.* The old globe, which was Universal's logo throughout the forties, hadn't been used by the studio in over twenty-five years.

Robert Shaw, Robert Redford, Paul Newman

THE LAST DETAIL

A Columbia Picture; Directed by Hal Ashby; Produced by Gerald Ayres; Screenplay by Robert Towne; Based on the novel by Darryl Ponicsan; Photography by Michael Chapman; Associate producer: Charles Mulvehill; Production designed by Michael Haller; Music by Johnny Mandel; Assistant directors: Gordon Robinson, Wes McAfee, and Al Hopkins; Costumes by Ted Parvin; Film editor: Robert C. Jones; Filmed in Metrocolor; An Acrobat Film; Running time: 104 minutes

CAST:
Buddusky (JACK NICHOLSON), *Mulhall* (Otis Young), *Meadows* (Randy Quaid), *Young prostitute* (Carol Kane); *M.A.A.* (Clifton James); *Kathleen* (Kathleen Miller), *Donna* (Luana Anders), *Marine O.D.* (Michael Moriarty), *Nancy* (Nancy Allen), *Surly bartender* (Don McGovern), *Taxi driver* (Michael Chapman), *Henry* (Gerry Salsberg)

At a southern naval outpost, seamen Buddusky (Jack Nicholson) and Mulhall (Otis Young) are

Jack Nicholson, Otis Young

ordered to transport a young sailor named Meadows (Randy Quaid) to Portsmouth Prison. To their amazement, they are told Meadows has been sentenced to eight years for stealing $40 from a polio collection box, and the reason for the stiff sentence is that the Admiral's wife is a member of the charity.

Since they are given two weeks to carry out the order, Buddusky and Mulhall agree to deliver Meadows as quickly as possible, so they may squeeze in a few days of carousing on the way back. Boarding the train that will take them through Washington and New York to Portsmouth, Buddusky and Mulhall begin feeling sorry for the hapless but likable Meadows, and, realizing he is about to have eight years taken out of his life, they decide to show him one last good time.

Arriving in Washington, the three sailors begin their odyssey with a two-day beer-drinking marathon, during which Buddusky and Mulhall help Meadows shed some of his inhibitions. Sensing that the oversized, gawky youth has been a put-upon "milquetoast" all his life, Buddusky tells him that being a "Baddass" (which is Buddusky's nickname) is the only way to get by in the world. Under Buddusky's tutelage, Meadows becomes a bit more aggressive in his approach to life, and he surprises himself when he actually complains to a waiter about a meal that wasn't cooked to his liking.

In New York City, the sailors search for female companionship, and, settling in a small bar in the Village, Meadows is approached by Donna (Luana Anders), a pretty meditation student who invites him

Jack Nicholson, Randy Quaid

to a party. Meadows assumes it's a pick-up, and, eager for his first sexual experience, he swaggers over to his buddies, telling Buddusky and Mulhall to come along if they want some "action." At Donna's apartment, Buddusky and Mulhall try to make time with her friends, Kathleen (Kathleen Miller) and Nancy (Nancy Allen) but find that the girls want only to engage in mindless small talk. Donna, however, invites Meadows up to her bedroom when he tells her he's on his way to prison. Seating Meadows on the edge of her bed, Donna snuggles up to him, saying she's now going to do something that will be greatly important to him. Nervously anticipating his seduction, Meadows is dumbfounded when Donna says, "I'm going to chant for you. I'm going to chant for your escape." Then she kneels and begins chanting rapidly.

Seeing Meadows has been disappointed by this, Buddusky and Mulhall take him to a whorehouse, where he is introduced to sex by a young prostitute (Carol Kane). Afterward, he tells Buddusky, "I know it was an act for her, but I think she really liked me." Buddusky replies: "She probably did, kid; they have feelin's like everyone else." Satisfied they have allowed Meadows to squeeze a few years of living into two weeks, Buddusky and Mulhall deliver him to Portsmouth.

Five Easy Pieces made a superstar of Jack Nicholson. The actor's superb portrayal of Bobby Dupea captured the attention of audiences and critics alike, and remains one of the best all-around screen performances of the decade. Curiously, however, Nicholson followed this triumph by going behind the camera to co-write and direct a decidedly noncommercial little picture called *Drive, He Said* in 1971. The film, which dealt with the painful affair

Otis Young, Randy Quaid, Jack Nicholson

Otis Young, Randy Quaid, Jack Nicholson

novel *The Last Detail,* a gritty, humorous, and touching story concerning a hard-bitten career sailor who finds it his unpleasant duty to escort a young boot to Portsmouth Prison. Nicholson flipped over the book after reading it, realizing it would make a great film and he was the only actor in Hollywood who could successfully play the central character, Billy "Baddass" Buddusky.

The character had many of the fiercely rebellious yet charming qualities of Bobby Dupea, but he was also a little older and a little wiser. The actor was so inspired by the book that he immediately contacted his friend, writer Robert Towne, about the possibility of working up a screenplay. Interestingly, Nicholson originally wanted to do *The Last Detail* as a vehicle for himself and an actor friend of his, Rupert Crosse, who would co-star as Buddusky's sidekick, Mulhall. Shortly before the actual filming began, however, Crosse became ill and was replaced by Otis Young, who turned in an excellent performance.

The film emerged as one of the year's biggest hits, somewhat overshadowing another fine drama of life among the sailors, *Cinderella Liberty* (1973), which was also based on a Ponicsan novel. *The Last Detail* is a superb blend of comedy, drama, and pathos, and it allows Nicholson, Young, and Randy Quaid to shine as the three principles.

While the film gives Nicholson his share of serious dramatic moments, it also allows him to display his flair for comedy. He is hilarious during the scene in which he vainly tries to talk one of Donna's girlfriends into bed, proudly telling her how the tight

between a college basketball star and a professor's wife, was a critical and financial disaster, and was, perhaps, hampered by the fact that the popular Nicholson chose not to participate in it as an actor. His next starring film, 1971's *Carnal Knowledge,* was successful, but both *A Safe Place* (also 1971) and *The King of Marvin Gardens* (1972) were too esoteric for mass appeal, and neither film featured Nicholson in the kind of colorful, "rebel-hero" role with which audiences had come to identify him. After the disappointing response to *The King of Marvin Gardens,* Nicholson realized that what he needed was another strong vehicle like *Five Easy Pieces*—one that would not only provide him with a juicy role, but also would have good box-office potential.

During his search for such a property, Nicholson read the galleys of Darryl Ponicsan's forthcoming

Otis Young, Jack Nicholson, Randy Quaid

naval uniform calls attention to a certain part of his anatomy. The ensemble playing of Nicholson, Young, and Quaid perfectly captures the spirit of the three sailors who decide to transcend the unpleasantness of the detail by treating it like just another shore leave.

MAGNUM FORCE

A Warner Bros. Presentation of a Malpaso Company Film; Directed by Ted Post; Produced by Robert Daley; Screenplay by John Milius and Michael Cimino; Story by John Milius; Photography by Frank Stanley; Film editor: Ferris Webster; Assistant director: Wes McAfee; Music by Lalo Schifrin; Art direction: Jack Collins; From original material by Harry Julian Fink and R. M. Fink; Filmed in Technicolor; Running time: 124 minutes

CAST:
Harry Callahan (CLINT EASTWOOD), *Lt. Briggs* (Hal Holbrook), *Charlie McCoy* (Mitchell Ryan), *Early Smith* (Felton Perry), *Davis* (David Soul), *Sweet* (Tim Matheson), *Astrachan* (Kip Niven), *Grimes* (Robert Urich), *Carol McCoy* (Christine White), *Sunny* (Adele Yoshioka), *Sidney* (Albert Popwell), *Call girl* (Margaret Avery)

San Francisco. The mysterious shooting murders of several prominent mobsters are investigated by Inspector Harry Callahan (Clint Eastwood). He is ordered off the case, however, by Lt. Briggs (Hal Holbrook), who objects to Harry's methods ("We can't have the public screaming police brutality every time you go on the streets").

The murders continue, victimizing not only the higher-ups of organized crime but also petty criminals, such as a pimp who is shot six times at close range (a medical examiner remarks to Briggs that the killers are "trying to put the courts out of business").

Felton Perry, Clint Eastwood, Hal Holbrook

Robert Urich, Kip Niven, David Soul

Felton Perry

however, McCoy is killed while investigating another "Magnum" slaying, and Briggs tells Harry he suspects racketeer Frank Palanchio, but Harry disagrees ("It's not his style . . . it's too direct"). Briggs, however, orders Harry to arrest Palanchio.

Meanwhile, the SFPD pistol match is held, and the competition for champion narrows to Harry and Davis. Now suspecting Davis and his comrades of the killings, Harry lets him win, then asks to try the

Clint Eastwood, Hal Holbrook

After his reassignment to the case, Harry retreats to the underground firing range at the Hall of Justice for some practice. There he meets officers Davis (David Soul), Sweet (Tim Matheson), Astrachan (Kip Niven), and Grimes (Robert Urich), four rookie bike cops. Observing them on the firing line, Harry is awed by their shooting skill, which is the best he's ever seen. Meanwhile, Harry worries about his friend Charlie McCoy (Mitchell Ryan), an older traffic cop having a nervous breakdown.

The ballistic report on the pimp killing shows he was shot with a .357 Magnum, the same caliber used in the gang slayings. Harry's partner, Early Smith (Felton Perry) jokingly comments: "Maybe it's a cop . . . maybe it's Harry . . . no one hates hoodlums worse than he does." Although meant in fun, Smith's remark sticks in Harry's mind, and he begins suspecting Charlie McCoy of the murders. Later,

young officer's .357 revolver. Harry intentionally fires one of the slugs into a thick fencepost, retrieving it later that night. Running it through ballistics, Harry sees it matches the bullet that killed McCoy. His suspicions confirmed, Harry goes home and is confronted by the four vigilante cops, who explain that they're "simply ridding society of criminals who'd be caught and convicted anyway if the courts worked properly."

Harry refuses to condone their actions, explaining that what they're doing is still murder. Shortly afterward, Harry finds a plastic explosive in his mailbox, and, realizing it was planted by the young "death squad" members, he phones Briggs to tell him about it. An hour later, Briggs arrives and after examining the small bomb invites Harry to drive back to headquarters with him. Suddenly drawing his gun and pointing it at Harry, Briggs orders him to drive out of town.

After Briggs reveals it was he who engineered the vigilante killings, the quick-thinking Harry slams the brakes, causing Briggs to smash his head on the dashboard. Dumping Briggs into the street, Harry

Hal Holbrook, Clint Eastwood

notices the killer cops in the rear-view mirror and realizes they've been following the whole time. Driving to an abandoned pier, Harry confronts them one by one, managing to put each out of commission.

Dirty Harry proved to be Clint Eastwood's highest-grossing motion picture. It was superbly directed by Don Siegel, and featured Eastwood in one of his all-time best performances. Warners and Eastwood realized, after looking at the box-office receipts, that a sequel was definitely in order, and they put writers John Milius (who rewrote the original *Dirty Harry* substantially but was not credited for it) and Michael Cimino to work on a screenplay that would continue the adventures of Harry Callahan.

Taking their theme from a real incident, in which a group of Brazilian police officers took the law into their own hands and began killing criminals in cold blood, Milius and Cimino fashioned a script that pitted Harry against four fellow officers who were, in a sense, practicing an extreme perversion of his own philosophy. The screenplay was, appropriately enough, titled *Magnum Force,* and the film was shot

Clint Eastwood

on location in San Francisco by Ted Post, who had directed Eastwood's earlier hit, *Hang 'Em High,* an ode to the actor's "spaghetti westerns."

Magnum Force emerged as one of the most exciting, action-packed police dramas ever made. It was far more violent than the original had been, and it featured more gunplay than any three of Eastwood's westerns. Many critics disliked the film for this reason, citing that the shooting murders performed by the young vigilante cops (in which the victims are blown apart by close-range hits from .357 Magnums) were a little *too* graphic. What these critics failed to realize, however, is that the cold and brutal nature of the killings did nothing but enhance the dramatic impact of the story, which was certainly

Clint Eastwood

one of the most thought-provoking ever conceived for a film of this type.

Clint Eastwood's portrayal of Harry in *Magnum Force* is excellent, and he is ably supported by Hal Holbrook as his envious superior and Felton Perry as his likable young partner. Also well drawn are the characters of Davis, Sweet, Astrachan, and Grimes—the members of the police "death squad." These roles are acted with great skill, and David Soul, Tim Matheson, Kip Niven, and Robert Urich portray the officers as coldly cerebral young supermen, bound by a fanatical conviction that the law is wrong and they are right. From a physical standpoint, the actors suit the roles ideally, and their boyish, clean-cut looks present a chilling contrast to their deadly shooting skills.

Magnum Force grossed even more than the original *Dirty Harry,* and its success paved the way for 1976's *The Enforcer,* the third film in the series.

France. The honor of King Louis XIII (Jean-Pierre Cassel) is protected by his musketeers, Porthos (Frank Finley), Athos (Oliver Reed), and Aramis (Richard Chamberlain), who are at constant odds with Cardinal Richelieu (Charlton Heston) and Rochefort (Christopher Lee), who seek to seize the king's power by discrediting him.

During a skirmish with Rochefort's men, the musketeers are aided by a young rake named D'Ar-

THE THREE MUSKETEERS

A 20th Century-Fox Picture; Directed by Richard Lester; Produced by Alexander Salkind; Screenplay by George MacDonald Fraser; Based on the novel by Alexander Dumas; Photography by David Watkins; Film editor: John Victor Smith; Music by Michel Legrand; Filmed in Technicolor; Running time: 105 minutes

CAST:
Athos (OLIVER REED), *D'Artagnan* (MICHAEL YORK), *Aramis* (RICHARD CHAMBERLAIN), *Constance* (RAQUEL WELCH), *Rochefort* (CHRISTOPHER LEE), *Queen Anne* (GERALDINE CHAPLIN), *Milady* (FAYE DUNAWAY), *Cardinal Richelieu* (CHARLTON HESTON), *Porthos* (Frank Finlay), *Buckingham* (Simon Ward), *Louis XIII* (Jean-Pierre Cassel)

tagnan (Michael York), whose swordsmanship is equal to their own. Making him an "honorary" musketeer, the crusaders learn that France's Queen Anne (Geraldine Chaplin) is having an affair with Buckingham (Simon Ward) of England, and that Richelieu intends exposing her as an adultress. Through his contacts at the Palace, Richelieu learns the Queen recently gave Buckingham her diamond necklace as a remembrance. Sensing a juicy opportunity, the Cardinal hires Milady (Faye Dunaway), a treacherous adventuress, to journey to England and secure two of the necklace's diamonds as evidence.

Meanwhile, D'Artagnan falls in love with Constance (Raquel Welch), the Queen's trusted friend, who reveals Richelieu's plan. Relaying this to his comrades, D'Artagnan and the musketeers head for England, hoping to intercept Milady.

During their journey, however, they are ambushed by Rochefort's men, and Porthos, Athos, and Aramis "appear" to be killed in the skirmish. Sad-

Faye Dunaway, Charlton Heston

Michael York (right)

dened, D'Artagnan rides to England without them. Meanwhile, Milady uses her wiles to seduce Buckingham and obtain two diamonds from the Queen's necklace. Confident this will prove her Majesty's infidelity, Milady returns to France, presenting the diamonds to Richelieu, who then suggests to the King that the Queen should, in all propriety, wear her necklace to an upcoming ball.

In England, D'Artagnan is granted an audience with Buckingham, who examines the necklace after hearing the story. Finding that two of its diamonds are, indeed, missing, Buckingham visits a master jeweller, instructing him to fashion a duplicate of the necklace. Afterward, Buckingham gives the flawless copy to D'Artagnan, who races back to France.

Arriving on the night of the ball, D'Artagnan is delighted to see Porthos, Athos, and Aramis alive and well and waiting for him at the palace gate. The musketeers present the Queen with the imitation necklace, and, thanking them for saving her reputation, she strides confidently into the ballroom. Richelieu's scheme is stifled, and D'Artagnan is inducted as the fourth musketeer.

With the exception of *Dr. Jekyll and Mr. Hyde*, Alexander Dumas's *The Three Musketeers* is, perhaps, the most oft-filmed "classic" of literature. It is *the* original swashbuckling adventure, and possibly no other "classic" novel has had as many interpretations on the screen. It has been a favorite of filmmakers for over sixty years, and the musketeers have been portrayed by some of Hollywood's most colorful actors—Douglas Fairbanks, Gene Kelly, Van Heflin, Gig Young, Paul Lukas, Don Ameche, the Ritz Brothers, Walter Abel, and Eugene Pallette, to name but a few.

Despite the many screen versions produced over the years, however, this superb Richard Lester film, released in 1973, is by far the best; and it is, perhaps, the *only* one to truly capture the imagination of the public. In spite of some good sequences, the previous *Three Musketeers* films pale in comparison, and are generally unsatisfying for a number of reasons. Either the story was misinterpreted (as in the 1939 Ritz Brothers musical); or the vehicle was used to showcase a particular star (like the Douglas Fairbanks silent version, which seems, in retrospect, merely an excuse to highlight Fairbanks's athletic ability); or the approach was lacklustre (as in the painfully dull 1933 film). The makers of these films failed to realize that *The Three Musketeers* is neither comedy nor drama, but a finely balanced combination of the two, such as *The Adventures of Robin Hood*.

Happily, the Richard Lester film is the precise balance of comedy, romance, and swordplay needed to make the story work. It was a big, impressive production, featuring an all-star cast, sumptuous photography and settings, and a literate, witty screenplay by George MacDonald Fraser. A beautiful picture to watch and hear, it remains immensely popular.

THE DAY OF THE JACKAL

A Universal Picture; Directed by Fred Zinnemann; Produced by John Woolf; Photography by Jean Tournier; Screenplay by Kenneth Ross; From the book by Frederick Forsyth; Coproducers: Julien Derode and David Deutsch; Music by Georges Delerus; Film editor: Ralph Kemplen; Assistant directors: Louis Pitzele and Peter Price; Production designed by Willy Holt and Ernest Archer; Photographed in Technicolor; Running time: 142 minutes

CAST:
"The Jackal" (EDWARD FOX), *The minister* (Alan Badel), *Rolland* (Michel Auclair), *Lebel* (Michel Lonsdale), *Lloyd* (Terence Alexander), *Thomas*

Edward Fox

(Tony Britton), *The President* (Adrien Cayla-Legrand), *The gunsmith* (Cyril Cusack), *Denise* (Olga Georges-Picot), *Pascal* (Jacques François), *Colette* (Delphine Seyrig), *Colonel Rodin* (Eric Porter), *Caron* (Derek Jacobi), *St. Clair* (Barrie Ingham), *Bernard* (Anton Rodgers), *Bastien-Thiry* (Jean Sorel)

France. 1963. Armed members of the O.A.S. (an underground organization plotting the assassination of President Charles de Gaulle) wait by a deserted roadside for the President's limousine to drive past. However, the assassination attempt fails, and all but three of the underground members are captured and executed.

Retreating to their headquarters, the remaining O.A.S. men plan another attempt on De Gaulle's life, only this time they hire one of the world's most skilled assassins to do the job. He is "the Jackal" (Edward Fox), a young Englishman whose track record is so impressive that he commands $500,000 per job. His contacts in the international

Edward Fox, Cyril Cusack

underground are legion, and after reaching an amicable agreement with the O.A.S. he secures a forged French passport, identification card, and driver's license. As an added precaution, he steals the passport of a Swiss schoolteacher, so he'll have additional means of identification should anything happen to his own. Following this, he instructs an "underground" gunsmith (Cyril Cusack) to fashion a portable single-shot rifle capable of chambering explosive ammunition.

Meanwhile, French intelligence interrogates several O.A.S. informants, one of whom admits that a man known as "Jackal" is preparing an attempt on the President's life. The French minister (Alan Badel) instructs Inspector Lebel (Michel Lonsdale) to research all political assassinations of the past five years, in the hope of finding a clue to the Jackal's identity. Later, Lebel learns that a man named Charles Calthrop was responsible for a recent South American assassination, and that the first three letters of the killer's first and last names—*chacal*—is the French translation of *jackal*. A further investiga-

Edward Fox

tion reveals that "Calthrop" and "Jackal" are, indeed, the same man, and that he is planning to kill De Gaulle on French Liberation Day.

Realizing the authorities are onto him, Jackal masquerades as the schoolteacher, and using the stolen passport eludes detection. On Liberation Day, the authorities take great precaution to insure De Gaulle's safety, but the Jackal sneaks into a tall building disguised as a battered war veteran.

However, a policeman informs Lebel that a strange-looking man was seen entering the apartment house across from where De Gaulle is standing. Alarmed, Lebel bolts up the apartment stairs while, in a room on the top floor, the Jackal draws a bead on the President. The killer squeezes off one well-aimed shot, but at the last instant the President leans forward to shake hands with an admirer and the bullet misses. Before the Jackal can reload his weapon, Lebel bursts into the room, spectacularly killing the assassin with a barrage of machine gun fire.

One of the seventies' most popular political thrillers, *The Day of the Jackal* marked veteran director Fred Zinnemann's return to the screen after an absence of seven years, and is a motion picture especially noted for its vivid atmosphere. Following the completion of his Oscar-winning *A Man for All Seasons* (1966), Zinnemann spent several years preparing to make an epic film of André Malraux's *Man's Fate,* but sadly the production never came to fruition.

The Day of the Jackal was based on the best-selling novel by Frederick Forsyth, and most critics agreed that the film deftly re-created the book, and that it managed to keep all the heart-pounding thrills of the novel intact. Because the film dealt at length with political assassination, a particularly topical issue, *The Day of the Jackal* scored heavily at the box office.

Overall, however, the film was not without its flaws. Its plot was almost impossibly complex, plagued by hundreds of loose ends that made no sense until the climax, making it extremely difficult for the audience to follow what was happening on-screen a great deal of the time. Moreover, Zinnemann chose to approach the story in a rather low-key, understated manner, which robbed many scenes of the tension so important to a good suspense drama. Another major drawback is that *The Day of the Jackal* contains little action or excitement before the final reel, and before that seems almost like a long, meticulous documentary examining in minute detail the day-to-day activities of the assassin and his pursuers. The film, as a whole, is much too intricate and slow-moving.

Its strongest points are the excellent performances

Edward Fox

by a sterling international cast, most notably Edward Fox as the ingenious professional killer known as "The Jackal." In a superbly controlled performance, Fox weaves a portrait of a complex, enigmatic man whose crisp, businesslike approach to his deadly trade contrasts sharply with his outward charm and appearance. Also impressive is Cyril Cusack as the gunsmith who limits his clientele to the world's top assassins. In a performance reminiscent of his earlier work as captain of the firemen in Truffaut's *Fahrenheit 451* (1966), Cusack displays a chilling aloofness and calm when he asks the Jackal "Will you be trying for a head shot or a chest shot?" in reference to the assassination.

AMERICAN GRAFFITI

A Universal Picture; Directed by George Lucas; Produced by Francis Ford Coppola; Co-producer: Gary Kurtz; Screenplay by George Lucas, Gloria Katz, and Willard Huyck; Photography by Ron Eveslage and Jan D'Alquen; Film editors: Verna Fields and Mar-

Ronny Howard, Richard Dreyfuss,
Charlie Martin Smith

Candy Clark, Charlie Martin Smith

MacKenzie Phillips, Paul Le Mat

cia Lucas; Art direction: Dennis Clark; Costume designer: Aggie Guerard Rodgers; Set decorations: Douglas Freeman; Sound editing: James Nelson; Visual consultant: Haskell Wexler; Choreographer: Toni Basil; Dialogue coach: Gino Havens; Assistant directors: Ned Kipp and Charles Myers; Filmed in Technicolor; Running time: 110 minutes

CAST:
Curt (Richard Dreyfuss), *Steve* (Ronny Howard), *John Milner* (Paul LeMat), *Terry* (Charlie Martin Smith), *Laurie* (Cindy Williams), *Debbie* (Candy Clark), *Carol* (Mackenzie Phillips), *Disc jockey* (Wolfman Jack), *Joe* (Bo Hopkins), *Bob Falfa* (Harrison Ford), *Carlos* (Manuel Padilla, Jr.), *Ants* (Beau Gentry), *Peg* (Kathleen Quinlan), *Eddie* (Tim Crowley), *Mr. Wolfe* (Terry McGovern), *Blond in T-Bird* (Suzanne Somers), *Falfa's girl* (Debralee Scott), *Wendy* (Debbie Celiz), *Jeff* (Ron Vincent)

A small California town on a warm spring evening in 1962. A group of recent high school graduates gather at the local Mel's Drive-In in preparation for a long night of "cruising." They include Steve Bolander (Ronny Howard), a clean-cut, "all-American" boy who is going off to college the following day; Terry "The Toad" Fields (Charlie Martin Smith), an awkward, bespectacled kid whose greatest dream in life is someday to become a "cool dude"; Curt Henderson (Richard Dreyfuss), the intelligent and artistic "class philosopher" who's uncertain about his life's direction; and Laurie Henderson (Cindy Williams), Curt's sister and Steve's girlfriend, who is saddened by the prospect of Steve's leaving.

Since, instead of going for a "cruise," Steve and Laurie plan to spend their last night together at the high school's "farewell" dance, Terry borrows Bolander's beautiful '58 Impala for the night. While cruising down Main Street some time later, Terry spots a pretty nineteen-year-old named Debbie (Candy Clark), who agrees to go riding with him after he tells her that she's the image of Connie Stevens.

Also cruisin' through the night is Big John Milner (Paul LeMat), an older boy who is a kind of hero to Steve, Curt, and Terry. At 22, John refuses to grow up, and his life still revolves around his yellow '32 Ford Deuce Coupe and its ability to beat anything on wheels. Super-cool and fearless, John has for years been the town's undisputed king of drag racing. During his cruise, John encounters a car full of attractive girls and smoothly asks if one would like to be his date for the evening. Carol (Mackenzie Phillips), the youngest, eagerly volunteers, but when she enters his car John is disappointed to learn that she's only thirteen. Cute and feisty, however, Carol persuades Big John to let her cruise with him for a while.

Paul Le Mat

At the farewell dance, Laurie cries softly in Steve's arms, and, realizing that if he leaves the next day she'll be heartbroken, Steve decides to forsake his plans for college. Giving serious thought to his future, Curt, on the other hand, makes up his mind to attend a university, not wanting to "stay seventeen forever" like John.

Meanwhile, John gives Carol a tour of the local auto junk yard, showing her the wrecked cars of the town's legendary drag racers, who were all victims of fatal accidents. Carol and John then resume their cruise, and a wicked-looking '55 Chevy pulls up next to them, its engine revving ominously. In the car is Bob Falfa (Harrison Ford), a slick, cocky dragster who challenges John to a race. Taking Carol home, John grants Falfa's wish, and the two meet at Paradise Road with everyone converging to watch the race.

Bo Hopkins, Beau Gentry, Richard Dreyfuss

As the two cars speed down the highway, Falfa's takes a slight lead but blows a tire and crashes. Luckily, no one is hurt. Realizing he would have lost the race, a deflated John tells Terry: "He had me, man. He was pullin' away from me just before he crashed."

The following day, Curt departs for college, and we learn what eventually happened to the characters in the story—John Milner was killed by a drunk driver in June 1964. Terry Fields was reported missing in action near An Loc in December 1965. Steve Bolander became an insurance agent in Modesto, California. And Curt Henderson is now a writer living in Canada.

Ronny Howard, Candy Clark, Charlie Martin Smith

American Graffiti is a landmark motion picture. It ranks as the most successful film in history to have a budget of less than a million dollars, and its artistic and financial triumph allowed its director, George Lucas, to make *Star Wars*—the most popular film of all time. It launched more film and television careers than any other single movie, and aside from Lucas *American Graffiti* brought varying degrees of stardom to Richard Dreyfuss, Ronny Howard, Paul LeMat, Charlie Martin Smith, Cindy Williams, Candy Clark, Mackenzie Phillips, Bo Hopkins, Harrison Ford, Kathleen Quinlan, and Suzanne Somers. It was shot in just twenty-nine days in northern California on a budget of $750,000, and on much of the film George Lucas acted as his own director of photography.

American Graffiti's beautifully nostalgic flavor touched the hearts of audiences as few films have, and the universality of its many characters made it easy for audiences to identify with them. The film's flawless depiction of adolescent night life in a small California town is no accident; George Lucas was born and raised in Modesto, California, and has

often said that *American Graffiti* was an homage to his life as a car-obsessed teenager.

However, perhaps the most extraordinary thing about *American Graffiti* is that it became an enormous success despite the fact that its studio, Universal, had absolutely no faith in its commecial potential from the first day of shooting right up to its San Francisco premiere. The studio had been reluctant to back Lucas's project from the beginning. They felt that sophisticated audiences of the seventies would not pay to see a nostalgic combination of rock-and-roll songs and teenage fantasies. In addition, they realized that Lucas had only one commercial film to his credit—the bizarre and fascinating *THX-1138*—which had been a box-office failure despite its quality. Moreover, the studio felt uneasy about the fact that Lucas's cast for *American Graffiti* would be comprised of relatively unknown actors who had no box-office "pull" to speak of.

As a condition to their backing the project, Universal insisted that Lucas secure a "big name" talent to act in some capacity on *American Graffiti,* either on the technical or performing end. To comply with this demand, Lucas brought in his one-time mentor Francis Ford Coppola to act as the film's producer. Due to the phenomenal success of the director's recently released *The Godfather,* Coppola's name now carried considerable weight in the industry, and on the strength of Coppola's involvement Universal agreed to back *American Graffiti* with a rather modest $750,000 budget. Throughout the shooting schedule, however, the studio continued to display an indifferent attitude toward the project. For example, when, during the course of filming, Lucas asked the company for a paltry $10,000 to buy the rights to the many rock-and- roll "classics" he wanted to use as background music, the studio refused. (Ironically, when the film was released and became a sizable hit, Universal happily paid five times as much for the rights to the same songs.)

Upon the film's completion, *American Graffiti* made its bow at a "sneak preview" showing in San Francisco before an audience of about one thousand people. Also in attendance were Lucas, Coppola, and several higher-ups from the studio who had not yet seen the picture. Though the audience went wild over the film, the studio executives were a little less enthusiastic—they seemed distressed by the picture's low lighting and unorthodox style, and they declared that the film was, in its present form, completely unsatisfactory. Coppola, who believed in the film one hundred percent, was angered by this, and he offered to buy the picture from the studio on the spot and release it himself, but the representatives wisely declined. This later proved to be one of the smartest decisions the studio ever made.

1974

Michael York, Jacqueline Bisset

John Gielgud, Richard Widmark

Wendy Hiller, Rachel Roberts (extreme right)

MURDER ON THE ORIENT EXPRESS

A Paramount Picture; Directed by Sidney Lumet; Produced by John Brabourne and Richard Goodwin; Screenplay by Paul Dehn; From the novel by Agatha Christie; Photography by Geoffrey Unsworth; Film editor: Anne V. Coates; Music by Richard Rodney Bennett; Production design and costumes by Tony Walton; Art direction by Jack Stephens; Assistant director: Ted Sturgis; Photographed in Technicolor and Panavision; Running time: 127 minutes

CAST:

Inspector Hercule Poirot (ALBERT FINNEY), *Col. Arbuthnot* (SEAN CONNERY), *Greta Ohlsson* (INGRID BERGMAN), *Beddoes* (JOHN GIELGUD), *Ratchett* (RICHARD WIDMARK), *Princess Dragomiroff* (WENDY HILLER), *Mary Debenham* (VANESSA REDGRAVE), *Count Andrenyi* (MICHAEL YORK), *Countess Andrenyi* (JACQUELINE BISSET), *Hector McQueen* (ANTHONY PERKINS), *Mrs. Hubbard* (LAUREN BACALL), *Bianchi* (Martin Balsam), *Pierre Michel* (Jean-Pierre Cassel), *Hildegarde Schmidt* (Rachel Roberts), *Dr. Constantine* (George Coulouris), *Hardman* (Colin Blakely), *Foscarelli* (Denis Quilley)

The time is 1934. The story takes place aboard the *Orient Express* during a journey from Istanbul to Calais. The passengers making the trip include Hercule Poirot (Albert Finney), a French detective noted for his skill of "deductive reasoning"; Mr. Ratchett (Richard Widmark), a wealthy American businessman suspected of moonlighting in the criminal underworld; Colonel Arbuthnot (Sean Connery), a retired British military commander in the constant company of his mistress and wife-to-be Mary Debenham (Vanessa Redgrave); Ratchett's faithful secretary Hector McQueen (Anthony Perkins), a thin, neurotic man who caters to his employer's every whim; Count Andrenyi (Michael York), a young aristocrat whose only abnormality is the insane jealousy he feels for his beautiful new wife (Jacqueline Bisset); Greta Ohlsson (Ingrid Bergman), a fanatically religious missionary from Sweden; and Mrs. Hubbard (Lauren Bacall), a famous American stage actress traveling incognito.

On the first morning of the journey, Ratchett informs Poirot that, for some reason, he feels an attempt will be made on his life during the trip, and he offers the detective a large sum of money to protect Ratchett from harm. Well aware of Ratchett's shady background, Poirot refuses, explaining that he is a detective, not a bodyguard.

Sometime later, Ratchett is found murdered in his bed, and Poirot's investigation reveals that he was first drugged, then stabbed twelve times in the chest. At first, Poirot surmises that Ratchett was the victim of a Mafia revenge killing, but, not quite satisfied with this conclusion, the detective begins interrogating the passengers. Although they all seem to have airtight alibis, Poirot discovers, much to his astonishment, that the twelve passengers are all somehow related to the family of a child who had been kidnapped and murdered by Ratchett some years earlier.

As the journey draws to a close, Poirot assembles the passengers in the club car, where he unleashes a fantastic theory: the wounds in Ratchett's chest were the result of a ritualistic revenge slaying in which each of the passengers took their turn stabbing him after he'd been drugged by his valet Beddoes (John Gielgud), who, as it turns out, once served as chauffeur for the murdered child's family.

Hearing this, Mr. Bianchi (Martin Balsam), a railroad representative, tells Poirot that his theory is *too* incredible, and if it were ever made public it would not only cause the railroad great scandal, but would also bring disgrace to the passengers, who are all respected citizens. At Bianchi's request, Poirot forsakes his theory, and later reports to the police that Ratchett was, indeed, the victim of underworld vengeance.

Murder on the Orient Express rates a special niche in the history of seventies cinema for several reasons. First of all, it is perhaps the most satisfying screen adaptation of an Agatha Christie novel ever attempted. Second, it featured one of the most impressive casts yet assembled for a seventies motion picture. It also gave the members of its all-star cast uniformly good roles, as virtually all the characters in the story were highly complex and fascinating individuals. In particular, the film provided Albert Finney with one of his greatest screen roles to date, and the handsome, athletic actor was able to submerge himself completely beneath the guise of the small, gnomelike detective, Hercule Poirot. Most important, however, *Murder on the Orient Express* was almost singularly responsible for a seventies revival of the "old-fashioned" mystery movie which, unlike other traditional genres such as the horror film and the western, had up to this point remained sadly neglected by most of the decade's filmmakers.

As everyone is well aware, the "classic whodunit" mystery had been one of the great cinematic staples throughout the thirties and forties, when most of the major studios specialized in producing high-quality mystery pictures for audiences that were hungry for "escapist" entertainment. While the genre petered out to a drastic extent during the fifties, an attempt was made to revive it in 1963, when Kirk Douglas and

Albert Finney, John Gielgud, Rachel Roberts, Wendy Hiller

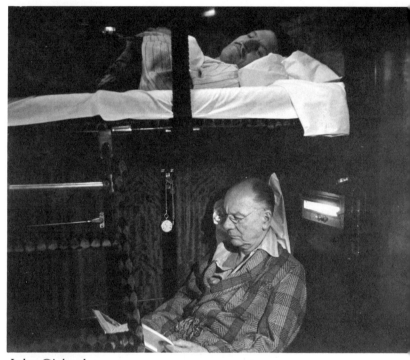

John Gielgud

Ingrid Bergman

Universal-International produced the stylish and gimmicky *The List of Adrian Messenger*. It was, purely and simply, an attempt to recapture both the look and feel of the mystery films of old, as it was photographed in darkly lit, razor-sharp black-and-white, and featured an array of bizarrely eccentric characters that made it strongly reminiscent of the Sherlock Holmes movies of twenty years earlier. Containing a superb performance by George C. Scott as a kind of super-sleuth composite of Ellery Queen, Bulldog Drummond, and Sherlock Holmes, it was an entertaining and atmospheric production. Despite its quality, however, *The List of Adrian Messenger* was only moderately successful, and for a long while it looked as though the traditional Hollywood mystery film was, indeed, a thing of the past.

Wendy Hiller, Rachel Roberts, Lauren Bacall, Sean Connery, Anthony Perkins, Martin Balsam

All this changed, however, when in 1974 Paramount released this splendid version of *Murder on the Orient Express.* Unlike *Adrian Messenger,* it was a blockbuster at the box office, and it proved conclusively that audiences were once again becoming interested in seeing a traditional mystery film that in both style and mood was modelled after the old "classics." Its success led to the production of such similar films as *The Seven-Per-Cent Solution* (1976), *Murder by Death* (1976), *Death on the Nile* (1978), *The Great Train Robbery* (1978), *Murder by Decree* (1978), and *Time After Time* (1979).

Anthony Perkins, Vanessa Redgrave, Sean Connery, Albert Finney, Michael York, Jacqueline Bisset, Lauren Bacall, Martin Balsam

96

THE GODFATHER, PART II

A Paramount Picture; Produced and directed by Francis Ford Coppola; Screenplay by Francis Ford Coppola and Mario Puzo; Based on *The Godfather* by Mario Puzo; Photography by Gordon Willis; Production designer: Dean Tavoularis; Film editors: Peter Zinner, Barry Malkin, and Richard Marks; Costumes: Theadora Van Runkle; Co-producers: Gary Frederickson and Fred Roos; Production manager: Michael S. Glick; Music by Nino Rota; Art direction: Angelo Graham; Assistant directors: Newton Arnold, Henry J. Lange, Jr., Chuck Myers, Alan Hopkins, Burt Bluestein, and Tony Brandt; Additional music: Carmine Coppola; Filmed in Technicolor; Running time: 200 minutes

CAST:
Michael (AL PACINO), *Tom Hagen* (ROBERT DUVALL), *Kay* (DIANE KEATON), *Vito Corleone* (ROBERT DE NIRO), *Connie* (Talia Shire), *Fredo* (John Cazale), *Hyman Roth* (Lee Strasberg), *Frank Pentangeli* (Michael V. Gazzo), *Al Neri* (Richard Bright), *Fanucci* (Gaston Moschin), *Genco* (Frank Sivero), *Mama* (Morgana King), *Deanna* (Marianna

Robert De Niro and family

B. Kirby, Jr., Robert De Niro

Hill), *Merle Johnson* (Troy Donahue), Willie Cicci (Joe Spinell), *Tessio* (Abe Vigoda), *Mrs. Marcia Roth* (Fay Spain), *Vito's mother* (Maria Carta), *Senator Geary* (G. D. Spradlin), *Vito Andolini as a boy* (Oreste Baldini)

1958. At his Lake Tahoe estate, Michael Corleone (Al Pacino), now the head of his father's criminal empire, is visited by U.S. Senator Geary (G. D. Spradlin), who is violently opposed to organized crime. During their meeting, the senator tells Michael that he resents the Mafia's intrusion into Nevada, and that he intends fighting the Corleones any way he can. Later, however, the clever Michael uncovers a dark secret from Geary's past involving the gruesome murder of a prostitute, and, threatened with scandal, the senator reluctantly agrees to stay out of Michael's way.

After surviving an attempt on his life, Michael travels to Cuba to open a plush casino-hotel in partnership with the powerful Hyman Roth (Lee Strasberg), a high-ranking Jewish gangleader. Although, after days of negotiating, the two reach an amicable business agreement, Michael distrusts Roth—fearing it was he who engineered the assassination attempt back in the States. Returning to America sometime later, Michael learns that his brother Fredo (John Cazale), resentful of having always been the "black sheep" of the family, set him up for Roth's hit men, and that Roth is, indeed, anxious to assume Michael's command by getting him out of the way.

Meanwhile, Michael's pregnant wife Kay (Diane Keaton) miscarries, and Michael is summoned to ap-

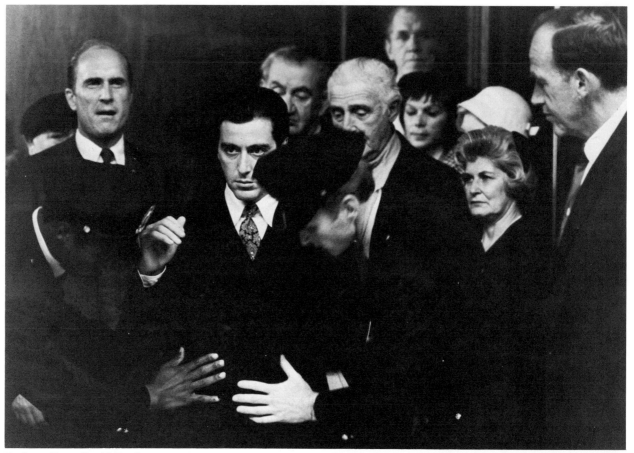

Robert Duvall, Al Pacino

pear before a Senate Investigation of organized crime. His father's former lieutenant, Frankie Pentangeli (Michael V. Gazzo), has vowed to give evidence against him and to reveal all the inner workings of the Mafia. At the last instant, however, Michael imports Pentangeli's revered brother from Italy to sit in on the investigation. During the subsequent hearing, Pentangeli sees the old family tie and is unable to betray Michael, much to the Senate's astonishment.

Afterward, Kay confesses that she aborted Michael's child because she didn't want it to grow up in her husband's corrupt world. This enrages Michael, and after slapping her repeatedly he vows never to see her again. Now free to act according to his principles, Michael sets about destroying his enemies one by one—his loyal aide Tom Hagen (Robert Duvall) persuades Pentangeli to vindicate himself by committing suicide; Hyman Roth is assassinated at an airport; and Fredo is shot in the back of the head while fishing near Michael's estate.

One of the most profitable films produced in the seventies, *The Godfather* was epic storytelling at its

Robert De Niro, Frank Sivero

Robert De Niro, Gaston Moschlin

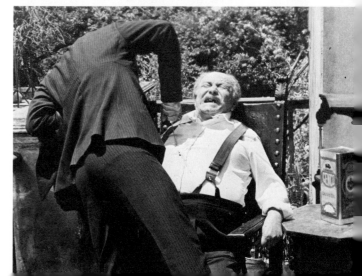

98

Al Pacino, Diane Keaton

best, and its success made Francis Ford Coppola a director whose services were highly in demand. It was such an impressive work that, at the time of its release, one could hardly imagine how it could be bested; but Coppola managed to do just that with *The Godfather, Part II,* one of the few film sequels of the seventies that actually improved upon the original.

Curiously, most of the sequels made during the decade turned out to be major disappointments for all concerned. The lavish, expensive follow-ups to films such as *The Exorcist, The Omen, The French Connection, Love Story,* and *Jaws* were far below the quality of the originals, and one of them—*Exorcist II: The Heretic*—lays substantial claim to being the decade's worst major film.

The Godfather, Part II, however, was something else again. While it easily matches the technical excellence of the original, it also contains a more intriguing plot line. Not only does *The Godfather, Part II* continue the Corleone saga where *The Godfather* left off, but it also gives the audience additional insight into the character of Don Vito by depicting his early life via flashbacks. It is a much slower, more analytical film than the original, lacking much of *The Godfather's* action and excitement. *The Godfather, Part II* is a film of enormous scope, as its story spans fifty years in the life of the Corleone family.

The many flashbacks to turn-of-the-century New York are especially well done, and Coppola and his photographer Gordon Willis wisely incorporated subtle changes in the tint of their Technicolor photography to give these scenes an authentic ''period'' flavor. The flashback sequences of Don Vito's early years have a soft, rich, almost glowing texture, which presents a sharp contrast to the hard,

realistic color scheme used for Michael's Senate Investigation.

The performances in *The Godfather, Part II* are uniformly fine, and Al Pacino as Michael presents a brilliant, larger-than-life portrait of a basically decent man so corrupted by power that he has become a monster. Robert De Niro is also splendid in his Oscar-winning portrayal of the young Don Vito, a role essayed completely in Italian. Thanks to Coppola's knowing direction, the film seems much shorter than its 200-minute running time, so fascinating are the characters and incidents. Not surprisingly, *The Godfather, Part II* was named Best Picture, also winning the year's Oscars for direction, screenplay, art direction, and music-scoring.

THE TOWERING INFERNO

A 20th Century-Fox–Warner Bros. Picture; Directed by John Guillermin; Produced by Irwin Allen; Action sequences directed by Irwin Allen; Photography by Fred Koenekamp and Joseph Biroc; Production designer: William Creber; Associate producer: Sidney Marshall; Music by John Williams; Film editors: Harold F. Kress and Carl Kress; Costumes by Paul Zastupnevich; Assistant directors: Wes McAfee, Newton Arnold, and Malcolm Harding; Screenplay by Stirling Silliphant; Based on the novels *The Tower* by Richard Martin Stern and *The Glass Inferno* by Thomas N. Scortia and Frank M. Robinson; Art direction by Ward Preston; Filmed in Panavision and DeLuxe Color; Running time: 165 minutes

99

CAST:
Doug Roberts (PAUL NEWMAN), *Michael O'Hallorhan* (STEVE McQUEEN), *James Duncan* (WILLIAM HOLDEN), *Susan Franklin* (FAYE DUNAWAY), *Harlee Claiborne* (FRED ASTAIRE), *Roger Simmons* (RICHARD CHAMBERLAIN), *Lisolette Mueller* (JENNIFER JONES), *Dan Bigelow* (ROBERT WAGNER), *Jernigan* (O. J. SIMPSON), *Patty Simmons* (SUSAN BLAKELY), *Senator Gary Parker* (ROBERT VAUGHN), *Scott* (Felton Perry), *Will Giddings* (Normann Burton), *Carlos* (Gregory Sierra), *Lorrie* (Susan Flannery), *Paula Ramsay* (Sheila Matthews), *Mayor* (Jack Collins), *Kappy* (Don Gordon)

The Glass Tower, the world's tallest building, is erected in San Francisco. To celebrate its completion,

Richard Chamberlain

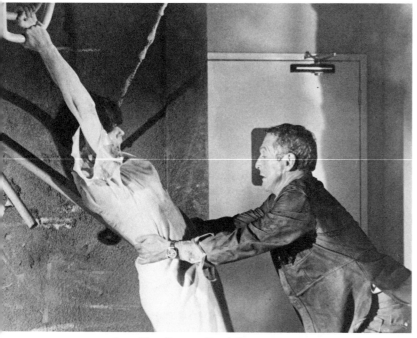

Jennifer Jones, Paul Newman

the architect, Doug Roberts (Paul Newman), and the builder, James Duncan (William Holden), hold a gala party on the 122nd floor. During the course of the evening, Roberts learns that Roger Simmons (Richard Chamberlain), Duncan's son-in-law and an electrical contractor, installed faulty wiring in the Glass Tower to save money. As a result of this, a fire breaks out in one of the storerooms; concerned, Roberts tells Duncan, who refuses to be bothered by a "minor fire."

The minor blaze soon becomes major, however, and Roberts is forced to enlist the aid of the fire department, headed by Chief Michael O'Hallorhan (Steve McQueen). To prevent panic and chaos, the chief instructs the partygoers to form a line leading to the elevators. Despite these precautions, many of the

William Holden

100

guests meet horrible deaths, including Simmons, who tries to escape out a window.

After much of the building is destroyed, O'Hallorhan and his men extinguish the inferno by exploding the Tower's million-gallon water tanks. Afterward, O'Hallorhan tells Roberts that tall buildings are fire risks, and that architects never seem willing to accept this.

Despite its silly script and stereotyped characters, 1972's *The Poseidon Adventure* was an enormous success. The film grossed over $100 million, making it one of the most profitable light entertainments in

pulse-pounding finale. It was also the kind of fast-moving thriller that would translate well to the screen.

However, Fox and Allen were never able to secure rights to the property—they were purchased by Warner Bros. for an astronomical amount. Not long afterward, however, Allen and Fox managed to buy the rights to a similar book, *The Glass Inferno* by Thomas N. Scortia and Frank M. Robinson. Realizing that Warners was no doubt preparing a "burning skyscraper" film of its own, Fox and Allen approached the rival studio with a unique idea. Fox proposed that, instead of working against each other on competing projects, the studios might be better off pooling their resources to produce one mammoth motion picture.

Warners went for the idea, and the result was 1974's *The Towering Inferno,* considered by many as the best disaster film of them all. Running just minutes short of *The Godfather,* this was an epic disaster drama, and it completely outclassed the decade's other entries. As had been the case with *The Poseidon Adventure,* the script of *The Towering Inferno* was not especially strong, but the rich production values, John Guillermin's skillful direction, the breathtaking special effects scenes and an all-star cast headed by Paul Newman and Steve McQueen more than compensated.

Steve McQueen, Ernie Orsatti

history. Shortly after its release, 20th Century-Fox and Irwin Allen began searching for another strong "disaster" story—one that could be turned into an equally profitable follow-up film.

During their search, Allen and Fox ran across a suspense novel called *The Tower* by Richard Martin Stern which Allen believed had definite possibilities. The book dealt with the spectacular burning of a sky-scraper, which was certainly as compelling a cir-cumstance as an overturned ocean liner. The book seemed to be everything Fox and Allen were looking for—its central incident was a major disaster, it con-tained a variety of colorful characters, and it had a

Paul Newman, Steve McQueen

Marty Feldman, Peter Boyle, Gene Wilder

YOUNG FRANKENSTEIN

A 20th Century-Fox Picture; Directed by Mel Brooks; Produced by Michael Gruskoff; Screenplay by Gene Wilder and Mel Brooks; Based on characters in the novel *Frankenstein* by Mary Shelley; Photography by Gerald Hirschfeld; Production designer: Dale Hennesy; Assistant directors: Marvin Miller and Barry Stern; Costumes by Dorothy Jeakins; Makeup by William Tuttle; Set decorations by Robert DeVestel; Special effects by Hal Millar and Henry Miller, Jr.; Music by John Morris; Lab equipment by Kenneth Strickfaden; Running time: 106 minutes

CAST:
Dr. Frankenstein (GENE WILDER), *Igor* (MARTY FELDMAN), *The monster* (PETER BOYLE), *Elizabeth* (MADELINE KAHN), *Frau Blucher* (CLORIS LEACHMAN), *Inga* (Teri Garr), *Herr Falkstein* (Richard Haydn), *Insp. Kemp* (Kenneth Mars), *Mr. Hilltop* (Liam Dunn), *Herr Waldman* (Leon Askin), *Jailer* (Oscar Beregi), *Medical student* (Danny Goldman), *Frightened villager* (Lou Cutell), *Village elder* (Arthur Malet), *Insp. Kemp's aide* (Richard Roth), *Little girl* (Anne Beesley), *Gravediggers* (Monte Landis, Rusty Blitz), *The blind hermit* (GENE HACKMAN)

Anxious to receive his legacy, Dr. Frederick Frankenstein (Gene Wilder) travels to the family estate in Transylvania. There he is given his grandfather Victor's notebook by Frau Blucher (Cloris Leachman), the infamous doctor's former mistress.

Inspired by what he reads, young Frederick decides to re-create Baron Victor's greatest experiment—the creation of a man—with the help of the hunchbacked Igor (Marty Feldman) and a shapely nurse named Inga (Teri Garr). Because Igor secures a criminal brain

Marty Feldman

Peter Boyle, Gene Hackman

Gene Wilder, Peter Boyle

instead of a normal one, the "being" turns out to be another monster (Peter Boyle). Naturally, the strange goings-on at the castle unnerve the villagers, and they send Inspector Kemp (Kenneth Mars) to investigate.

Some time later, the monster escapes and, like *his* famous ancestor, encounters a little girl (Anne Beesley) and a blind hermit (Gene Hackman) during his travels. Managing to retrieve his creation, the resourceful Frederick works up a song-and-dance act featuring the monster and himself.

Meanwhile, Frederick's fiancée Elizabeth (Madeline Kahn) arrives from America and is seduced by the monster, who delights her with the huge dimensions of a certain part of his anatomy (after the incident, Elizabeth breathlessly says: "Oh God, I think I *love* him"). Since Frankenstein originally planned to give the monster a scientist's brain, he swaps brains with it, and having Frederick's brain in the monster's body delights Elizabeth very much.

Despite the fact that they were wildly funny, Mel Brooks's first two screen comedies, *The Producers* (1968) and *The Twelve Chairs* (1970), were both failures at the box office, and it wasn't until 1974's *Blazing Saddles* that the director hit upon the formula that worked best for his brand of outrageous satire. It was a fast-paced, no-holds-barred spoof of Hollywood westerns of the thirties and forties, featuring such diverse performers as Gene Wilder, Madeline Kahn, Harvey Korman, Dom De Luise, Cleavon Little, and ex-football player Alex Karras in starring roles. The combination of Hollywood satire and crazy comedy proved to be a winning one, and much to Brooks's delight, *Blazing Saddles* became a formidable hit in no time at all.

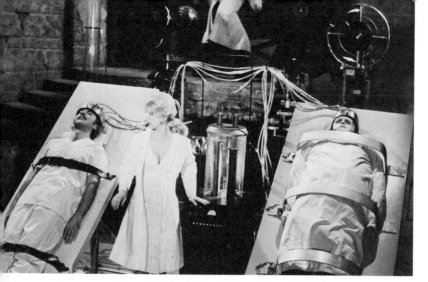

Gene Wilder, Teri Garr, Peter Boyle

Brooks then realized that if an outlandish western satire could be a success, so could spoofs of other "classic" film genres, and he proceeded to poke fun at horror films in *Young Frankenstein* (1974), silent films in *Silent Movie* (1976), and the Alfred Hitchcock thrillers in *High Anxiety* (1977). Of his four comic "tributes" to old Hollywood, *Blazing Saddles* is generally regarded as the funniest, but *Young Frankenstein* remains the one that most perfectly captures the essence of the genre it is spoofing.

It becomes quite obvious when viewing the film that Brooks went to extraordinary lengths to give *Young Frankenstein* the genuine look and feel of the Universal horror "classics." Not only did Brooks shoot *Young Frankenstein* in dark, ominous black-and-white, but he also injected the screenplay (written in collaboration with the film's star Gene Wilder) with visual and dramatic elements from many of the original films. Of course, the most obvious of these are Igor's giving the monster a criminal brain and the monster's encounter with a blind hermit, which are parodies of incidents in *Frankenstein* (1931) and *The Bride of Frankenstein* (1935). In addition, *Young*

Teri Garr, Gene Wilder

Frankenstein's Inspector Kemp was modeled after the character Lionel Atwill played in *Son of Frankenstein* (1939), and the idea of giving the monster a scientist's brain was taken from *The Ghost of Frankenstein* (1942). Also, *Young Frankenstein*'s laboratory scene, in which Frederick and the monster are strapped to adjacent tables, is visually reminiscent of the climax of *Frankenstein Meets the Wolf Man* (1942). Incidentally, the laboratory equipment in *Young Frankenstein* was the work of Kenneth Strickfaden, who designed the electronic gadgets for the original Frankenstein series.

PHANTOM OF THE PARADISE

William Finley

A Fox-Rank Picture; Written and directed by Brian De Palma; Produced by Edward R. Pressman; Photography by Larry Pizer; Production designer: Jack Fisk; Set decorations: Sissy Spacek; Special effects by Greg Auer; Assistant directors: Michael Dmytryk and Robert Enrietto; Costumes by Rosanna Norton; Choreography by Harold Oblong; Sound recording by James Tanenbaum; Associate costume designer: Peter Jamison; Production managers: Thomas Lightburn and Gary Kent; Color by Movielab; Running time: 91 minutes

CAST:
Swan (PAUL WILLIAMS), *Phoenix* (Jessica Harper), *Winslow Leach* (William Finley), *Beef* (Gerrit Graham), *Philbin* (George Memmoli), *Warden* (Gene Gross), *Night watchman* (Henry Calvert)

Swan (Paul Williams), head of Death Records and a powerful rock impresario, wants a "new sound" to inaugurate his plush rock palace, the Paradise. Winslow Leach (William Finley), a young composer, is writing a rock opera based on *Faust*, and after hearing the lead song Swan offers to buy it. Arriving at the offices of Death Records to sign a contract,

William Finley

Phoenix sing the lead song. Later, the dubious Swan walls Leach up in a recording booth and hires a famous glitter rock star, Beef (Gerrit Graham), to sing the song instead. Afterward, Leach escapes and disposes of Beef, clearing the way for Phoenix.

The opening of the Paradise is a triumph, and Phoenix is a smash. Her success intoxicates her, however, and she falls under Swan's spell, making love to him at his castle later that night. Seeing the two in bed together through a castle window, Leach goes berserk and stabs himself, but the wound mysteriously heals. Swan later tells Leach he can't die because he's under "eternal" contract to Swan, who's under "eternal" contract to the Devil. Sneaking into the files at Death Records, Leach plays a video tape revealing that Swan's pact with Satan calls for the taped image to age while Swan stays eternally young.

Meanwhile, the ruthless Swan plans to marry Phoenix on the Paradise stage, then have her assassinated to provide spectacular entertainment for his audience. During the ceremony, however, Leach

Gerrit Graham

Winslow meets and falls in love with Phoenix (Jessica Harper), a young singer waiting to audition for Swan. Unbeknownst to Leach, Swan intends stealing his music, and later frames the composer on a drug charge to get him out of the way.

Sent to prison, Leach watches his song become a big hit for Swan and, determined to get revenge, later escapes. He raids the Death Records offices to sabotage tapes of his stolen music, but in the process he gets his head caught in a record press. Horribly disfigured, Leach dons a birdlike space helmet and black cape, and begins "haunting" the Paradise.

Swan later confronts Leach, persuading him to finish the *Faust* score in time for the Paradise's gala opening. Leach agrees, insisting, however, that

Paul Williams, William Finley

burns the tape and attacks Swan, who withers and dies. The evil spell broken, Leach's knife wound opens and he dies in Phoenix's arms.

One of the decade's most fascinating entertainment phenomena was the "glitter rock" scene of the early seventies. Pioneered by top-flight performers like David Bowie and Alice Cooper, it combined rather loud and savage rock music with outrageous costumes and makeup. While "glitter rock" was enormously popular for a time, it lacked the style and poetry of Elvis, the Beatles, and the rock music of the sixties, and it ultimately gave way to the even more bizarre and decadent "punk rock" of the late seventies.

The "glitter" era was satirized in a 1973 stage play called *The Rocky Horror Show*, which became an enormous hit both in the U.S. and abroad. It was filmed in 1976, and *The Rocky Horror Picture Show* continues to play at special "midnight" screenings around the country, at which the audience dresses in outlandish costumes modelled after those in the film. Surprisingly, this rather garish, noisy item has become the most popular "cult" movie of the decade, and many members of its devoted following have seen it over one hundred times.

A much better rock satire, Brian De Palma's *Phantom of the Paradise* never caught on as well, which is, indeed, a pity, for this underrated little masterwork is one of the seventies' most enjoyable films. De Palma is one of the cinema's great engineers, and his films are usually marked by dazzling, imaginative camerawork and special effects that seldom fail to spellbind the observer. He is particularly well known for his idolization of Alfred Hitchcock, after whom he has patterned much of his style, and most De Palma films contain a few Hitchcock "in jokes" that add to the overall fun.

In 1974, De Palma wrote and directed this colorful jab at the rock industry, combining elements of *Phantom of the Opera* with the *Faust* legend. Though it was not greatly successful, *Phantom of the*

Paul Williams

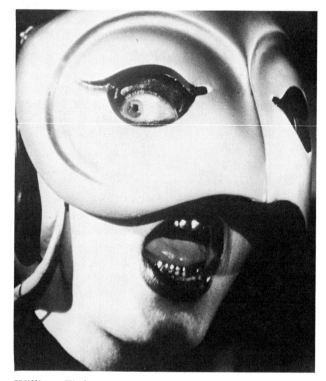

William Finley

William Finley

Paradise is, perhaps, De Palma's best film to date, and its flashy visuals and clever story line established him as one of Hollywood's most inventive young directors. The film contained a surprisingly deft portrayal by composer Paul Williams as the ruthless, omnipotent Swan, and it featured some genuinely good rock performances, most notably Beef's powerful "Frankenstein" number at the opening of the Paradise.

CHINATOWN

A Paramount Picture; Directed by Roman Polanski; Produced by Robert Evans; Screenplay by Robert Towne; Photography by John Alonzo; Production designer: Richard Sylbert; Film editor: Sam O'Steen; Costumes by Anthea Sylbert; Associate producer: C. O. Erickson; Music by Jerry Goldsmith; Art direction: W. Stewart Campbell; Assistant directors: Howard W. Koch, Jr. and Michele Ader; Filmed in Panavision and Technicolor; Running time: 131 minutes

CAST:
J. J. Gittes (JACK NICHOLSON), *Evelyn Mulwray* (FAYE DUNAWAY), *Noah Cross* (JOHN HUSTON), *Yelburton* (John Hillerman), *Escobar* (Perry Lopez), *Ida Sessions* (Diane Ladd), *Mulvihill* (Roy Jenson), *Hollis Mulwray* (Darrell Zwerling), *Man with knife* (Roman Polanski), *Loach* (Dick Bakalyan), *Walsh* (Joe Mantell), *Sophie* (Nandu Hinds), *Duffy* (Bruce Glover), *Maid* (Beulah Quo), *Lawyer* (James O'Reare), *Gardener* (Jerry Fujikawa), *Evelyn's butler* (James Hong)

Los Angeles, 1937. Private eye J. J. Gittes (Jack Nicholson) is hired by Mrs. Mulwray to investigate her husband's affair with a younger woman. Gittes begins tailing Mr. Mulwray and his young paramour, and snaps several incriminating photos of the couple. He turns the pictures over to Mrs. Mulwray, but for some reason they are published in a news tabloid several days later. The scandal now public, Mr. Mulwray's corpse is later found in a dried-up reservoir on the outskirts of town. Meanwhile, Gittes learns the woman who hired him was an imposter, and that the real Mrs. Mulwray (Faye Dunaway) is suing him on her late husband's behalf.

Finding out Mulwray was murdered, Gittes investigates his background, and discovers that he and the powerful Noah Cross (John Huston) once owned Los Angeles' water supply, and that Mulwray had recently prevented construction of a dam that would have provided the city with more water. Furthermore, Gittes learns that the dam was the brainchild

Jack Nicholson, Dick Bakalyan, Faye Dunaway

Roman Polanski, Jack Nicholson, Roy Jenson

John Huston, Roy Jenson

Jack Nicholson

John Huston, Jack Nicholson

108

Jack Nicholson, Faye Dunaway

of Cross, owner of vast orchard properties that would have benefitted from its construction.

Determined to convince her he had nothing to do with the photos' being published, Gittes visits Mrs. Mulwray, a beautiful, mysterious woman. Attracted to Gittes, she drops the lawsuit, and later reveals she's Noah Cross's daughter. That night, she and Gittes make love, but she insists on leaving before sun-up. Following her to a secluded house, Gittes watches through a side window as she argues with her husband's young mistress. Later, Mrs. Mulwray confesses to Gittes that the girl is both her sister and her daughter—the result of an incestuous rape by her father Noah. She tells Gittes she is hiding the girl from Cross, who is determined to claim her.

Gittes hides Mrs. Mulwray and the girl in a Chinatown apartment, then has a showdown with Cross, who freely admits to hiring the imposter, printing the scandal, and killing Mulwray. At the point of a gun, Gittes reluctantly leads Cross to Mrs. Mulwray. Determined to prevent Cross from taking the girl, Mrs. Mulwray makes a frantic escape attempt, but the corrupt police (who are on Cross's payroll) shoot her in the back. While Cross tries to comfort his hysterical "granddaughter," a stunned Gittes is told by police to ". . . forget it. It's Chinatown."

Roman Polanski's *Chinatown* is one of the seventies' most popular and celebrated films, and remains an exceptional entertainment. The screenplay, written by Robert Towne, is among the most complex and fascinating conceived for a film of this type, and the acting of Jack Nicholson, Faye Dunaway, and John Huston is superlative.

A brooding, atmospheric detective drama in the *Big Sleep–Maltese Falcon* vein, *Chinatown* perfectly captures the mood and appearance of an old Hollywood "classic"; aside from the acting, direction and screenplay, this is, perhaps, the most intriguing thing about the film. The rich, darkly shaded Technicolor photography of John Alonzo strongly resembles that used in the thirties and forties, and the opening titles—art deco lettering set against a pale green backdrop—could have easily been designed for a forties mystery. Jerry Goldsmith's music score, dominated by the haunting trumpet strains of the main theme, likewise has a "period" flavor. And the settings of W. Stewart Campbell look as though they were lifted from 1944's *Murder, My Sweet*, one of the best of the Phillip Marlowe films.

Interestingly, the screenplay for *Chinatown* sprang from a simple, one-line story idea which writer Towne offhandedly mentioned to producer Robert Evans in 1973. Evans, who had just left his post as the production chief at Paramount, was at that time looking for a solid vehicle to launch his career as an independent producer. Intrigued by Towne's idea and certain it would make a great film, Evans instructed him to work up a script, and Towne spent the next eighteen months writing the massive *Chinatown* screenplay, which eventually won him his first Academy Award.

Faye Dunaway

Jack Nicholson, Perry Lopez

1975

FACE TO FACE

A Paramount Pictures Release; Produced and directed by Ingmar Bergman; Original screenplay by Ingmar Bergman; Production design by Anne Hagegard; Photography by Sven Nykvist; Film editor: Siv Lundgren; Musical passages by Mozart; Photographed in Eastmancolor; Running time: 136 minutes

CAST:

Dr. Jenny Isaksson (LIV ULLMANN), *Dr. Thomas Jacobi* (Erland Josephson), *Grandpa* (Gunnar Bjornstrand), *Grandma* (Aino Taube-Henrikson), *Dr. Erik Isaksson* (Sven Lindberg), *Veronica* (Kristina Adolphson), *Maria* (Kari Sylwan), *Elizabeth Wankel* (Siv Ruud), *The lady* (Tore Segelcke), *Dr. Wankel* (Ulf Johansson), *Michael Stromberg* (Gosta Ekman)

Dr. Jenny Isaksson (Liv Ullmann), a psychiatrist, spends her holiday at her grandparents' home in the country. During this time, the tomb-like desolation of the house takes its toll on Jenny, and she begins suffering peculiar mental symptoms, including depression, hysteria, and hallucinations involving the ghostly spectre of an old woman.

Longing to be around people her own age, Jenny attends a party given by her high-living friend Elizabeth (Siv Ruud). Here she meets Dr. Thomas Jacobi (Erland Josephson), a handsome physician. Though Jenny makes it clear she's a married woman, Jacobi invites her home for a drink, and once there he tries to seduce her, without success. Despite this, Jenny and Thomas make love the following week. In the middle of the night, however, Jenny suffers an emotional breakdown (a terrifying interlude in which her wracking sobs and screams seem like they'll never stop), but she recovers with Thomas's help.

Returning to her grandparents' house the following day, she relaxes for the first time in weeks, feeling her ordeal at Thomas's has purged whatever madness was welling up inside her. Her mental state returns to panic, however, when she again hallucinates a ghostly old woman, resembling her grandmother, with an evil look on her face. Shattered, Jenny takes an overdose of sleeping pills. Sinking into unconsciousness, she has a bizarre dream—dressed like "Little Red Riding Hood," she glides about a surreal landscape encountering people from her past. Meeting her deceased parents, Jenny curses them for the strict upbringing that left her a disturbed adult, then feels pity upon realizing how vacant their lives were. She awakens in a hospital bed, learning that Thomas saved her in the nick of time.

After a slow, painful recovery, Jenny has one final seizure, pouring out her feelings about the painful relationship between her mother and grandmother.

Again using Thomas as a soundingboard, Jenny reveals that her mother (who raised Jenny with Gestapo-like strictness) and grandmother would often have violent arguments, during which the older woman's face would assume a terrifying, inhuman quality. Realizing these memories were at the root of her illness, Jenny returns home to try and rebuild her life.

Originally filmed as a four-part television series in Sweden, *Face to Face* was edited into a theatrical feature by Ingmar Bergman in the same manner as his *Scenes from a Marriage* (1973), which also featured Liv Ullmann and Erland Josephson in the

Liv Ullmann

leading roles. A long, harrowing account of a female psychiatrist whose visit to her childhood home triggers a severe nervous breakdown, *Face to Face* is generally regarded as Bergman's most brutal exploration of the human psyche to date, and the detached and clinical manner in which it explores Jenny's plight is a far cry from the poetic, ethereal flavor of his earlier "psychodrama," *Cries and Whispers*.

Despite good supporting performances from Erland Josephson as Jenny's compassionate lover and Bergman veteran Gunnar Bjornstrand as her ailing grandfather, Liv Ullmann's powerhouse por-

trayal of the unfortunate Jenny completely dominates the picture, and *Face to Face* represents, perhaps, the peak of the actress's work in seventies
cinema. The segments depicting Jenny's breakdown
(in which Ullmann erupts with the twisted emotions
that have been buried for a lifetime—at one point actually re-creating a dialogue from the past between
Jenny and her mother, first speaking the mother's
stern commands, then replying sheepishly in a
childlike voice) have a realism and intensity rarely
witnessed in the cinema; this often makes them painfully difficult to sit through. While the effectiveness
of these scenes is mostly due to Ullmann's marvelous
acting, they were also enhanced by the work of
Bergman's photographer Sven Nykvist, who filmed
Face to Face in a mercilessly bright and ugly shade of
Eastmancolor that gives it an added dimension of
reality.

While critics continue praising Ingmar Bergman as
a filmmaker, usually very little is said about his skills
as a film*writer*. The fact remains that Bergman also
writes most of the films he directs, and many of his
triumphs contain some of the most thought-pro-

Erland Josephson, Liv Ullmann

Liv Ullmann, Siv Ruud

Liv Ullmann

Ingmar Bergman, Liv Ullmann

voking dialogue ever written for the screen. *Face to Face* is no exception, and Jenny's speech about how, during family arguments, her grandmother's facial expression would mysteriously change from benign to demonic is both penetrating and disturbing.

SHAMPOO

A Columbia Picture; Directed by Hal Ashby; Produced by Warren Beatty; Screenplay by Robert Towne and Warren Beatty; Photographed by Laszlo Kovacs; Music by Paul Simon; Production designer: Richard Sylbert; Art direction by Stu Campbell; Film editor: Robert C. Jones; Assistant director: Art Levinson; Filmed in Technicolor; Running time: 109 minutes

CAST:
George (WARREN BEATTY), *Jackie* (JULIE CHRISTIE), *Jill* (GOLDIE HAWN), *Felicia* (LEE GRANT), *Lester* (Jack Warden), *Johnny Pope* (Tony Bill), *Senator* (Brad Dexter), *Lorna* (Carrie Fisher), *Norman* (Jay Robinson), *Bank officer* (George Furth), *Producer* (William Castle)

1968. George (Warren Beatty) is the most popular hairstylist in Beverly Hills. An extremely attractive man in his late thirties, his skill at making women more beautiful is exceeded only by his ability to please them in the bedroom, and many of his clients see him "after hours" on a regular basis. George is absolutely obsessed with "pleasing" women, which is the main reason he became a hairstylist in the first place.

Though he has "made it" with nearly all his customers, the three main relationships in George's life are with Jackie (Julie Christie), his former girlfriend; Jill (Goldie Hawn), his fiancée; and Felicia (Lee Grant), an attractive older woman with whom he sleeps. The triangle becomes even more intriguing when it is revealed that Jackie is also mistress to Felicia's wealthy husband Lester (Jack Warden), who plans to leave Felicia for the younger woman.

Tired of the constant nagging of his neurotic boss Norman (Jay Robinson), George begins making plans to open his own shop, and after failing to qualify for a bank loan visits Lester at Felicia's suggestion. Impressed with George's drive and ambition, Lester agrees to finance the venture, but the deal falls through when he learns of George's involvement with Felicia and Jackie. Accompanied by two hulking bodyguards, Lester visits George at his small apartment, and threatens to have him beaten to a pulp unless he can come up with a reasonable explanation.

Goldie Hawn, Warren Beatty

Julie Christie, Goldie Hawn

George tells Lester that both women need more than one man in their lives, and that he fills that need. Although he manages to talk himself out of trouble with Lester, he is not so lucky with Jill, who, after learning of George's infidelity, calls him a heartless bastard incapable of really loving anyone. Though George assures her that he'll try to mend his ways, Jill leaves him for her boss, Johnny Pope (Tony Bill).

Realizing that, at thirty-seven, his days as a "stud" are numbered, George later begs Jackie to marry him, but she is unable to pass up the financial security offered by Lester. At the conclusion, George is left

Julie Christie, Warren Beatty

with the prospect of perhaps never having a meaningful relationship.

Curiously, many of the seventies' most successful films were not produced with the idea that they would reap tremendous profits, and their eventual triumph at the box office came as a surprise to the people that made them. Perhaps the most obvious example of this was *Star Wars,* a film that was expected to do moderately well but one that was not really produced with big box office in mind. Its director George Lucas and its producer Gary Kurtz merely hoped the picture would make enough money to justify 20th Century-Fox's investment, but neither of them dreamed the film would become a mammoth success (quite ironically, George Lucas was so afraid *Star Wars* would not do well that he retreated to Hawaii the week it premiered).

William Castle, Julie Christie, Warren Beatty

There were, on the other hand, several films produced during the decade that were specifically designed to make a killing at the box office, and one of the best was *Shampoo,* a film that, aside from being a huge moneymaker, was also something of a personal triumph for its star, Warren Beatty. The actor has every reason to be proud of *Shampoo,* as he not only starred in it but also served as producer and co-wrote the screenplay with the formidable Robert Towne, whose screenwriting credits include two of Jack Nicholson's best films—*The Last Detail* and *Chinatown.*

Aside from his artistic involvement with the film, Beatty also proved with *Shampoo* that he was one of the shrewdest and most skillful businessmen in Hollywood. Though primarily regarded as a slick, well-mounted satire on the political tone and sexual freedom of the late sixties, *Shampoo* is, more than

anything else, a brilliantly designed commercial product geared to sell itself to a mass audience, and Beatty's perfect packaging of the vehicle accounts more for its success than any message it might contain.

In every respect, Beatty fashioned *Shampoo* to attract as many paying customers as possible, in the same way an ad agency designs a beautiful, swank, and sexy television commercial to sell a particular product to viewers. He cast it with some of the most attractive and gifted people in Hollywood, most notably Julie Christie, Goldie Hawn, and Lee Grant as the three main women in George's life. While the actresses delivered splendid performances, Beatty made certain that their physical attractiveness would also be highlighted throughout, and several scenes in the film display the actresses at their absolute sexiest, which added enormously to the box-office appeal.

Julie Christie, Goldie Hawn, Tony Bill, Warren Beatty

Also, *Shampoo* dealt openly and candidly with the sex lives of the rich and beautiful, a subject that has fascinated millions of readers over the years but one that, until *Shampoo,* had never been brought to the screen with any success. For the most part, the many film versions of the Jacqueline Susann and Harold Robbins best-sellers were rather poorly made despite their big budgets, often containing laughable performances and bad scripts which gave them little appeal to audiences. *Shampoo,* however, contained all the erotic flavor of films such as *The Love Machine* and *Once Is Not Enough,* but it was also an excellent movie, blessed with a literate script, fine performances, and superb direction. The fact that it was a high-quality motion picture that also happened to be very, very sexy made it a natural winner with audiences, and *Shampoo* grossed some $60 million during its original run in the United States.

THE FOUR MUSKETEERS

A 20th Century-Fox Picture; Directed by Richard Lester; Produced by Alexander Salkind; Screenplay by George MacDonald Fraser; Based on *The Three Musketeers* by Alexander Dumas; Photography by David Watkins; Music by Lalo Schifrin; Film editor: John Victor Smith; Filmed in DeLuxe Color; Running time: 107 minutes

CAST:
Athos (OLIVER REED), *D'Artagnan* (MICHAEL YORK), *Aramis* (RICHARD CHAMBERLAIN), *Milady* (FAYE DUNAWAY), *Constance* (RAQUEL WELCH), *Cardinal Richelieu* (CHARLTON HESTON), *Rochefort* (CHRISTOPHER LEE), *Queen Anne* (GERALDINE CHAPLIN), *Duke of Buckingham* (Simon Ward), *Porthos* (Frank Finlay), *Louis XIII* (Jean-Pierre Cassel), *The maid* (Nicole Calfan)

Michael York

Seeking revenge because her plan to discredit the Queen (Geraldine Chaplin) was thwarted by the musketeers, Milady (Faye Dunaway) plots the downfall of D'Artagnan (Michael York), Constance (Raquel Welch), and Buckingham (Simon Ward). Turning to D'Artagnan first, Milady lures him into an affair, which causes the young musketeer to forget his beloved Constance. Catching D'Artagnan "offguard" for a brief instant, the evil temptress tries to do him in, but he luckily escapes and regains his senses.

Having failed to eliminate D'Artagnan, Milady instructs Rochefort (Christopher Lee) to kidnap Constance, then journeys to England and purposely allows herself to be arrested at Buckingham Palace. Imprisoned, Milady feigns a passionate interest in the Bible in order to establish rapport with Buckingham's chaste, fanatically religious jailer. Using her wiles, she seduces the man into submission, and later convinces him that Buckingham seeks to overthrow religion in England. Completely under her spell, the jailer frees her, then assassinates the duke by plunging a dagger into his heart.

Meanwhile, D'Artagnan learns that Buckingham has been killed and Constance has been taken to a nun's retreat near the coast of Italy. The four musketeers ride to Italy and storm the retreat, which is heavily guarded by Rochefort's men. Inside the retreat, D'Artagnan encounters Rochefort and engages him in a furious duel, during which Rochefort is run through. In an upstairs chamber, D'Artagnan finds the body of Constance, who has been murdered by Milady.

Charlton Heston, Jean-Pierre Cassel

116

Michael York, Richard Chamberlain, Frank Finlay,
Oliver Reed

Seizing Milady sometime afterward, the musketeers decide she must be executed for her crimes, and they hire a ghoulish headsman to carry out the sentence.

At the end of *The Three Musketeers,* Richard Lester whetted his audience's appetite by showing several exciting scenes from the forthcoming sequel, which promised to be even better than the original. When *The Four Musketeers* emerged two years later, audiences were, indeed, treated to one of the great adventure films of the decade. It was superior to *The Three Musketeers* in almost every respect, and was much more interesting because its bawdiness was offset by a great deal of serious drama.

Unlike the first film, in which the frivolity was merely punctuated from time to time by scenes of intrigue at the King's palace, the sequel's lightheartedness is contrasted by strong dramatic interludes, such as those involving the violent deaths of several popular characters from the original. At the same time, the comedy in *The Four Musketeers* is actually broader than in the first film, which makes its drama all the more effective. About midway through the story, for example, there's a hilarious duel between D'Artagnan and Rochefort on a slippery frozen lake. This tongue-in-cheek skirmish presents a nice contrast to their final confrontation in the nun's retreat, which is as dramatic as the one between Errol Flynn and Basil Rathbone in *The Adventures of Robin Hood,* and which ends with Christopher Lee gruesomely impaled on D'Artagnan's sword. Unlike the grand finale of the first film, the ending of *The Four Musketeers* is surprisingly downbeat, as the heroes hire an evil-looking headsman to carry out Milady's execution.

THE DAY OF THE LOCUST

A Paramount Picture; Directed by John Schlesinger; Produced by Jerome Hellman; Screenplay by Waldo Salt; Based on the novel by Nathanael West; Photography by Conrad Hall; Film editor: Jim Clark; Music by John Barry; Costumes by Ann Roth; Assistant Directors: Barry Stern, Tim Zinnemann, Charles Ziarcho, and Arnie Schmidt; Art direction by John Lloyd; Production designed by Richard MacDonald; Filmed in Technicolor and Panavision; Running time: 140 minutes

CAST:
Homer (DONALD SUTHERLAND), *Faye Greener* (KAREN BLACK), *Harry Greener* (BURGESS MEREDITH), *Tod* (William Atherton), *Big Sister* (Geraldine Page), *Earle* (Bo Hopkins), *Miguel* (Pepe Serna), *Abe* (Billy Barty), *Claude Estee* (Richard A. Dysart), *Director* (William Castle), *Mary Dove* (Lelia Goldoni), *Adore* (Jackie Haley), *Mrs. Johnson* (Madge Kennedy), *Joan* (Nita Talbot), *Mr. Odlesh* (Norm Leavitt), *Mrs. Odlesh* (Jane Hoffman), *Mrs. Loomis* (Gloria LeRoy), *Butler* (Alvin Childress), *Ned Grote* (John Hillerman), *Helverston* (Paul Stewart), *Dick Powell* (Dick Powell, Jr.)

The thirties. Faye Greener (Karen Black), an aspiring actress, lives in a Hollywood bungalow with her father Harry (Burgess Meredith), a former vaudeville pitchman. Though pretty and talented, Faye has never secured even a bit role in films, and soon realizes that compromising her virtue is the only way to get anywhere. With the help of an actress friend, Faye joins a stable of girls who make themselves sexually available to producers in exchange for bit parts.

Richard Chamberlain

Donald Sutherland

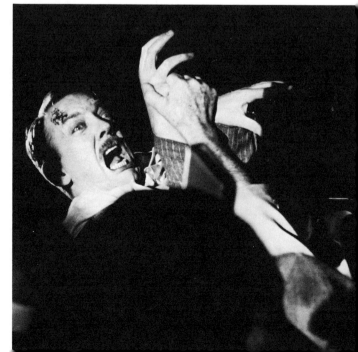

Karen Black

Donald Sutherland, Karen Black

Suddenly finding her services as a bit player in demand, Faye makes some new friends among the film colony, including an idealistic art director, Tod (William Atherton), who falls in love with her. Sensing this, Faye toys with his emotions, telling him, "I could never love a man who wasn't criminally handsome" in response to his marriage proposal. Aside from Tod, whom Faye considers "too nice" to take seriously, she also begins spending a great deal of time with two robust stuntmen, Earle (Bo Hopkins) and Miguel (Pepe Serna), who compete for her sexual favors.

Sometime later, Faye's father dies and, unable to live on a bit player's wages, she moves in with Homer (Donald Sutherland), an awkward, buffoonish man who is nonetheless financially well-off. Because of his great size and clumsy manner, Homer is a natural object of ridicule, and he is often taunted by an evil neighborhood child (Jackie Haley). Beneath his ridiculous appearance, however, Homer is a gentle soul with a childlike need for love and trust. Though they share the same roof, the relationship between Faye and Homer remains platonic, and he is content to take care of her out of gratitude for her companionship. He even allows her friends Tod, Earle, and Miguel to stay over for a weekend party, and though

Miguel and Earle mock their host, Tod develops a kinship toward Homer.

Tod at last realizes his love for Faye was a boyish illusion and that she's hardly the ideal he had built up in his mind. Witnessing the vulgar sensual rapport between Faye and the grimy Miguel, Tod finally sees her as a sluttish woman who feels nothing but contempt for tender souls like Homer and himself. While Tod survives the realization, Homer is not so lucky, and, accidentally seeing Faye and Miguel having sex, he suffers an emotional breakdown. In tears, Homer later tells Tod of his inability to comprehend the cruelty of people, saying that "people just won't understand that people need love."

Several nights later, Tod attends a crowded film premiere, and is alarmed to see Homer wandering the streets. Seeing Homer is very disturbed, Tod leads him away from the commotion to a deserted parking lot. Sitting on the fender of a black limousine, the pathetic Homer agrees to let Tod take him home after the premiere. Instead of staying with Homer, however, Tod leaves him alone and returns to the crowded streets, hoping to catch a glimpse of the Hollywood luminaries in attendance.

Unfortunately for Homer, his wicked child-nemesis is also present, and seeing the gentle giant sitting by himself, she starts tormenting him once again. Little realizing that Homer is on the verge of psychosis, she strikes him with a rock, causing him to go berserk and attack her. Venting his anguish in a curiously triumphant frenzy, Homer stomps her to death as several crowd members watch in horror.

The news that "some big creep just killed a kid" quickly spreads, and the crowd turns into a bloodthirsty mob. Like angry locusts, they engulf Homer, who is slaughtered like some great sacrificial bull. The crowd destroys everything in its path, and

Karen Black

Burgess Meredith, Karen Black

several people, including Tod, are maimed. Lying wounded in the street, Tod observes the ghastly spectacle, realizing that he and Homer have, all along, been the victims of a cruel and sadistic world.

First published in the thirties, Nathanael West's novel of old Hollywood finally reached the screen in this brilliant, powerful film, directed by John Schlesinger and featuring Karen Black, Donald Sutherland, and Burgess Meredith in perhaps the finest performances of their careers. West's book, written during his days as a fledgling screenwriter, was a searing drama of human cruelty set against the background of thirties Hollywood, and it beautifully captured the glamour, decadence, and soullessness of the film capital during its "Golden Era."

Though an excellent story property, filmmakers avoided *The Day of the Locust* for years, fearing that the novel's complexities might make it impossible to transfer to the screen. It wasn't until 1975, nearly forty years after its publication, that the book was finally filmed by Paramount. John Schlesinger was, perhaps, the ideal choice to direct the film, since the central theme of *The Day of the Locust* was how cruelty and corruption often bring about the downfall of the young, the sensitive, and the idealistic. Schlesinger had dealt with this theme a number of times in the past, most notably in *Midnight Cowboy* (1969), the story of a naive young Texan who has his dreams of glory shattered by the harsh realities of life.

Released during the early part of 1975, *The Day of the Locust* emerged as a stark and harrowing film, which probably prevented it from becoming the enormous success it should have been. It is certainly among the finest films of the decade, and it has become well known for some of the most darkly haunting images in contemporary cinema.

120

JAWS

A Universal Picture; Directed by Steven Spielberg; Produced by Richard D. Zanuck and David Brown; Screenplay by Peter Benchley and Carl Gottlieb; Based on the novel by Peter Benchley; Photography by Bill Butler; Production designer: Joseph Alves, Jr.; Film editor: Verna Fields; Music by John Williams; Underwater photography by Rexford Metz; Assistant directors: Tom Joyner and Barbara Bass; Filmed in Technicolor and Panavision; Running time: 125 minutes

CAST:
Brody (ROY SCHEIDER), *Quint* (ROBERT SHAW), *Hooper* (RICHARD DREYFUSS), *Ellen Brody* (Lorraine Gary), *Vaughn* (Murray Hamilton), *Meadows* (Carl Gottlieb), *Hendricks* (Jeffrey C. Kramer), *Chrissie* (Susan Backlinie), *Cassidy* (Jonathan Filley), *Estuary victim* (Ted Grossman), *Michael Brody* (Chris Rebello), *Sean Brody* (Jay Mello), *Mrs. Kintner* (Lee Fierro), *Alex Kintner* (Jeffrey Voorhees), *Ben Gardner* (Craig Kingsbury), *Medical examiner* (Dr. Robert Nevin), *Interviewer* (Peter Benchley)

Amity Island, a popular resort, is suddenly plagued by a series of shark attacks in which several people are killed. Fearing bad publicity, the mayor (Murray Hamilton) orders local fishermen to hunt the culprit, and they eventually capture a medium-sized shark. The mayor then publicly reassures all visitors to Amity that the shark problem has been solved.

Later, however, Roy Hooper (Richard Dreyfuss), a young icthyologist, arrives to investigate and, after examining the evidence, tells Police Chief Brody (Roy Scheider) that he's not sure the right shark was captured. He tells Brody the attacks sound more like the work of a Great White shark, the largest and most deadly of the species. Another fatal attack forces Chief Brody to agree, and much to the mayor's dismay Brody and Hooper hold a town meeting to decide what should be done. None of the local fishermen relish the idea of stalking a Great White, but a rugged, crusty seafarer named Quint (Robert Shaw) volunteers to capture and kill the monster for a large fee. The town council agrees to Quint's terms, and several days later Quint, Brody, and Hooper board Quint's boat *The Orca* to begin their shark hunt.

Roy Scheider, Richard Dreyfuss

Roy Scheider, producer Richard Zanuck and director Steven Spielberg

Roy Scheider, Lorraine Gary

After a few days at sea, they finally catch a glimpse of the villain: a gigantic, twenty-eight-foot latter-day prehistoric beast (after seeing the shark, Brody tells Quint, "I think you'll need a bigger boat"). In an effort to weaken the creature, Quint harpoons it several times, to no avail. After a while, the Great White seems to sense that it's being hunted, and begins to "fight back" by pulling the boat farther out to sea. During a lull in the action, the three men get drunk one evening, and Quint and Hooper affectionately swap "scar" stories about their many hazardous adventures at sea.

The next day, the Great White begins stalking *them,* and Quint, Hooper, and Brody realize they're in for a life-and-death struggle. During the ensuing battle, the giant shark almost capsizes the boat as it leaps on deck to devour Quint while Brody and Hooper topple overboard. Brody finally disposes of the shark by exploding an air tank in its mouth, after which he and Hooper swim to safety.

Before *Star Wars* broke all existing box-office records in the summer of 1977, *Jaws* ranked as the number one money making film of all time. It was based on the best-selling novel by Peter Benchley, and like the book it recounted with almost brutal realism a series of harrowing shark attacks on a small seaside resort. It was a well-made, exciting movie, directed with superb precision by the then twenty-seven-year-old Steven Spielberg and featuring a fine cast headed by Robert Shaw, Richard Dreyfuss, and Roy Scheider—all of whom became major screen stars as a result of *Jaws.* It was the subject of one of the most extensive publicity campaigns in history, and to this day its studio, Universal, freely admits that they sold *Jaws* as an "event" first and a motion picture second.

During the eight months prior to its release, its producers Richard D. Zanuck and David Brown, its writer Peter Benchley, and its editor Verna Fields embarked on a remarkable nationwide tour to promote what the Universal publicity department called "*Jaws*-consciousness." The ad campaign on radio and television was especially well devised, and it continually emphasized the fact that, unlike *The Exorcist* and similar films of the decade, *Jaws* dealt with a very *real* horror—relentless Great White shark attacks like those in the story could, after all, very easily happen in real life. These ads became known for the at once catchy and chilling slogan "None of men's fantasies of evil can compare with the reality of *Jaws*." The film had a staggering promotional budget of over two and a half million dollars, and it began a trend that was to later become an integral part of the merchandising of future "megahits" like *Star Wars, Close Encounters of the Third Kind,* and *Superman.*

To coincide with the picture's release, consumer products such as T-shirts, tote bags, and lunch boxes were marketed and sold by the millions, each featuring the familiar logo of a shark's head rising from the water. The poster for *Jaws* added greatly to the film's selling power, featuring, as it did, art work combining the two elements that never fail to attract customers—sex and violence. The poster consisted of a giant, phallic shark's head rising toward a nude female swimmer, with the title *Jaws* stamped below in hard, red lettering.

Of course, no amount of publicity could have sold the film if it wasn't a good one. When it was finally released in the summer of 1975, it proved to be more

Robert Shaw

Roy Scheider, Robert Shaw

Robert Shaw, Roy Scheider, Richard Dreyfuss

than worthy of all the commercial hullabaloo, and emerged as an excellent combination of horror film, suspense drama, and adventure story. The shark itself, an enormous mechanical creation measuring twenty-four feet and weighing one and a half tons, was designed by the film's production designer Joe Alves at the cost of $250,000. Affectionately nicknamed "Bruce" by the members of the crew, the giant model certainly ranks as one of the most terrifying creatures ever conceived for a motion picture. Unlike the even larger shark designed for the sequel, *Jaws II,* Bruce did not look the least bit mechanical on screen, and thanks to Spielberg's splendid manipulation of it remained a thoroughly believable and horrifying menace throughout.

Ronee Blakley, Henry Gibson

Gwen Welles, Keenan Wynn

Christina Raines, Keith Carradine

NASHVILLE

A Paramount Picture; Produced and directed by Robert Altman; Screenplay by Joan Tewkesbury; Photography by Paul Lohmann; Executive producers: Martin Starger and Jerry Weintraub; Music by Richard Baskin; Associate producers: Robert Eggenweiler and Scott Bushnell; Assistant directors: Tommy Thompson and Alan Rudolph; Wardrobe by Jules Melillo; Film editors: Sidney Levin and Dennis Hill; Titles by Dan Perri; Sound editor: William A. Sawyer; Sound recording: Jim Webb and Chris McLaughlin; Filmed in Panavision and MGM Color; Running time: 159 minutes

CAST:
Tom Frank (Keith Carradine), *Barbara Jean* (Ronee Blakley), *Connie White* (Karen Black), *Haven Hamilton* (Henry Gibson), *Delbert Reese* (Ned Beatty), *Linnea Reese* (Lily Tomlin), *Sueleen Gay* (Gwen Welles), *Mary* (Cristina Raines), *Opal* (Geraldine Chaplin), *L.A. Joan* (Shelley Duvall), *Norman* (David Arkin), *Kenny Fraiser* (David Hayward), *Pfc. Glenn Kelly* (Scott Glenn), *Tommy Brown* (Timothy Brown), *John Triplette* (Michael Murphy), *Bud Hamilton* (Dave Peel), *Mr. Green* (Keenan Wynn), *Lady Pearl* (Barbara Baxley), *Jimmy Reese* (James Dan Calvert), *Donna Reese* (Donna Denton), *Barnett* (Allen Garfield), *Star* (Bert Remsen)

To coincide with the annual music festival, a political rally is planned in Nashville for presidential candidate Hal Phillip Walker. The organizers of the rally, John Triplette (Michael Murphy) and Delbert Reese (Ned Beatty), want several Grand Ole Opry stars to perform at it, including country-and-western favorite Haven Hamilton (Henry Gibson) and Barbara Jean (Ronee Blakley), a popular folksinger recently recovered from a nervous breakdown.

During the week of the festival, Nashville is besieged by performers from all parts of the country who have come to seek their fame and fortune. One of the more talented hopefuls is Tom Frank (Keith Carradine), leader of a fledgling folk trio. A notorious ladies' man, he is having an affair with his partner's wife Mary (Cristina Raines), and during his stay in Nashville he embarks on brief flings with two other women—Delbert Reese's wife Linnea (Lily Tomlin) and Opal (Geraldine Chaplin), an attractive English girl covering the event for the BBC.

Meanwhile, the still unstable Barbara Jean botches her opening concert, and her manager-husband assures her angry fans she'll make up for it by giving a free one in a few days. Hearing of this and sensing a great opportunity, the enterprising Reese persuades Barbara Jean to fulfill the promise by performing at the upcoming political rally.

Later, Sueleen Gay (Gwen Welles), a shapely waitress with singing ambitions, is hired to perform at a political stag gathering organized by Reese and Triplette. When the guests hear her embarrassingly bad singing, however, they holler for her to strip, and Reese promises her a shot at the rally if she complies. Wanting desperately to sing at the rally, Sueleen performs a stilted strip-tease, and later that night Reese tries to talk her into bed, without success.

On the day of the rally, Haven and Barbara Jean are a smash, but while taking their bows Barbara is shot by a disturbed drifter (David Hayward). As Barbara Jean is carried off by medical attendants, an ambitious unknown seizes the on-stage microphone

ever brought to the screen. It was a highly unconventional script, telling not one but a myriad of stories involving over twenty major characters. Moreover, the characters weaved in and out of each other's lives in scenes that were rather brief and episodic, and the plot was a mixture of such diverse elements as humor, tragedy, and social commentary—all played against the background of a major music festival. The complex, multileveled nature of the script would probably have been more than the average director could have handled, but Altman relished the challenge of once again stringing many characters and incidents together in a single film, as he had done in his first major success, 1969's *M.A.S.H.* Altman

Ronee Blakley

Keith Carradine

and starts performing while, in the wings, Sueleen Gay waits patiently for the opportunity that will never come.

Robert Altman's *Nashville* is, by any standard, an exceptional piece of cinema, and is one of the few seventies films that manages to be thought-provoking and entertaining at the same time. The screenplay for the film, written by Altman's close friend Joan Tewkesbury, was masterful, and every one of its characters, from the principles to the tiniest bit part, was acted with skill by the enormous cast.

Though brilliant, Tewkesbury's screenplay must also rank as one of the most difficult story properties

succeeded admirably with *Nashville,* turning it into 159 minutes of fascinating, topical entertainment.

Altman also managed to elicit uniformly splendid performances from his cast, and while he made all the characters in the story memorable, two of them emerged as standouts. Ronee Blakely turns in a superb performance as the tragic, doomed Barbara Jean, and she glides hesitantly through the film like a sensitive, wounded sparrow trying desperately to mend itself. It is a tribute to Altman's skill that, although it is never even hinted at before the climax, the audience somehow senses throughout the story that Barbara Jean is in terrible danger, and therefore

David Hayward, Scott Glenn, Geraldine Chaplin

Lily Tomlin

Ronee Blakley, Keenan Wynn

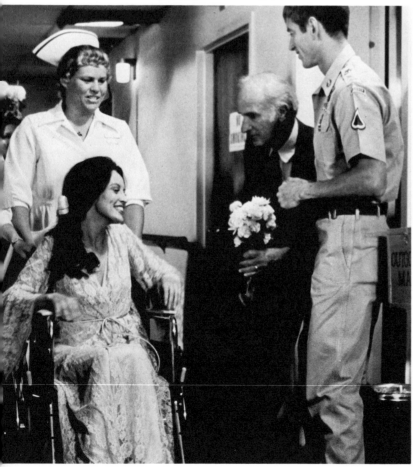

Henry Gibson

her assassination, while shocking, is hardly a surprise. Also excellent is Gwen Welles as Sueleen Gay, a simple, good-hearted young woman whose dreams of stardom are forced to withstand a series of cruel realities (like her indignities at the stag party and her final wait at the rally for the "big break" that doesn't materialize).

Interestingly, the actors in the film wrote many of their own songs, and Keith Carradine won an Academy Award for the gentle "I'm Easy."

Robert Mitchum

Charlotte Rampling, Robert Mitchum

FAREWELL, MY LOVELY

An Avco Embassy Picture; Directed by Dick Richards; Produced by Jerry Bruckheimer and George Pappas; Screenplay by David Zelag Goodman; Based on the novel by Raymond Chandler; Photography by John Alonzo; Executive producers: Elliott Kastner and Jerry Bick; Assistant directors: David Sonsa and Henry Lange; Music by David Shire; Production designed by Dean Tavoularis; Film editors: Joel Cox and Walter Thompson; Art direction by Angelo Graham; Filmed in color; Running time: 97 minutes

CAST:
Phillip Marlowe (ROBERT MITCHUM), *Mrs. Grayle* (Charlotte Rampling), *Nulty* (John Ireland), *Mrs. Florian* (Sylvia Miles), *Moose Malloy* (Jack O'Halloran), *Brunette* (Anthony Zerbe), *Tommy Ray* (Walter McGinn), *Jonnie* (Sylvester Stallone), *Mr. Grayle* (Jim Thompson), *Amthor* (Kate Murtagh), *Marriott* (John O'Leary), *Billy Rolfe* (Harry Dean Stanton), *Nick* (Joe Spinell), *Georgie* (Jimmy Archer)

Released from prison in the summer of 1941, Moose Malloy (Jack O'Halloran), a giant-sized thug, hires private eye Phillip Marlowe (Robert Mitchum)

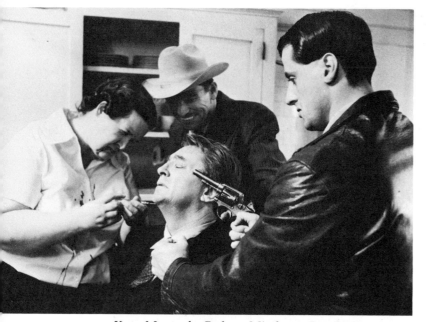

Kate Murtagh, Robert Mitchum, Burt Gilliam,
Sylvester Stallone

Robert Mitchum

to find his long-lost girlfriend, Velma Valento. Moose tells Marlowe that Velma once worked in a dime-a-dance joint called Florian's, which has since become an all-black nightclub.

Hoping to find a clue to Velma's whereabouts, Marlowe visits Florian's and is told the only person who might know anything is Tommy Ray (Walter McGinn), a trumpet player who once worked with Velma at Florian's. Housed in a sleazy hotel across from the club, Tommy tells Marlowe to see Mrs. Florian (Sylvia Miles), the alcoholic wife of the dive's former owner, who has kept in touch with Velma over the years. Marlowe learns from Mrs. Florian that Velma is in an insane asylum following a nervous breakdown.

Believing this closes the case, Marlowe returns to his office and is visited by the wealthy, effeminate Mr. Marriott (John O'Leary), who wants Marlowe to help him recover a stolen jade piece. Marriott tells Marlowe the valuable stone belongs to Mrs. Grayle (Charlotte Rampling), a wealthy friend of his, and that it is being held for ransom by thugs. Fascinated by the story, Marlowe takes the case, but during the attempt to recover the piece, Marriott is killed and Marlowe is knocked out.

Days later, Marlowe visits Mrs. Grayle, a beautiful, sensuous woman, who admits to finding him very attractive despite her marriage to an aged millionaire. Her lust for Marlowe is such that she tries seducing him on the spot, but he rebuffs her, explaining it wouldn't be right with her husband in the next room. Promising to phone her in a few days whether he finds out about the jade piece or not, Marlowe is later kidnapped by thugs, who take him to Amthor (Kate Murtagh), a gross whorehouse madame. Insisting Marlowe give her the whereabouts of Moose Malloy, Amthor injects Marlowe with a

Sylvia Miles, Robert Mitchum

Robert Mitchum

Raymond Chandler's Phillip Marlowe novels, published during the forties, are among the toughest, most atmospheric detective stories ever written. They continue to be popular to this day, and several of them have been made into exceptional motion pictures. In 1944, *Farewell, My Lovely,* perhaps the most famous of the lot, was filmed under the title *Murder, My Sweet,* which featured a superb performance by Dick Powell as Marlowe and clever, rather gimmicky direction by Edward Dmytryk. The celebrated Humphrey Bogart–Lauren Bacall version of *The Big Sleep* followed in 1946, and two years later Robert Montgomery directed and starred in a screen adaptation of *The Lady in the Lake.* In 1959, there was a short-lived television series starring the rugged Phillip Carey, followed ten years later by a slick, sexy film version of *The Little Sister* with James Garner.

Despite the many interpretations of Marlowe over the years, however, the movies did not find their *ideal* Marlowe until 1975, when Robert Mitchum played the character in a remake of *Farewell, My Lovely.* Mitchum, then in his late fifties, projected a resigned, world-weary cynicism that was just perfect for the character, and his performance is one of the best of his long career.

From a technical standpoint, *Farewell, My Lovely* is also intriguing, and production designer Dean Tavoularis, art director Angelo Graham, and photographer John Alonzo (*Chinatown*) obviously worked closely to create a properly dingy and rundown ambience for the story. Marlowe's is a dark, shoddy, nocturnal world utterly devoid of warmth or sunlight, and it is a credit to Alonzo that he lensed the sleazy hotel and nightclub settings in muted, shadowy tones that truly capture the feel of Phillip Marlowe's drab nightworld.

powerful drug when he refuses. The effect is devastating, but after living through three days of nightmarish hallucinations, Marlowe escapes. Later, he learns that Tommy Ray and Mrs. Florian have been murdered.

Afterward, he gets a call from Mrs. Grayle, who tells him to meet her at a plush nightspot owned by the shady Mr. Brunette (Anthony Zerbe), who later offers Marlowe $1,500 if he brings Malloy to a yacht party the following week. Marlowe wonders why Moose is suddenly so popular, but he is distracted when Mrs. Grayle insists they head for the nearest bedroom.

Sometime afterward, Moose tells Marlowe that he was in prison for stealing $80,000 and only he knows where the loot is hidden. Realizing Amthor and Brunette are after the money, Marlowe tells Moose to lay low for a while, but Moose insists Marlowe take him to the party. Aboard Brunette's yacht, Marlowe learns that Mrs. Grayle is the long-lost Velma and that Tommy and Mrs. Florian were killed because they might betray her true identity. Marlowe realizes Brunette, Amthor, and Velma have conspired to cheat Moose out of his booty, and he warns the giant not to reveal its whereabouts. Still in love with Velma, however, Moose stupidly tells her where it is, after which she coldly guns him down. Creating a distraction, the quick-thinking Marlowe shoots Velma, then turns Brunette over to the chief of detectives.

DOG DAY AFTERNOON

A Warner Bros. Picture; Directed by Sidney Lumet; Produced by Martin Bregman and Martin Elfand; Screenplay by Frank Pierson; Based on a magazine article by P. F. Kluge and Thomas Moore; Photography by Victor J. Kemper; Assistant directors: Burt Harris and Alan Hopkins; Associate producer: Robert Greenhut; Film editor: Dede Allen; Production design by Charles Bailey; Costumes by Anna Hill Johnstone; Art direction by Doug Higgins; Filmed in Technicolor; Running time: 130 minutes

CAST:
Sonny (AL PACINO), *Sal* (John Cazale), *Mulvaney* (Sully Boyar), *Sheldon* (James Broderick), *Moretti*

Carol Kane (second from left), Sully Boyar, Al Pacino

Al Pacino

(Charles Durning), *Leon* (Chris Sarandon), *Jenny* (Carol Kane), *Sylvia* (Penny Allen), *Margaret* (Beulah Garrick), *Deborah* (Sandra Kazan), *Miriam* (Marcia Jean Kurtz), *Maria* (Amy Levitt), *Angie* (Susan Peretz), *Vi* (Judith Malina), *Carmine* (Carmine Foresta), *Murphy* (Lance Henriksen), *Bobby* (Gary Springer), *Maria's boyfriend* (Chu Chu Malave), *Pizza boy* (Lionel Pina), *Limo driver* (Dick Williams)

On a hot summer afternoon, the First Savings Bank of Brooklyn is held up by Sonny (Al Pacino) and Sal (John Cazale), two down-and-out characters. Although the bank manager (Sully Boyar) and female tellers agree not to interfere with the robbery, Sonny finds that there's actually nothing much to steal, as most of the cash has been picked up for the day.

As if this weren't enough, Sonny gets an unexpected phone call from Police Captain Moretti (Charles Durning), who tells him the place is surrounded by the city's entire police force. Having few options under the circumstances, Sonny nervously bargains with Moretti, demanding safe escort to the airport and a plane out of the country in return for the bank employees' safety.

Meanwhile, Sonny's transvestite lover Leon (Chris Sarandon) arrives on the scene and talks with Sonny via police telephone. Leon tries to persuade Sonny to surrender peacefully but Sonny refuses, telling Leon he attempted the robbery only to provide Leon with money for the sex change he always wanted. Later, FBI Agent Sheldon (James Broderick) also tries to talk Sonny out, but Sonny insists on his original plan, and the authorities finally submit.

Amazed when an airport shuttle bus pulls up in front of the bank, Sonny, Sal, and the hostages walk slowly onto the street. Entering the bus, Sonny and his companions are then driven to the airport. At the last instant, however, the driver (really an FBI agent) whirls around and shoots Sal dead, and Sonny is taken into custody. The hostages, all unharmed, gratefully return to their families.

The Godfather, Part II contained what many consider to be Al Pacino's finest screen work, but making the epic film had proven an emotionally trying

Charles Durning

Dog Day Afternoon, a film that gave him one of his best roles and which reunited him with his director from *Serpico,* Sidney Lumet. Though he has never been entirely happy working in films, Pacino admits that he finds it difficult to resist what he considers a winning screenplay, and after reading Frank Pierson's treatment for *Dog Day Afternoon,* Pacino was unable to refuse the part.

Like *Serpico, Dog Day Afternoon* was the dramatization of a real-life story—in this case the famous incident from the early seventies in which the Chase Manhattan Bank in Flatbush, Brooklyn, was held siege by a gay robber determined to steal enough for his male lover to undergo a sex change operation. Interestingly, *Dog Day Afternoon* emerged as a more clinical, objective film than *Serpico,* and it showed neither the robbers nor the law enforcement personnel in a particularly flattering light.

The film had an almost serio-comic flavor, enhanced by the colorful playing of Chris Sarandon as Sonny's lover Leon and the "sad sack" appearance and dialogue of Sonny's pathetic sidekick Sal (asked by Sonny which country he'd like to escape to, Sal glumly replies, "Wyoming"). John Cazale, who portrayed Sal, also played Pacino's treacherous weakling brother Fredo in both *Godfather* films.

John Cazale, Al Pacino

experience for the actor. The character's many complexities, coupled with the sheer magnitude of the role, put Pacino in the hospital for exhaustion about midway through the filming. Following the picture's completion, Pacino stated that *The Godfather, Part II* was going to be his last motion picture for a while and that, weary of the laborious process of filmmaking, he wanted to return to the (for him) less demanding and more fulfilling world of the New York stage.

Before Pacino was able to do this, however, he was lured back in front of the cameras once again for

ONE FLEW OVER THE CUCKOO'S NEST

A United Artists Picture; Directed by Milos Forman; Produced by Saul Zaentz and Michael Douglas; Screenplay by Lawrence Hauben and Bo Goldman; Based on the novel by Ken Kesey; Photography by Haskell Wexler, William Fraker, and Bill Butler;

Film editors: Richard Chew, Lynzee Klingman, and Sheldon Kahn; Production designer: Paul Sylbert; Associate producer: Martin Fink; Assistant directors: Irby Smith and William St. John; Music by Jack Nitzsche; Filmed in color; Running time: 129 minutes

CAST:
R. P. McMurphy (JACK NICHOLSON), *Nurse Ratched* (LOUISE FLETCHER), *Billy Bibbit* (Brad Dourif), *Chief Bromden* (Will Simpson), *Two girls* (Marya Small, Louisa Moritz), *Harding* (William Redfield), *Ellis* (Michael Berryman), *Dr. Spivey* (Dean R. Brooks), *Col. Matterson* (Peter Brocco), *Miller* (Alonzo Brown), *Turkle* (Scatman Crothers), *Warren* (Mwako Cumbuka), *Martini* (Danny De Vito), *Sefelt* (William Duell), *Bancini* (Josip Elic), *Nurse Itsu* (Lan Fendors), *Washington* (Nathan George), *Beans Garfield* (Ken Kenny), *Harbor*

Jack Nicholson, Josip Elic, Will Sampson

Danny DeVito, Brad Dourif, Jack Nicholson

Jack Nicholson, Marya Small

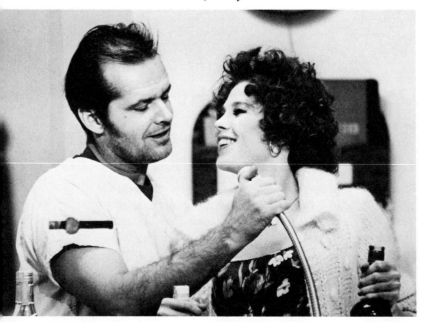

master (Mel Lambert), *Cheswick* (Sydney Lassick), *Night supervisor* (Kay Lee), *Taber* (Christopher Lloyd)

To escape the monotony of a prison work farm, Randle P. McMurphy (Jack Nicholson) feigns madness and is transferred to a mental hospital. An outspoken "free spirit," he immediately clashes with the strict, authoritarian head nurse, Mrs. Ratched (Louise Fletcher), and discovers his fellow patients to be relatively normal people ("no crazier than any other s.o.b. on the street," in McMurphy's words).

After a few weeks at the hospital, McMurphy realizes most of the patients are not insane at all, but merely helpless emotional misfits who were hospitalized primarily because they couldn't get along in the outside world. Their instability makes them easy targets for the hospital's rather sadistic staff, particularly Ratched, who delights in wielding cruel punishment for the slightest misconduct. Determined to "liven things up," McMurphy organizes card games (with pornographic decks), sports activities, and field trips, breathing life into the dreary hospital. Nurse Ratched, however, objects to the patients' enjoying themselves, and, seeing him as a threat to her own position, she determines to break McMurphy.

The patients grow to love him, however, affectionately calling him "Mac", and he continues to

Louise Fletcher

disregard the rules by taking his new friends on a boating holiday, which does them more good than being in the hospital. It isn't long before the patients' love for Mac outweighs their fear of Ratched, and when several of them disobey her at Mac's instigation, he is given electroshock in retaliation. Meanwhile, Mac befriends Chief Bromden (Will Sampson), a huge Indian who, like McMurphy, faked insanity to escape an unpleasant situation on the outside. The two plan an escape from the hospital, and as the fateful day approaches they throw a midnight celebration, smuggling two girls (Marya Small and Louisa Moritz) and a case of whiskey into the ward.

A patient who idolizes Mac is young Billy Bibbit (Brad Dourif), whose emotional disturbance stems from a domineering mother. Billy is acutely withdrawn (though Mac has brought him "out of his shell" to a great extent) and has spent so much time in the hospital that he has never made love (at one point, McMurphy tells him: "Hey, you're a young guy. You should be out drivin' cars and bird-doggin' chicks"). Determined to give his young friend a taste of life's fruit, Mac persuades one of the girls, Candy, to sleep with Billy. The next morning, however, Ratched finds Billy and Candy in bed together and, threatening to tell his mother, drives Billy to suicide.

Angered beyond control, McMurphy tries to strangle Ratched and is later lobotomized as punishment. Transformed into a pitiful catatonic by the surgery, McMurphy is mercifully smothered by Bromden, who then makes a glorious escape.

Ken Kesey's *One Flew Over the Cuckoo's Nest,* the story of Randle P. McMurphy's heroic struggle for human rights and dignity inside an oppressive mental hospital, was enormously successful as a novel, a play, and a film. The exclusive rights to the vehicle had been purchased by Kirk Douglas in the early sixties, and the actor appeared as McMurphy in the original Broadway production. Following the stage run, Douglas wanted to film *One Flew Over the Cuckoo's Nest* through his own company, Bryna Productions, but a heavy schedule of commitments made this impossible. In the early seventies, Douglas, who was now too old to play McMurphy, gave the property to his son Michael who, in addition to being a hot young actor (as a result of his work on television's *The Streets of San Francisco*), was also an aspiring producer.

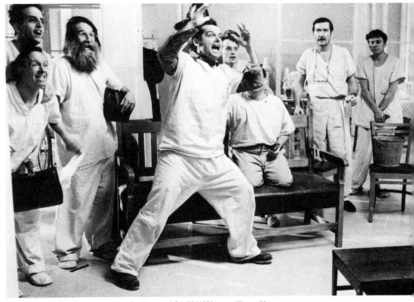

Jack Nicholson, Brad Dourif, William Duell

In 1975, the younger Douglas produced this stunning film version, directed by Milos Forman and starring Jack Nicholson as McMurphy. Like the novel and play, the film was a deeply affecting comment on the human condition, and Nicholson won the year's Best Actor Oscar for what is, perhaps, the most powerful performance of his career.

Nicholson made McMurphy an outspoken rebel-hero in the same mold as his earlier characters, Bobby Dupea in *Five Easy Pieces* and Billy Buddusky in *The Last Detail.* Despite the obvious similarities of the three, however, Nicholson made perhaps, his strongest impression on audiences with McMurphy, not only because of the acting, but also because it was the one time a Nicholson rebel-hero ultimately

133

lost his battle against "the system." Both Dupea and Buddusky were free to express their contempt for society without punishment, and Nicholson's memorable brawls with the surly waitress (in *Five Easy Pieces*) and the bigoted bartender (in *The Last Detail*) left him unscathed because they took place in the outside world, where his adversaries had no real power over him. His situation in *Cuckoo's Nest* is another matter entirely. In this case, Nicholson's rebel-hero is trapped in a small, corrupt domain ruled by sadists who despise him for his individuality and who eventually destroy him for attempting to bring something positive and beautiful into their negative little universe.

A finely made, disturbing film, *One Flew Over the Cuckoo's Nest* won all the major Oscars for 1975—Best Picture, Actor, Actress, Direction, and Screenplay.

THE MAN WHO WOULD BE KING

An Allied Artists Picture; Directed by John Huston; Produced by John Foreman; Screenplay by John Huston and Gladys Hill; Based on the story by Rudyard Kipling; Photography by Oswald Morris; Film editor: Russell Lloyd; Production designer: Alexander Trauner; Wardrobe by Edith Head; Associate producer: James Arnett; Assistant director: Bert Batt; Music by Maurice Jarre; Art direction: Tony Inglis; An Allied Artists/Columbia Pictures Production; Filmed in Panavision and Technicolor; Running time: 129 minutes

CAST:
Daniel Dravot (SEAN CONNERY), *Peachy Carnehan* (MICHAEL CAINE), *Rudyard Kipling* (Christopher PLUMMER), *District Commissioner* (Jack May), *Billy Fish* (Saeed Jaffrey), *Kafu-Selim* (Karroum Ben Bouih), *Roxanne* (Shakira Caine), *Ootah* (Doghmi Larbi), *Mulvaney* (Paul Antrim), *Babu* (Mohammed Shamsi), *Ghulam* (Albert Moses)

In 1880's India, Daniel Dravot (Sean Connery) and Peachy Carnehan (Michael Caine), two roguish con men, storm into the office of newswriter Rudyard Kipling (Christopher Plummer), asking him to witness a contract. Agreeing to swear off women and liquor, Dravot and Carnehan plot a daring adventure—to be the only white men to enter ancient Kafiristan since Alexander the Great, who first conquered it. Leaving Kipling's office, the two embark on a long journey, finally making it to Kafiristan after numerous adventures.

Once there, they luckily acquire an interpreter (Saeed Jaffrey) and several rifles to ward off hostile

Sean Connery

Sean Connery, Michael Caine

Michael Caine

Michael Caine, Sean Connery

Sean Connery

Christopher Plummer, Michael Caine

natives who resent their intrusion. During a skirmish with native tribes, Dravot is shot with an arrow, which sticks in his bandolier, making him appear invulnerable. Declared a "god" by the impressionable natives, Dravot is sent to the holy city of Sikandergul, where he is given a king's treasure as an offering.

Feeling it's all too good to last, Carnehan pleads with Dravot to leave, but Daniel insists on playing his god-king role to the hilt, and he later takes a beautiful native princess, Roxanne (Shakira Caine), for his queen. During their marriage ceremony, however, the apprehensive girl bites Dravot's hand, drawing blood, and the natives realize he's a fraud. As punishment for their deception, Dravot is killed and Carnehan crucified. By chance, Carnehan survives, and the holy men let him go.

Years later, Carnehan visits Kipling to tell him the incredible tale of "the man who would be king."

The Man Who Would Be King, a short story written by Rudyard Kipling in his early twenties, had fascinated John Huston ever since the director first read it as a sickly, bedridden boy of fourteen. For twenty years, Huston dreamed of bringing the story to the screen, and there were several abortive attempts at it before the project was finally realized in this lavish, wonderful motion picture.

The director first envisioned it as the perfect vehicle for Clark Gable and Humphrey Bogart, who had never worked together on screen, and whose teaming would almost certainly have meant big box office. The monumental teaming was, however, made impossible by Bogart's death in 1957. In the mid-sixties, Huston thought of Richard Burton and Peter O'Toole, who had proven such a winning combination in *Beckett,* but curiously this never materialized due to Huston's inability to find financial backing.

Then, ten years later, John Foreman, the producer of Huston's *The Life and Times of Judge Roy Bean* and *The Mackintosh Man,* became greatly interested in doing *The Man Who Would Be King,* and the idea finally got off the ground. Foreman obtained the backing of Allied Artists, who budgeted the film at a relatively modest $8 million. Huston originally wanted to make the picture in Afghanistan, where the Kipling story takes place, but various setbacks prevented this, and Huston ended up making the film on location in Morocco.

Upon the film's completion, Allied Artists began a vigorous publicity campaign for *The Man Who Would Be King,* and the film, perhaps the finest action-adventure drama to hit the decade's screens, became greatly successful. Sean Connery and Michael Caine turned in superb performances in the lead roles, and the actors seemed so perfectly cast as Dravot and Carnehan that it is doubtful any of the previously planned versions would have been nearly as good.

135

THE SUNSHINE BOYS

An MGM Picture; Directed by Herbert Ross; Produced by Ray Stark; Screenplay by Neil Simon; Based on his own play; Photography by David M. Walsh; Film editor: John F. Burnett; Set decorations by Marvin March; Production designer: Albert Brenner; Assistant directors: Jack Roe and Gary Daigler; Sound by Jerry Jost and Harry W. Tetrick; Costumes by Pat Norris; Titles designed by Wayne Fitzgerald; Filmed in Metrocolor; Running time: 111 minutes

CAST:
Willie Clark (WALTER MATTHAU), *Al Lewis* (GEORGE BURNS), *Ben Clark* (Richard BENJAMIN), *"Nurse"* (Lee Meredith), *Mechanic* (F. Murray Abraham), *Real nurse* (Rosetta Le Noire), *TV director* (Jim Cranna), *Commercial director* (Howard Hesseman), *Helen* (Jennifer Lee), *Stage manager* (Garn Stephens), *Doris* (Carol Arthur), *Desk clerk* (Santos Morales), *Man at audition* (Fritz Feld), *Man at audition* (Jack Bernardi), *Patient* (Sid Gould), *Man on street* (Sammy Smith), *Mr. Ferranti* (Dan Resin)

Veteran vaudeville comic Willie Clark (Walter Matthau) now relies on his agent-nephew Ben

George Burns, Lee Meredith, Walter Matthau

(Richard Benjamin) to find him occasional work in television commercials. However, while auditioning for a potato chip commercial one morning, Willie flubs his lines and, embarrassed, decides to retire from show business.

Ben, however, wants Willie to continue performing and books the old trouper into an upcoming television special, in which he'll be reunited with his old partner, Al Lewis (George Burns). Once the hottest act in vaudeville (known as "The Sunshine Boys"), Lewis and Clark have been "on the outs" for years, and Willie cringes when Ben mentions a possible reunion. After much persuasion, however, Willie agrees to give it a try. He and Al arrive at the television station for a rehearsal, but during a run-through of their old "The Doctor Will See You Now" sketch, Al angers Willie, who storms off the stage. Willis has a heart attack in the wings and is rushed to the hospital; he later recovers.

Richard Benjamin, Walter Matthau

Returning home, Willie is told by Ben that he's been invited to live out his days in comfort at the Old Actors' Home in New Jersey. Later, Al visits Willie and the two talk over old times. They reconcile, and to his surprise Willie learns that Al is also moving to the Old Actors' Home.

Neil Simon was especially well served by the film versions of his plays in the seventies. All were translated to the screen—*Barefoot in the Park* (1967), *The Odd Couple* (1968), *Plaza Suite* (1971), *The Sunshine Boys* (1975), *The Prisoner of Second Avenue* (1975), and *Chapter Two* (1980)—and all were solid hits with audiences and critics alike. During the decade, Simon also made his mark as a screenwriter, and his two original scripts—*Murder by Death* (1976) and *The*

George Burns, Walter Matthau

Goodbye Girl (1977)—were both made into top-notch movies. Of the Simon stageworks brought to the screen during the seventies, *The Sunshine Boys* is one of the best and most entertaining. Like most Simon comedies, it is both funny and heartwarming, and MGM and producer Ray Stark (*Funny Girl*) gave it a lavish and faithful screen treatment in 1975.

The story of two old vaudeville troupers who are given a chance to make a comeback, *The Sunshine Boys* was originally planned as a vehicle for George Burns and Jack Benny, but Benny's death in 1974 prevented this. Walter Matthau, who was much younger than either of the characters in the story, was hired to play the Benny role, Willie Clark, and the actor was required to wear extensive age makeup throughout the film.

Incredibly, *The Sunshine Boys* marked George Burns's first screen role since 1939, when he co-starred with Gracie Allen in the largely forgotten *Honolulu*. His charming, touching portrayal of Al Lewis won him the year's Best Supporting Actor Oscar, and it launched Burns on a brand new screen career at the age of eighty-one.

The honors Burns received should not, however, obscure Matthau's bravura acting as the stubborn, cantankerous Willie Clark. Deftly playing a man many years his senior, Matthau got a rare chance to display his skill at vocal characterization during the hilarious "The Doctor Will See You Now" sketch. In the routine, Matthau used a high, thickly accented, cartoonlike character voice for the slightly nutty physician he was playing.

George Burns, Walter Matthau, Richard Benjamin

1976

TAXI DRIVER

A Columbia Picture; Directed by Martin Scorsese; Produced by Julia and Michael Phillips; Screenplay by Paul Schrader; Photography by Michael Chapman; Music by Bernard Herrmann; Associate producer: Philip Goldfarb; Art direction by Chuck Rosen; Film editor: Marcia Lucas; Costumes by Ruth Morley; Assistant director: Peter Scoppa; Filmed in Panavision and color; Running time: 113 minutes

CAST:
Travis Bickle (ROBERT DE NIRO), *Betsy* (Cybile Shepherd), *Iris* (Jodie Foster), *Sport* (Harvey Keitel), *Wizard* (Peter Boyle), *Charles Palantine* (Leonard Harris), *Tom* (Albert Brooks), *Charlie T* (Norman Matlock), *Personnel officer* (Joe Spinnell), *Doughboy* (Harry Northrup), *Man in taxi* (Martin Scorsese)

New York City. Cab driver Travis Bickle (Robert De Niro) constantly, almost obsessively, reflects on the ugly corruption of life around him, and becomes increasingly disturbed over his own loneliness and alienation. In nearly every phase of his life, Bickle remains a complete outsider, failing to make emotional contact with anyone (even his attempt to converse with the ticket girl at a sleazy porn theater is met with cold rejection). Unable to sleep night after night, Travis haunts the local pornography emporiums to find diversion, and begins desperately thinking about an escape from his depressing existence.

Cybill Shepherd, Robert De Niro

Robert De Niro, director Martin Scorsese

One afternoon, he sees Betsy (Cybile Shepherd), a pretty political volunteer who works at the posh headquarters of presidential candidate Charles Palantine (Leonard Harris). At first, Travis observes her only from a distance, worshipping her as an untouchable ideal amid all the filth and degradation of the streets. Gathering his courage, Travis asks her for a date one night after work, and is surprised when she accepts. However, when he takes her to see a pornographic film, she becomes offended and storms out of the theater. His attempts to apologize are met with repeated, unreasoning rejection, and it becomes obvious to Travis that she was merely playing with him from the start.

His ideal shattered, Travis falls into a deep depression, and the meaninglessness of his life starts eating away at him. Slowly, inexorably, his mind begins to

Albert Brooks, Cybill Shepherd

disintegrate, and he later buys an arsenal of handguns from an underground dealer. Without really knowing why, Travis embarks on an intense regimen of physical training and begins practicing daily with his guns at a firing range to become a crack shot. Later, he tells his friend and fellow taxi driver Wizard (Peter Boyle) that he's afraid he'll do something violent unless he can release the pent-up anger and frustration within him.

Hoping that a sexual encounter might ease some of the strain, Travis visits Sport (Harvey Kietel), a small-time pimp, and buys fifteen minutes with Iris (Jodie Foster), a thirteen-year-old prostitute. Drawn to the lovely young girl, Travis refuses her services and strikes up a friendship instead. Disgusted by Iris's circumstance, Travis offers to finance her escape from Sport, whom he calls the "lowest scum on the face of the earth." Touched by his genuine concern for her welfare, Iris agrees to let him help her return home to her parents.

Sometime later, however, Iris again falls under Sport's velvety spell, and she resumes her life on the streets. Upon learning of this, Travis's mind finally snaps, and, arming himself to the teeth, he drives to the apartment building which houses Sport's prostitution ring. Confronting Sport, Bickle baits him with insults before shooting him point-blank in the stomach. Inside the building, Travis kills two of Sport's gangster accomplices before attempting to shoot himself. However, his gun turns out to be empty, and, exhausted from his ordeal, he simply sits down amid the carnage to wait for the arrival of the police.

Later it is revealed that, by chance, Travis's nightmare of madness and violence has, ironically, made him into a local hero, applauded by the media for saving an innocent young girl from the clutches of Sport and his gang. Now something of a celebrity around town, Travis turns the tables on Betsy by rejecting her after she enters his cab one evening and tries to get back in his good graces.

Taxi Driver seemed an unlikely candidate for box-office success. The bleak and uncompromising script by Paul Schrader dealt with the psychotic breakdown of a lonely cab driver in New York City. Its protagonist, Travis Bickle, was a man completely alienated from the mainstream of life, and the unbearable drabness of his existence eventually drives him to madness and murder. Many of its key scenes took place in especially dreary New York locations—sleazy porn theaters, run-down apartment houses, and dirty streets illuminated by chintzy neon signs. Also, it featured one of the goriest bloodbaths in the history of cinema when, at the climax of the story, Travis slaughters a group of pimps and gangsters to prevent them from further corrupting a thirteen-year-old prostitute he has befriended. All in all, *Taxi Driver* was not the stuff that hits are made of, even in the somber seventies.

When he first completed the script, Schrader took it to the production team of Julia and Michael Phillips, who had produced the popular *The Sting* several years earlier. Despite the stark and raw nature of the story, the Phillipses thought it had great potential if produced properly, and they immediately tried to find a major studio to back the project. However, they eventually found that the only way they could get it produced would be in a package deal involving the rather inappropriately wholesome Jeff Bridges as Bickle under the direction of Robert Mulligan, whose past films included *To Kill a Mockingbird* (1962), *Up the Down Staircase* (1967), and *Summer of '42* (1971). Not surprisingly, Schrader felt that such a combination would not befit his rather downbeat story, and he knew full well that if *Taxi Driver* was to be brought to the screen effectively, it would need the ideal star-director combination to do it justice.

Robert De Niro, Cybill Shepherd, director Martin Scorsese

By chance, Schrader saw the 1974 film *Mean Streets* and knew instantly that Martin Scorsese and Robert De Niro were the ideal choices for *Taxi Driver*. The saga of young racketeers on the streets of New York's Little Italy, *Mean Streets* was a fine example of Scorsese's superb flair for color, and his excellent use of neon light throughout the story gave the film the kind of dreamlike, surreal atmosphere that Schrader wanted for *Taxi Driver*. Likewise, De Niro's portrayal of the crazy Johnny Boy, one of the young thugs, exhibited the proper balance of sensitivity and madness needed for Travis Bickle. The Phillipses agreed with Schrader's judgment, and after securing the services of De Niro and Scorsese they persuaded Columbia to back the film.

Heralded by an excellent publicity campaign that included extensive airing of the film's "trailer" on network television, *Taxi Driver* was released in 1976 with all its harsh realism and brutality intact, and to everyone's surprise became an instant success. The potentially depressing tale of Travis Bickle had been transformed by Scorsese into a compelling, strangely beautiful film, its fiery, intense, almost rapturous color scheme acting as a constant buffer to the negative subject matter. De Niro's performance as Bickle was applauded as one of the best of the decade, and his sensitive playing made the character sympathetic despite his actions. He portrayed Bickle as a basically honest, kind, and decent man, which made his disintegration into madness all the more disturbing.

MARATHON MAN

A Paramount Picture; Directed by John Schlesinger; Produced by Robert Evans and Sidney Beckerman; Screenplay by William Goldman; From his novel; Photography by Conrad Hall; Art direction by Jack DeShields; Assistant directors: Howard W. Koch, Jr. and Burt Harris; Music by Michael Small; Film editor: Jim Clark; Production designed by Richard MacDonald; Filmed in Metrocolor; Running time: 120 minutes

CAST:
Babe Levy (DUSTIN HOFFMAN), *Szell* (LAURENCE OLIVIER), *Doc Levy* (ROY SCHEIDER),

Dustin Hoffman, Marthe Keller

Janeway (William Devane), *Elsa* (Marthe Keller), *Professor* (Fritz Weaver), *Mr. Levy* (Allen Joseph), *Erhard* (Marc Lawrence), *Rosenbaum* (Lou Gilbert), *Melendez* (Tito Goya), *LeClerc* (Jacques Marin)

New York. Babe Levy (Dustin Hoffman) trains daily in hope of one day becoming an Olympic marathon runner. A graduate student in history, his desire for a gold medal is eclipsed only by his determination to vindicate his father, a respected teacher who committed suicide when his reputation was tarnished during the McCarthy witch hunts.

Babe's older brother Doc (Roy Scheider) is a top-ranking secret agent. Though his job with U.S. Intelligence pays well, he begins a clandestine involvement with Szell (Laurence Olivier), an ex-Nazi seeking to claim his late brother's diamond fortune, locked in a safe deposit box in a New York bank. For a large fee, Doc sneaks Szell into America, but when he stupidly demands more money for continued silence, Szell stabs him. Having strength enough to crawl to Babe's apartment, Doc attempts to tell what happened but dies before uttering a word.

Later, Babe is kidnapped by Szell's thugs, who take him to an abandoned warehouse. Strapped tightly to a chair, Babe is puzzled when Szell enters the room and begins setting up all manner of dental equipment. A skilled dentist, Szell often used the tools of his trade to torture concentration camp victims, and he now intends doing the same to Babe to find out if Doc said anything before he died. After Szell bores into an exposed oral nerve with an electric drill, Babe still insists that Doc said nothing, and Szell concludes that he must be telling the truth. Later, Babe escapes, and thanks to his superb condition runs across Manhattan to his apartment, where he picks up his .45 automatic.

Meanwhile, Szell obtains the diamonds, then makes the mistake of visiting a pawnbroker to have them assessed. Suddenly realizing the man is a former victim, Szell hastily exits. On the street, an old Jewish woman also recognizes Szell, and begins

Dustin Hoffman

Roy Scheider

Laurence Olivier

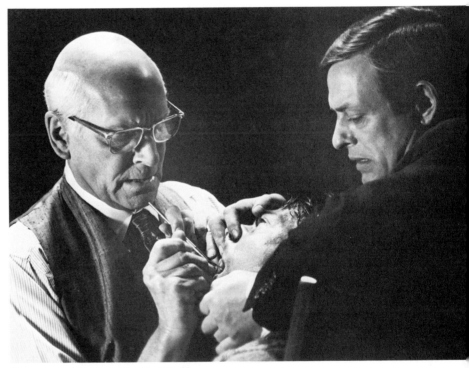

Laurence Olivier, Dustin Hoffman

Roy Scheider, Laurence Olivier

Dustin Hoffman, Laurence Olivier

ranting about "the human monster on the streets of Manhattan."

Scurrying away, Szell is confronted at gunpoint by Babe, who orders him into a deserted indoor reservoir. Forcing the Nazi to open his briefcase, Babe looks at the sparkling treasure, and tells Szell he can keep all the diamonds he can swallow. Painfully gulping only one of the gems, Szell lunges at Babe, and in the scuffle the diamonds spill into the water. In a desperate attempt to retrieve them, Szell falls down and is fatally stabbed with his own knife.

Marathon Man is one of the great suspense films of the seventies, featuring an excellent cast, a literate, high-tension screenplay, and tight, fast-paced direction by John Schlesinger. Usually a director of serious, "heavy" dramatic pictures (such as *Midnight Cowboy* and *The Day of the Locust*), Schlesinger was greatly enthused about tackling a pure thriller, and he made *Marathon Man* a stylish, pulse-pounding entertainment.

The film was based on the highly successful novel by William Goldman, and movie rights to the book had been purchased by producer Robert Evans shortly after he read the galleys. The subsequent film, though grim and violent, was a box-office hit—audiences were mesmerized by the acting of Dustin Hoffman and Laurence Olivier, and by Schlesinger's virtuoso direction.

The critics, however, were not particularly impressed by *Marathon Man,* citing that the story line was confusing and its excessive mayhem bordered on being tasteless. Another complaint was that *Marathon Man* let a full hour go by before introducing the major conflict of the story (Szell's desire to recover the diamonds and his involvement with Doc and Babe). Most critics said the film wasted far too much time on exposition, and that the segments during its first hour (Babe's practice runs; the flashbacks about his father; an explosive car crash involving two old men, one a German and the other a Jew; and Doc's brutal encounter with a hulking assassin in a Paris hotel room) had little to do with what *Marathon Man* was really about. These incidents were, however, rather important to the film's mood, as they all contained an aura of dread foreboding (especially the fiery collision involving the old war enemies), which perfectly set the stage for the eventual appearance of the evil Szell.

In one of his finest performances in recent years, Laurence Olivier captures the complex emotional makeup of the Nazi, who has mastered the art of both psychological and physical torture (before subjecting Babe to the drill, Szell drives him to distraction by repeating the meaningless phrase "Is it safe?" over and over again).

THE OUTLAW JOSEY WALES

A Warner Bros. Presentation of a Malpaso Company Film; Directed by Clint Eastwood; Produced by Robert Daley; Associate producers: Jim Fargo and John G. Wilson; Screenplay by Phil Kaufman and Sonia Chernus; From the novel *Gone to Texas* by Forrest Carter; Photography by Bruce Surtees; Film editor: Ferris Webster; Assistant director: Jim Fargo; Production designer: Tambi Larsen; Music by Jerry Fielding; Filmed in Panavision and DeLuxe Color; Running time: 135 minutes

CAST:
Josey Wales (CLINT EASTWOOD), *Laura Lee* (Sondra Locke), *Lone Watie* (Chief Dan George), *Fletcher* (John Vernon), *Terrill* (Bill McKinney), *Little Moonlight* (Geraldine Keams), *Grandma Sarah* (Paula Trueman), *Jamie* (Sam Bottoms), *Chief* (Will Sampson), *Head carpetbagger* (Woodrow Parfrey)

At the height of the Civil War, Josey Wales (Clint Eastwood), a peaceful farmer, becomes an outlaw when his family is murdered by Union scavengers. Joining a band of Confederate vigilantes headed by a man named Fletcher (John Vernon), Wales engineers several attacks on Union Army posts, and soon the mention of his name is enough to frighten the bluecoats.

At the war's conclusion, Fletcher and his men surrender, but Wales refuses to joint them, swearing to continue fighting as an "army of one." Captain Terrill (Bill McKinney), a Union officer and one of the men who killed Wales's family, offers a handsome reward for his capture. Undaunted by the price on his head, Wales heads for Texas, along with Lone Watie (Chief Dan George) and Little Moonlight (Geraldine Keams), two Indians he has befriended.

On their arrival in Texas, Wales rescues a family of homesteaders from a gang of ravaging carpetbaggers. Grateful, Grandma Sarah (Paula Trueman) insists Josey and the Indians stay on, and to his surprise Wales is elected head of the family. His reunion with family life dissolves his awful memories, and he finds further contentment when he falls in love with Sarah's granddaughter, Laura Lee (Sondra Locke). Sensing his idyll will be short-lived, however, Wales instructs his new family in the use of firearms, and converts their small house into a fortress.

Later, Captain Terrill and his men, who've been trailing Wales, surround him in front of the house, unaware the family is armed and ready to come to his aid. A furious gun battle ensues, and all the bountyhunters are killed except Terrill, who escapes on

Clint Eastwood

Clint Eastwood

horseback with Josey in pursuit. The chase ends in a windswept ghost town and (in a scene obviously inspired by *Dirty Harry*) Wales draws a point-blank bead on his enemy, then tauntingly snaps the triggers on his giant Colt Dragoons (the Old West equivalent of the .44 Magnum), leaving Terrill to guess whether either gun contains a live round. Both are empty, however, and Josey kills Terrill by running him through with his own saber.

By 1976, Clint Eastwood had proven himself a director of style and imagination in films such as *Play Misty for Me* (1971), *High Plains Drifter* (1973), *Breezy* (1973), and *The Eiger Sanction* (1975). In all of these, Eastwood revealed a keen cinematic eye and a definite "feel" for creating the proper atmosphere as well as the ability to direct himself, which is a rare talent indeed. Though Eastwood the actor is primarily known for his "superhero" roles in several large-scale westerns and police dramas, Eastwood the director was able to make his mark in several different kinds of pictures, and showed himself capable of handling a psychological horror story, a brooding Western, a gentle love story, and a contemporary spy drama with equal skill.

After directing and starring in *The Eiger Sanction*, Eastwood began work on his most ambitious project as a director to date. It was a sprawling, epic western

opus that would, in many ways, recall the mood and spirit of the John Ford–Howard Hawks "classics" of the late forties. *The Outlaw Josey Wales* made its debut in late 1976, and though most critics agreed that Eastwood's performance as the peace-loving farmer turned vigilante was his all-time best, they remained sharply divided as to the merits of the film

Will Sampson, Clint Eastwood

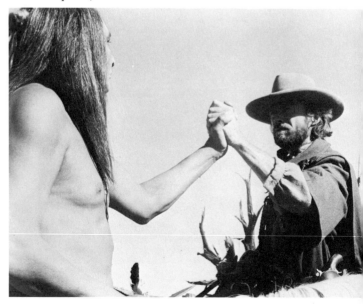

itself. Some hailed it as one of the ten best films of the year, while others found it merely boring, over-long, and hopelessly uneven.

While it must be admitted that *The Outlaw Josey Wales* contains more than its share of rough spots and that the opening scenes of the Union ravagers attacking Josey's farm have a curiously vague quality, the film, as a whole, is superbly realized. As an illustration of Eastwood's eye for detail, most of the set pieces in the film (such as Josey's burning cabin and a rustic riverside trading post Josey visits later in the story) were constructed slightly smaller than normal size; coupled with their dark, timberlike appearance, this gave them a truly authentic "frontier" flavor. Unlike the earlier *High Plains Drifter*, which featured Eastwood as a mysterious gunslinger seeking revenge on the men who once tried to kill him, *The Outlaw Josey Wales* is not an attempt by Eastwood to pay tribute to Sergio Leone and the "man-with-no-name" character. While Josey Wales is also a character strongly motivated by revenge, Eastwood gives him a warmth and humanity that the enigmatic stranger of his earlier westerns never had (during the burial of Wales's murdered son, the usually stoic Eastwood actually weeps).

Eastwood's skills as a director are clearly evident throughout the picture, but none of his images equal the one in which a group of carpetbaggers prepare to defile Laura Lee (Sondra Locke) after pillaging the homesteader's camp. Discovering her cowering in a small wagon, the filthy scavengers eye her hungrily, and Eastwood injects the episode with supreme tension as the camera cuts back and forth between the girl and her would-be rapists. The contrast between the fawnlike beauty of Sondra Locke and the sub-human griminess of her attackers is almost more than an audience can take, which is exactly the effect Eastwood wanted.

THE OMEN

A 20th Century-Fox Picture; Directed by Richard Donner; Produced by Harvey Bernhard; Screenplay by David Seltzer; Photography by Gilbert Taylor; Film editor: Stuart Baird; Set decorations: Tessa Davies; Sound recording: Gordon Everett; Executive producer: Mace Neufeld; Associate producer: Charles Orme; Special effects by John Richardson; Music by Jerry Goldsmith; Assistant directors: David Tomblin and Steve Lanning; Filmed in DeLuxe Color and Panavision; Running time: 111 minutes

CAST:
Robert Thorn (GREGORY PECK), *Katherine Thorn* (LEE REMICK), *Mrs. Baylock* (Billie Whitelaw), *Jennings* (David Warner), *Damien* (Harvey Stephens), *Bugenhagen* (Leo McKern), *Father Brennan* (Patrick Troughton), *Father Spiletto* (Martin Benson), *Priest* (Tommy Duggan), *Monk* (Robert Rietty), *Dr. Becker* (Anthony Nicholls), *Nanny* (Holly Palance), *Mrs. Horton* (Sheila Raynor), *Horton* (Robert MacLeod), *Reporter* (Roy Boyd), *Psychiatrist* (John Stride), *Nurse* (Nancy Manningham), *Marine* (Nicholas Campbell)

Gregory Peck

High-ranking U.S. diplomat Robert Thorn (Gregory Peck) and his wife Katherine (Lee Remick) anxiously await the birth of their child in a Rome hospital. When Katherine miscarries, Thorn is allowed by hospital officials to substitute another baby whose mother has died in delivery. Christened Damien (Harvey Stephens), the adopted child grows into a healthy, seemingly normal youngster, but at his fifth

Lee Remick, Harvey Stephens

147

Gregory Peck, Billie Whitelaw

birthday party his nanny inexplicably hangs herself, much to the Thorns' horror.

Father Brennan (Patrick Troughton), a priest dying of cancer, visits Thorn sometime afterward, warning him that he has adopted the son of Satan, and that the child will someday take over the world from a position of political power. He tells Thorn to seek the advice of an old monk named Bugenhagen (Leo McKern), an exorcist who knows the secret ritual by which the Devil's offspring can be destroyed.

Meanwhile, Mrs. Baylock (Billie Whitelaw), a governess with excellent references, becomes Damien's new nanny, and watches over the child day and night. Later, Father Brennan meets a bizarre death, not unlike that of Damien's former nanny. After hearing of Brennan's strange demise, Thorn is visited by Jennings (David Warner), the news photographer who covered Damien's birthday party. He tells Thorn that pictures he took of the child's nanny and Father Brennan contained shadowy marks revealing the angle from which they were eventually killed.

After Jennings reveals that he accidentally snapped a photo of himself containing similar marks, he and Thorn travel to Italy, hoping to locate Bugenhagen. They find him in an old monastery, and after hearing of the weird events in Thorn's life, Bugenhagen tells Thorn that he has, indeed, adopted the son of the Devil and that the only way to eliminate Damien is to slay him sacrificially on the altar of a church. He also informs Thorn that Mrs. Baylock is no doubt a Satanic emissary whose duty is to protect Damien from harm.

Meanwhile, Katherine is murdered by Mrs.

Baylock and Jennings dies in the manner prophesized by the photograph. Returning home, Thorn kills Mrs. Baylock and takes Damien to a nearby church in order to carry out Bugenhagen's order. Before he has the chance to dispose of Damien, however, Thorn is shot by police for "attempting to kill his son." Now an orphan, Damien is adopted by Robert Thorn's good friend, the President of the United States.

The horror films of the seventies were a uniformly frightening lot. The era's technical innovations in special effects, sound recording, and makeup, coupled with the fact that most of the decade's shockers were big-budget, major-studio affairs, allowed horror-film makers to indulge in effects bloodcurdling enough to make the old Frankenstein, Dracula, Wolf Man, and Mummy films look tame by comparison.

Though many critics and historians continue to believe that the most effective horror pictures are those which leave something to the imagination, the most successful fright movies of the seventies were noted for their lack of subtlety, sledgehammer shock effects, and blatant gruesomeness. Though the decade's shockers dealt with a variety of themes traditional to the genre—psychotic murderers preying on helpless, primarily female victims in *Black Christmas* (1976) and *Halloween* (1978); vampirism in *Martin* (1978) and *Dracula* (1979); the living dead in *Dawn of the Dead* (1979); a hostile life form from another world in *Alien* (1979); and monsters created by ecological imbalance in *Prophecy* (1979)—the most popular theme seemed to be the possession of a young child by a demonic spirit.

Lee Remick, Harvey Stephens

This was, of course, first explored in William Friedkin's *The Exorcist*, a film so terrifying and profitable that it inspired a whole string of cheap imitations, all of which tried to re-create the formula that had made *The Exorcist* such a hit. Most of these films failed to generate any enthusiasm, partly because audiences were well aware that the producers were trying to capitalize on someone else's success, and also because the films themselves were quickly made, rather chintzy items, lacking the style and imagination of the film that inspired them.

Although 1976's *The Omen* deals with a theme similar to that of *The Exorcist*, it is very much its own movie. It actually went *The Exorcist* one better in that it did not deal with the demonic possession of a child, but rather with the young son of Satan

Gregory Peck

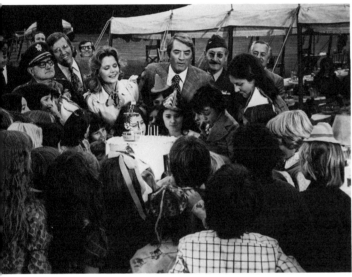

Lee Remick, Gregory Peck, Harvey Stephens

himself. An expensive, lavishly made, and thoroughly enjoyable picture that, despite its subject matter, had its tongue firmly in its cheek, *The Omen* became, along with films such as *The Exorcist* and *The Sentinel*, one of the decade's most representative horror pictures. Like the other two and countless lesser movies, *The Omen* dealt with clerical men doing battle with the forces of the Devil. But whereas *The Exorcist* and *The Sentinel* relied on horrific, sometimes *repulsive* shock scenes to achieve their moods, *The Omen* is a far more subtle exercise. Unlike the possessed Regan in *The Exorcist* or the hideous armies of Hell in *The Sentinel*, the chief "monster" in *The Omen* is Damien, a harmless-looking five-year-old who never transforms into a demon or actually does anything wicked, but whose seemingly innocent presence inspires dreadful things to happen around him. Unlike the other two, *The Omen* is regarded primarily as a "fun" horror movie that never takes itself too seriously (the ridiculous aspects of its plot would prevent this anyway).

Despite this, however, director Richard Donner did manage to achieve some chilling effects in *The Omen*, and Robert Thorn's nocturnal encounter with a group of vicious "devil dogs" in an old cemetery is a fine pastiche of terror, recalling in atmosphere some of the more famous "graveyard" scenes from the Universal horror "classics" of old. Likewise, the spectacular deaths of Damien's nanny (by hanging), the photographer (beheaded by a large pane of glass), Katherine (falling through the hood of an ambulance after being pushed out a window by Mrs. Baylock), and Father Brennan (run through by a falling church steeple) are superbly startling. Moreover, Donner is successful in making Damien's nanny Mrs. Baylock (Billie Whitelaw) a frightening, Satanic individual who, during her climactic struggle with Gregory Peck toward the end of the film, resembles a murderous, bloodthirsty animal.

Lee Remick, Gregory Peck

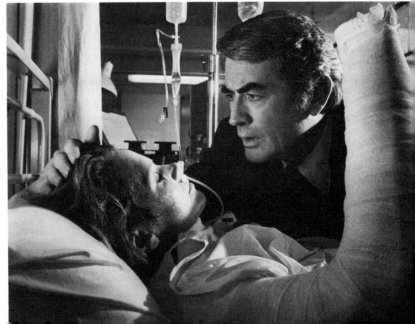

BOUND FOR GLORY

A United Artists Picture; Directed by Hal Ashby;
Produced by Robert F. Blumofe and Harold Leventhal; Screenplay by Robert Getchell; Based on the autobiography of Woody Guthrie; Photography by Haskell Wexler; Art direction by James H. Spencer and William Sully; Assistant director: Charles A. Myers; Film editors: Robert Jones and Pembroke J. Herring; Production designed by Michael Haller; Photographed in Deluxe Color; Running time: 147 minutes

CAST:
Woody Guthrie (David Carradine), *Mary Guthrie* (Melinda Dillon), *Pauline* (Gail Strickland), *Ozark Bule* (Ronny Cox), *Slim Snedeger* (Ji-Tu Cumbuka), *Locke* (John Lehne), *Luther Johnson* (Randy Quaid), *Liz Johnson* (Elizabeth Macey), *Talent agent* (Allan Miller)

David Carradine

1936. Feeling the crunch of the Great Depression, penniless singer Woody Guthrie (David Carradine) hops a freight to California, hoping to find steady employment out west. Thrown off somewhere in Arizona, he hitches a ride with a group of Oklahoma farm workers, exiles from their own land, who pray that California is the "land of milk and honey" it's supposed to be. Arriving at the California border, they are not permitted entry because of the excessive migration into the state.

Woody, however, sneaks across on foot and makes his way to Los Angeles, where he meets farm worker Luther Johnson (Randy Quaid), who, like thousands of others, is looking for work in California's fields. Becoming friends, Woody and Luther spend the night in one of the overcrowded labor camps set up to accommodate the unemployed masses. Here, Woody gets a taste of the terrible oppressions these people are forced to endure. Having little hope of ever finding work, they look forward only to the periodic visits of folksinger Ozark Bule (Ronny Cox), whose delightful songs keep their spirits from being broken.

150

During one of Ozark's songfests at the camp, Woody joins in, and Ozark is so impressed that he offers him a singing job at a Los Angeles radio station. Soon, the on-air combination of Ozark and Woody proves so popular that they begin touring the country. Despite his success, Woody develops a gnawing social conscience, and he begins singing about the farm workers' oppression on his broadcasts.

When his radio program gets a new sponsor, Woody is order to drop the controversial songs, but he refuses. After repeated warnings, Woody is fired, but is offered a star shot at the Cocoanut Grove if he agrees to commercialize himself. Finding the idea distasteful, however, Woody hops a freight bound for New York, hoping to bring joy to all oppressed people he meets along the way.

For some reason, the decade's screen biographies of entertainment personalities did not fare especially well at the box office. The year 1976 saw the production of three such films—*Gable and Lombard, W. C. Fields and Me,* and *Bound for Glory*—none of which managed to attract audiences. In the case of the first two, it is easy to understand why they failed, as neither of them was particularly well made. *Gable and Lombard,* one of the seventies' most spectacular flops, was almost laughably bad, and despite the fine acting of Rod Steiger in the title role, *W. C. Fields and Me* suffered from a weak and cliché-ridden script, which made it impossible for an audience to become involved in the story.

Gail Strickland, David Carradine

David Carradine

David Carradine

Woody Guthrie, David Carradine

Ji-Tu Cumbaka, David Carradine

Bound for Glory, the screen adaptation of Woody Guthrie's autobiography, was, however, an excellent motion picture, beautifully written, directed, and acted—featuring a strong performance by David Carradine in the role of Guthrie. The actor's own rebellious, slightly eccentric nature gave his portrayal of Guthrie a striking element of truth, and he was splendid as the talented, gutsy, irreverent folksinger whose many songs helped bring a spirit of joy and hope to Depression-ravaged America during the thirties.

A wholly satisfying film never given the recognition it so richly deserves, *Bound for Glory* was also noted for the marvelous cinematography of Haskell Wexler (recalling, in many ways, the vibrant look of old three-strip Technicolor) and for the flavorful direction of Hal Ashby. Despite its many qualities, however, *Bound for Glory* was not the success it should have been.

ROCKY

A United Artists Picture; Directed by John G. Avildsen; Produced by Irwin Winkler and Robert Chartoff; Screenplay by Sylvester Stallone; Photography by James Crabe; Art direction: James H. Spencer; Film editor: Richard Halsey; Executive producer: Gene Kirkwood; Music by Bill Conti; Performed by Valentine; Production design by Bill Cassidy; Assistant directors: Fred Gallo and Steve Perry; Filmed in color; Running time: 119 minutes

CAST:
Rocky Balboa (SYLVESTER STALLONE), *Adrian* (Talia Shire), *Mickey* (Burgess Meredith), *Paulie* (Burt Young), *Apollo Creed* (Carl Weathers), *Gazzo* (Joe Spinell), *Mike* (Jimmy Gambina), *Jergens* (Thayer David), *Cut man* (Al Silvani), *Fight announcer* (Bill Baldwin), *Marie* (Jodi Letizia), *Dipper* (Stan Shaw), *Bartender* (Don Sherman), *Pet store owner* (Jane Marla Robbins), *Fats* (Jack Hollander), *Club fighter* (Pedro Lovell), *Apollo's trainer* (Tony Burton), *Apollo's cornerman* (Hank Rolike), *Timekeeper* (Frank Stallone), *Secretary* (Shirley O'Hara), *Paulie's date* (Kathleen Parker), *Drunk* (Lloyd Kaufman)

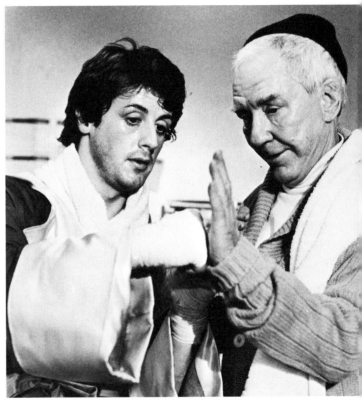

Sylvester Stallone, Burgess Meredith

Club fighter Rocky Balboa (Sylvester Stallone) lives in a small Philadelphia apartment with mementos of a ring career that never got off the ground. Past his prime, Rocky earns his living by strong-arming for a "numbers" racket, and limits his boxing to unimportant bouts at the local settlement house. He still trains daily to stay in shape, and his former trainer, Mickey (Burgess Meredith), constantly rides him for never realizing his potential. ("You had it in you to be a great fighter," Mickey says, "but you were lazy!")

Meanwhile, Rocky falls in love with Adrian (Talia Shire), a shy pet-store clerk; and her brother Paulie (Burt Young), a meatpacker, invites Rocky to Thanksgiving dinner. With great effort, Rocky persuades Adrian to step out with him, and after getting acquainted on a deserted ice rink they go to Rocky's

152

apartment. Adrian's discomfort is evident ("I've never been in a man's apartment before . . .") but Rocky's warmth wins her over, and they become lovers.

Later, Apollo Creed (Carl Weathers), the world heavyweight champion, dreams up a novel publicity idea—he will fight a complete unknown, giving the fellow a once-in-a-lifetime shot at the title. Skimming through the boxing registry, Creed chooses Rocky. Of course, Creed regards the whole thing as a joke, but Rocky begins training arduously, toughening his blows by hammering punches into large slabs of meat in Paulie's freezer.

Though realizing he can't win, Rocky knows that "going the distance" will prove that he "isn't just another bum from the neighborhood." The fight is a brutal, fifteen-round slugfest, during which Rocky breaks the champ's ribs. Creed retains his title, however, and tells Rocky he won't get a rematch, to which Rocky replies: "I don't want one." Confident he has proven himself, Rocky embraces Adrian.

Sylvester Stallone, who wrote the screenplay for *Rocky* in addition to playing the lead role, is possibly the most remarkable cinematic success story of the decade. The film, the pleasantly sentimental tale of a down-and-out club fighter who is given a once-in-a-lifetime shot at the heavyweight title, won the Academy Award as Best Picture of 1976, and remains one of the seventies' most popular films. Rocky Balboa's triumphant struggle to better himself and to prove that he wasn't "just another bum from the neighborhood," coupled with the beautiful, touching romance between Rocky and his girlfriend Adrian (Talia Shire), made the film a natural winner with audiences, and, interestingly, the story of Rocky

Sylvester Stallone

Sylvester Stallone, Carl Weathers

Balboa's victory over incredible odds closely parallels that of his creator, Sylvester Stallone.

Stallone's success was a literal "rags-to-riches" fairy tale (rare in Hollywood nowadays) as he shot from bits and supporting roles to worldwide fame and recognition. He is probably the only major film actor of the seventies to make the transition from unknown to superstar in such a grand manner (even John Travolta was an established television personality before *Saturday Night Fever*), and as such his story is unique. A mere two years before *Rocky*'s release, Stallone had been a starving, down-and-out actor and would-be screenwriter living in New York who, to try and change his luck, moved west on the small salary he received for his role in the movie *The Lords of Flatbush*. In Hollywood, however, things did not improve in the slightest, and he tried repeatedly without success to sell the few scripts he had written between minor acting assignments.

By chance, however, one evening Stallone happened to see the telecast of the famous heavyweight bout between Muhammed Ali and Chuck Wepner, in which Wepner (a "part-time" professional fighter from New Jersey) was rated an incredible underdog, not even expected to last four rounds. The determined Wepner went the distance, however, which so inspired Stallone that he dreamed up the character of Rocky Balboa who, like Wepner, would be a common man given a shot at the heavyweight title. Excited by his idea, Stallone worked feverishly on the script, completing it in three days (which, for a screenplay, is amazingly fast).

Stallone's agent read the script and was sufficiently impressed to turn it over to Gene Kirkwood, who eventually served as *Rocky*'s executive producer. Kirkwood presented it to Irwin Winkler and Robert Chartoff who, after insisting on minor changes, offered Stallone $75,000 for it. Hearing that they wanted to use the property as a vehicle for an es-

Carl Weathers, Sylvester Stallone, Burgess Meredith

Sylvester Stallone, Burgess Meredith
Sylvester Stallone, Carl Weathers

tablished star, Stallone (who wanted to play the role himself) refused, and the bidding eventually climbed to $265,000. However, Stallone would not accept any amount unless the producers agreed to cast him as Rocky. Finally, Winkler and Chartoff persuaded United Artists to gamble on Stallone, whose finished performance, arguably, made Rocky Balboa the most beloved screen character of the seventies.

NETWORK

A United Artists Picture; Directed by Sidney Lumet; Produced by Howard Gottfried; Story and screenplay by Paddy Chayefsky; Photography by Owen Roizman; Associate producer: Fred Caruso; Production design by Phillip Rosenberg; Film editor: Alan Heim; Music by Elliot Lawrence; Costumes by Theoni V. Aldredge; Assistant directors: Ralph Singleton and Jay Allan Hopkins; Filmed in Metrocolor and Panavision; Running time: 120 minutes

CAST:
Diana Christensen (FAYE DUNAWAY), *Max Schumacher* (WILLIAM HOLDEN), *Howard Beale* (PETER FINCH), *Frank Hackett* (ROBERT DUVALL), *Arthur Jensen* (Ned Beatty), *George Bosch* (John Carpenter), *Joe Donnelly* (Ed Crowley), *Mary Ann Gifford* (Kathy Cronkite), *Harry Hunter* (Jordan Charney), *Nelson Chaney* (Wesley Addy), *Louise* (Beatrice Straight), *Caroline* (Cindy Grover), *Barbara Schlesinger* (Conchata Ferrell), *Bill Herron* (Darryl Hickman), *The Great Ahmed Kahn* (Arthur Burghardt), *TV director* (Bill Burrows), *Edward Ruddy* (William Prince)

Howard Beale (Peter Finch), news anchorman for the UBS television network, is informed he is being fired after twenty-five years. Unable to cope with this, Beale suffers a breakdown on the air, informing his audience he will blow his brains out on the next week's broadcast. Naturally, the ratings skyrocket, and Beale receives fan mail from all parts of the country.

The following week's show garners the highest rating in network history, but instead of shooting himself Beale unleashes a tirade about the sorry state of mankind. At the end of his speech, Beale rises and spreads his arms wide apart like some great prophet, inviting his audience to "stand up wherever you are, go to the nearest window and yell as loud as you can: 'I'm mad as hell, and I'm not going to take it anymore!' " The response is overwhelming, and all across America a frightened and fed-up citizenry can be heard screaming away their frustrations.

Sensing a great opportunity, Diana Christensen (Faye Dunaway), a ruthless program executive, conceives the idea of a weekly series featuring Beale as a kind of modern-day messiah. This is, however, met with strong opposition by Max Schumacher (William Holden), vice-president of network news and Beale's friend, who finds the idea of capitalizing on Howard's mental problem grotesque. However, the network higher-ups accept Diana's concept, and Max is fired. The resulting "Howard Beale Crusade" is a bizarre combination of news, weather, sports, and prophecy—at the end of each program, Howard strides in front of the cameras to give his audience a devastating piece of social commentary.

Meanwhile, Diana prepares her second show, a dramatic series centering on a group of terrorist guerillas who will, of course, appear as themselves to boost ratings. Later, Diana bumps into Max, and the two become involved romantically. Deciding to leave his wife, Max moves in with Diana and begins work on a memoir about his broadcasting career. Though Max grows to love Diana, he finds she is impossible to reach emotionally, her feelings forever locked behind a mask of cold cynicism. Knowing he cannot survive in a relationship that gives him no emotional feedback, Max walks out on Diana and returns to his wife Louise (Beatrice Straight).

Meanwhile, Howard Beale denounces the monetary system on one of his broadcasts, which angers members of the conglomerate that owns UBS. The head of the conglomerate, an imposing man named Arthur Jensen (Ned Beatty), summons Beale into his office and proceeds to devastate the newsman with a hypnotic speech on the omnipotence of money and the unimportance of individual people. Reduced to human putty by this and completely under Jensen's spell, Howard stops championing human rights and begins alienating his viewers by telling them how meaningless their lives are.

Beale's ratings slacken, and, during an emergency production meeting, Diana and the network executives agree the most colorful way to end Howard's career is to have him assassinated on the air.

In 1971, screenwriter veteran Paddy Chayefsky wrote the script for a brilliant satirical film, *The Hospital*, which dealt with the bureaucracy and insanity of large-city health care. The film featured George C. Scott as a harried, bitterly discouraged doctor trying desperately to maintain balance and order amid the chaos of hospital routine. It contained all the madcap lunacy of a Marx Brothers comedy, yet *The Hospital* made a serious, compelling statement about contemporary life, and Chayefsky's script won him the Oscar for best original screenplay of the year.

William Holden
Peter Finch

155

Peter Finch, William Holden

Robert Duvall, William Holden

Peter Finch

William Holden, Faye Dunaway

Five years after *The Hospital*, Chayefsky wrote a similar satire of the television industry called *Network* which was, once again, a serious comment couched in the form of outrageous satire. The film, perhaps the biggest hit of 1976, dealt with the awesome power that television exerts over the lives of its viewers, and it contained a marvelous performance from Peter Finch as the "modern-day prophet" Howard Beale. *Network*, like *The Hospital*, won several major Oscars, including Best Picture; and Finch became the first actor in history to be given an Academy Award posthumously.

Network's script was even more radically satirical than the one Chayefsky wrote for *The Hospital*, and several incidents in the film push its credibility dangerously to the limit (the idea that a major television network would hire a group of terrorists to appear as themselves in a prime-time series is almost *too* absurd). Overall, however, *Network* is superbly realized, and will likely remain the cinema's definitive spoof of the television industry.

As an interesting sidelight, the Howard Beale character—whose compelling on-air speeches denouncing all of life's iniquities from poverty to urban alienation drew applause from some audiences—was so convincingly and passionately acted by Finch that, for many members of the audience, Beale actually did become a kind of revered spokesman for oppressed people, and it was, thus, deeply disturbing for some to see the character later mesmerized into submission by the conglomerate head (Ned Beatty).

In one of the film's most memorable moments, the "spokesman for the people" is chastised by the powerful business magnate for deriding the financial system on his program. Beatty is stunning in this scene, as he begins his speech by ranting about how money is the center of the universe and then, with silken gentleness, persuades Howard to spread the message that the individual is no longer important to society. The effect of this sequence is awesome.

Ned Beatty

THE ENFORCER

A Warner Bros. Presentation of a Malpaso Company Film; Directed by James Fargo; Produced by Robert Daley; Screenplay by Stirling Silliphant and Dean Reisner; Story by Gail Morgan Hickman and S. W. Schurr; Based on characters created by Harry Julian Fink and R. M. Fink; Photography by Charles W. Short; Art direction by Allen E. Smith; Film editors: Ferris Webster and Joel Cox; Assistant directors: Joe Cavalier, Joe Florence, and Billy Ray Smith; Music by Jerry Fielding; Filmed in Panavision and DeLuxe Color; Running time: 96 minutes

CAST:
Harry Callahan (CLINT EASTWOOD), *Kate Moore* (Tyne Daly), *Capt. McKay* (Bradford Dillman), *Lt. Bressler* (Harry Guardino), *Bobby Maxwell* (DeVeren Bookwalter), *DiGeorgio* (John Mitchum), *The mayor* (John Crawford), *Big Ed* (Albert Popwell)

Clint Eastwood

San Francisco. Inspector Harry Callahan (Clint Eastwood) investigates the activities of a terrorist group led by Bobby Maxwell (DeVeren Bookwalter), a psychotic Vietnam vet. Preparing for urban-guerilla warfare, the terrorists raid a munitions warehouse, stealing all manner of weaponry from bazookas to hand grenades. Harry's partner, Frank DiGeorgio (John Mitchum), has been tailing the group, and he enters the warehouse with his gun drawn, commanding them to freeze. Maxwell, however, sneaks behind Frank and stabs the unsuspecting cop with a hunting knife. Taken to the hospital, Frank tells Harry he recognized his attacker as Maxwell, a well-known pimp before he became a terrorist. DiGeorgio dies, and Harry is less than pleased when his new partner turns out to be a lady cop, Kate Moore (Tyne Daly).

Later, Maxwell and his gang kidnap the mayor (John Crawford) and demand a huge ransom for his release. Meanwhile, Harry, disguised as a gullible tourist, visits a nude-encounter parlor hoping to get a lead on Wanda, a girl Maxwell once pimped for. Later, he meets with Big Ed (Albert Popwell), a black militant who keeps an eye on underground activities. Ed tells Harry that a local priest, known for his fierce liberalism, probably knows where Maxwell is keeping the mayor. Meanwhile, Harry's oafish superior, Captain McKay (Bradford Dillman), wants to pay the ransom, which Harry thinks is foolish. Harry goes to see the priest who, after much coercion, tells him that Maxwell has taken the mayor to Alcatraz Island.

Clint Eastwood, Tyne Daly

Clint Eastwood

Storming Alcatraz, Harry and Kate shoot it out with Maxwell and his troops, and Kate is killed saving Harry's life. Maxwell climbs an observation tower to get out of range, while Harry secures one of the bazooka-like rocket launchers Maxwell's group lifted from the warehouse. Firing it into the tower, Harry blows Maxwell to pieces, and the mayor thanks Harry for coming to his rescue. The carnage on Alcatraz presents a strange contrast to the police copter hovering above, with McKay's voice coming over a loudspeaker, assuring the criminals he has their ransom money.

Typical of many Clint Eastwood pictures, both *Dirty Harry* and *Magnum Force* proved to be enor-

mously popular with audiences and enormously unpopular with critics. Though most reviewers conceded that the films were exciting, well-made action dramas, both were heavily denounced for their excessive violence. In particular, *Magnum Force* was criticized for its overt mayhem, and most critics were quick to point out that even the film's opening titles reflected its rather brutal nature (the cast and credits were played against a shot of Harry's hand holding the enormous .44 Magnum; at the conclusion of the theme music, the gun is cocked and pointed at the audience, while on the soundtrack we hear the famous ''This is a .44 Magnum . . .'' speech, after which the gun is fired. Though both films still rank as Eastwood's biggest box-office hits to date, for a long while the actor insisted that *Magnum Force* would be the only sequel. He soon realized, however, that

Clint Eastwood

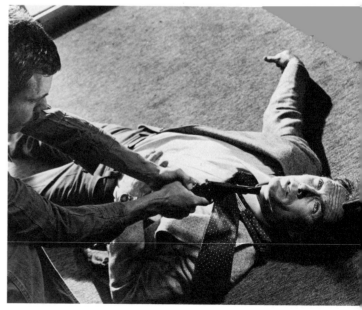

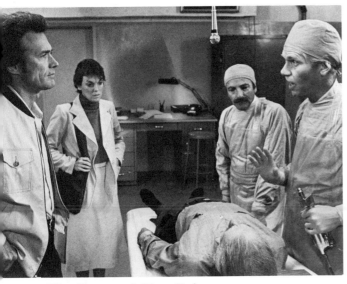

Clint Eastwood, Tyne Daly

Callahan's overwhelming popularity with audiences demanded further adventures, and a third film was eventually made.

However, when *The Enforcer* opened during the latter part of 1976, it became obvious that it was a very different kind of Dirty Harry adventure, for though the story took place in San Francisco and again pitted Harry against deadly criminals and a particularly dimwitted superior (played this time by Bradford Dillman), the violence in *The Enforcer* was toned down considerably. Moreover, to prevent the Callahan character from becoming stale in his third outing, the writers romanticized him to a certain degree. They softened his personality and outfitted him in stylish, expensive suits and jackets, as opposed to the bland sports clothes of the first two films. Also, the photography in *The Enforcer* was

Clint Eastwood

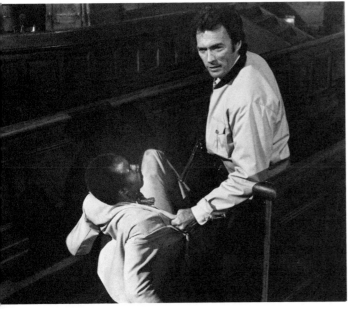

especially lush and striking, and its deep flesh tones gave Harry an uncharacteristic tan. This gave him something of a man-about-town image, which proved an entertaining change of pace from the tough, cynical loner of the other films.

As a further departure, the writers invented a unique undercover bit, in which Callahan disguises as an amiable fool (licking an ice-cream cone and sporting a too-small San Francisco Giants cap) in order to search the "nude encounter" parlors for Wanda. He pretends to be a naive customer, and when the girl refuses to tell him about Wanda, he gets angry and she calls the brawny manager, who mistakes Callahan for the creampuff he's pretending to be. Of course, this proves to be a costly error, as Callahan grabs the fellow and hisses: "Listen, *little man . . .* to me you're nothing but an insect who sells dirty pictures."

Clint Eastwood

CARRIE

A United Artists Picture; Directed by Brian De Palma; Screenplay by Lawrence D. Cohen; Based on the novel by Stephen King; Produced by Paul Monash; Associate producer: Louis Stroller; Photography by Mario Tosi; Film editor: Paul Hirsch; Music by Pino Donaggio; Costumes by Rosanna Norton; Art direction: William Kenny and Jack Fisk; Photographed in color; Running time: 97 minutes

CAST:
Carrie (SISSY SPACEK), *Margaret White* (PIPER LAURIE), *Tommy Ross* (William Katt), *Sue Snell*

159

(Amy Irving), *Billy Nolan* (John Travolta), *Chris Hargenson* (Nancy Allen), *Miss Collins* (Betty Buckley), *Mrs. Snell* (Priscilla Pointer), *Freddy* (Michael Talbot), *Mr. Morton* (Stefan Gierash), *Mr. Fromm* (Sydney Lassick), *Norman Watson* (P. J. Soles), *George* (Harry Gold), *Cora* (Cindy Daly), *The Beak* (Doug Cox), *Kenny* (Rory Stevens), *Ernest* (Anson Downes), *Boy on bicycle* (Cameron De Palma)

At Bates High School, Carrie White (Sissy Spacek), an awkward and withdrawn girl, is constantly ridiculed by her fellow students. Her only friends on campus are Miss Collins (Betty Buckley), the girls' gym teacher, and Sue Snell (Amy Irving), daughter of a well-to-do family. While most students at Bates come from upper-middle-class backgrounds, Carrie lives in a ramshackle house on the outskirts of town with her mother Margaret (Piper Laurie), a religious fanatic.

Carrie's problems stem from acute shyness (the result of her stern upbringing), and if properly groomed she'd be very attractive. Another thing setting her apart from others is her telekinetic power, which enables her to move objects and people through sheer force of her mind. Tommy Ross (William Katt), the most popular boy on campus, often dates Sue, who asks him to take Carrie to the senior prom. At first reluctant, Tommy eventually asks Carrie, and after much coaxing she says yes.

Meanwhile, two of Carrie's enemies, Chris (Nancy Allen) and Billy (John Travolta), plan an elaborate scheme to ruin Carrie's prom night. They first go to a pig farm, where they slaughter one of the animals,

Sissy Spacek, William Katt

John Travolta, Nancy Allen

Sissy Spacek, Piper Laurie

Sissy Spacek, William Katt

pouring its blood into a large bucket. The day before the prom, they bribe their fellow students to elect Tommy and Carrie king and queen, then place the bucket of pig blood above the auditorium's small stage. When Carrie and Tommy walk up to receive congratulations, Carrie will be right in the "line of fire."

Meanwhile, Carrie prepares for the big night, donning a lovely homemade dress that makes her feel pretty for the first time. This disturbs her mother, who tells Carrie to take her makeup off and "pray for forgiveness." Mrs. White is so disturbed by Carrie's beautiful appearance that she tries to forcibly stop her daughter from leaving. Using her telekinetic power to gently "shove" Margaret aside, Carrie runs to greet Tommy, who is amazed at her loveliness. At the prom, all the other students are equally impressed with Carrie, and, as the evening wears on, Tommy becomes genuinely attracted to her. At nine o'clock they are chosen king and queen, and Tommy escorts Carrie onto the stage while, below, Chris and Billy eagerly prepare to pull the cord that will overturn the bucket.

Sue is pleased to see Carrie enjoying herself, but she notices the cord and tries to tell Miss Collins. For some reason, Miss Collins refuses to listen and orders Sue out of the auditorium. Seconds later, Chris pulls the cord; Carrie is drenched in blood, while Tommy is knocked out by the falling bucket. At first shocked, the crowd bursts out laughing, and even Miss Collins can't help chuckling at Carrie's embarrassment.

This is too much for Carrie, who exacts a horrible revenge by psychically generating a holocaust of fire

Piper Laurie

161

and destruction leading to the deaths of all concerned. Making her way home sometime afterward, Carrie turns to her mother for comfort, but finds that Mrs. White has gone totally insane. Producing an enormous carving knife, she declares that Carrie must now pay for her sins with her life. Stabbing Carrie in the lower back, Mrs. White follows her as she falls down the stairs into the kitchen. As Mrs. White prepares to stab her again, Carrie summons her powers, making the knives and forks on a wall rack fly across the room and into her mother's body. Following this, Carrie uses her powers to destroy the house by fire.

Months later, Sue (the only survivor of the incident at Bates) begins having a recurring nightmare—she dreams of placing a bouquet of flowers on the rubble of Carrie's house when, suddenly, Carrie's bloodied hand shoots out of the ground and grabs her by the wrist.

Stephen King is, perhaps, history's most successful horror novelist. His books—*Carrie, 'Salem's Lot, The Shining, Night Shift, The Stand,* and *The Dead Zone*—have all been runaway best-sellers, and their cumulative sales have made King one of the wealthiest contemporary fiction writers. King's first major success was *Carrie*, the chilling tale of a misfit schoolgirl who uses her telekinetic powers to gain revenge on her cruel classmates.

The book was filmed by Brian De Palma in 1976, and the director turned it into one of the decade's most effective shockers. De Palma brought the novel vividly to life, injecting it with the same colorful, flamboyant cinematics that he used to such great effect in the earlier *Phantom of the Paradise.* He drew brilliant performances from Sissy Spacek as Carrie and Piper Laurie as her mother, and, rather typically, imbued the picture with several devices intended, once again, to pay homage to his idol, Alfred Hitchcock. The Hitchcock motifs in *Carrie* are obvious—"Bates" High School, brief snatches of Bernard Herrmann's famous "shower scene" music underlining key moments, and the similarities of Margaret White and Mrs. Bates (both were unbalanced zealots locked away in a musty, old house, continually expounding on the evils of sex and pleasure).

Carrie White's telekinetic destruction of Bates' faculty and student body is one of the "classic" horror scenes of the decade, and the ending, when Carrie's bloodied hand suddenly rises from the rubble, had audiences literally jumping out of their seats. The film was hugely successful, and Brian De Palma followed it with an even more elaborate journey into the realm of telekinesis, 1977's *The Fury.*

162

A STAR IS BORN

A Warner Bros. Picture; Directed by Frank Pierson; Produced by Jon Peters; Executive producer: Barbra Streisand; Screenplay by Joan Didion, John Gregory Dunne, and Frank Pierson; Based on the story by William Wellman and Robert Carson; Photography by Robert Surtees; Production designed by Polly Platt; Film editor: Peter Zinner; Art direction: William Hiney; Assistant directors: Stu Fleming, Michele Ader, and Ed Ledding; Choreography by David Winters; Song: "Evergreen," by Barbra Streisand and Paul Williams; Filmed in Panavision and Metrocolor; Running time: 140 minutes

CAST:
Esther Hoffman (BARBRA STREISAND), *John Norman Howard* (KRIS KRISTOFFERSON), *Bobby Ritchie* (Gary Busey), *Gary Danziger* (Oliver Clark), *Quentin* (Marta Heflin), *Oreos* (Vanetta Fields, Clydie King), *Bebe Jesus* (M. G. Kelly), *Freddie* (Joanne Linville), *Photographer* (Sally Kirkland), *Brian* (Paul Mazursky), *Mo* (Uncle Rudy)

Once one of the brightest and most popular stars in the rock industry, John Norman Howard (Kris Kristofferson) has lately taken to the bottle to help relieve the pressures of superstardom. His drinking becomes so severe that, on several occasions, it renders him incapable of delivering a good performance, and the rumor quickly spreads throughout the rock world that Howard is finished. After one particularly embarrassing concert appearance during which the drunken Howard unleashes a hostile tirade

Kris Kristofferson

at his fans, the singer retreats to his favorite night spot to try and get a grip on himself. There, he observes an all-girl trio called the Oreos, and he is struck by the beauty and talent of the lead singer, Esther Hoffman (Barbra Streisand).

After the performance, Howard calls Esther to his table and tells her she has a wonderful talent. Much to Esther's astonishment, Howard offers to act as her mentor, and he later arranges an audition for Esther that leads to a recording contract. When her first album is released some months later, it quickly sells out, and Esther soon becomes a star in her own right.

She and Howard fall in love and marry, but as her unique singing style gradually takes the country by storm, Howard's career goes further and further downhill. This begins to bother him, and John starts resenting his wife's success. When she wins a Grammy Award for her new recording, a beautiful love song called "Evergreen," John staggers into the ceremony drunk, and purposely spoils her acceptance speech.

Deciding they both need to get away from show business for a while, Esther and John buy a spacious

Kris Kristofferson, Barbra Streisand

Barbra Streisand

ranch in the country, and for a time they live an idyllic life. Soon afterward, however, John's personal demons begin to surface again, and he falls deeper and deeper into alcoholic despair. Sometime later, Esther is shattered by the news that John has been killed in a car crash.

It could be argued that Barbra Streisand was the decade's most popular show business personality.

Since first coming on the scene in the mid-sixties, Streisand's career continued to flourish throughout the seventies, during which she continually ranked among the top recording and motion picture stars. While her film career is limited to relatively few movies, all were enormously successful, and each revealed an extraordinary acting talent as well as a definite screen presence, which is something many other popular singers do not have.

A Star Is Born, a lavish musical updating of the old "classic," is, perhaps, the quintessential Streisand film of the seventies, and it is also of special interest because it teamed her with another recording star who successfully made the transition to films, Kris Kristofferson. When the picture was first released, it was rather unfairly lambasted by certain reviewers, who complained that it was merely an expensive but shallow showcase for the singing talents of its two stars.

While it is not a great film, and perhaps does not compare with the earlier, more dramatic versions of the time-worn story, *A Star Is Born* is nonetheless a glamorous and colorful entertainment that managed to thoroughly delight the filmgoing public. While Streisand's singing and acting are up to their usual standard of excellence, the star is also well served by the lush Panavision photography of veteran cinematographer Robert Surtees, and she certainly never looked quite so lovely in any other film. Although the picture is 140 minutes long (a length virtually unheard of for an "original" film musical), *A Star Is Born* moves swiftly, and perhaps its only major flaw is the ending when, after Kristofferson's dramatic death scene, the camera cuts to a lengthy and incongruous Streisand song sequence. This was something of an anti-climax, and it robbed the film of the more poignant ending it would have had by simply fading out after Kristofferson's demise.

Still, the film is an enjoyable one, and its Oscar-winning lead song, "Evergreen" (composed by Streisand and Paul Williams) is one of the decade's best screen tunes.

Kris Kristofferson, Barbra Streisand

Kris Kristofferson

Kris Kristofferson, Barbra Streisand

Kris Kristofferson, Barbra Streisand

THE SEVEN-PER-CENT SOLUTION

A Universal Picture; Produced and directed by Herbert Ross; Screenplay by Nicholas Meyer; Based on his novel; Executive producers: Alex Winitsky and Arlene Sellers; Associate producer: Stanley O'Toole; Photography by Oswald Morris; Music by John Addison; Art direction by Peter Lamont; Film editor: Chris Barnes; Assistant director: Scott Wodehouse; Costumes by Alan Barrett; Production designer: Ken Adam; Filmed in Panavision and color; Running time: 113 minutes

CAST:

Sherlock Holmes (NICOL WILLIAMSON), *Sigmund Freud* (ALAN ARKIN), *Dr. Watson* (ROBERT DUVALL), *Lola Deveraux* (VANESSA REDGRAVE), *Professor Moriarty* (LAURENCE OLIVIER), *Mary Watson* (Samantha Eggar), *Lowenstein* (Joel Grey), *Mycroft Holmes* (Charles Gray), *Baron Von Leinsdorf* (Jeremy Kemp), *Mrs. Freud* (Georgia Browne), *Mrs. Holmes* (Jill Townsend), *The pasha* (Gertan Klauber), *Mrs. Hudson* (Alison Leggatt), *Berger* (John Bird), *Freda* (Anna Quayle), *Madame* (Régine)

Laurence Olivier

Concerned because he hasn't seen his friend Sherlock Holmes (Nicol Williamson) in quite some time, Dr. Watson (Robert Duvall) visits the old flat at 221-B Baker Street and is shocked to find Holmes incapacitated by his drug addiction. Throughout their

years as a crime-fighting team, Watson had become accustomed to Holmes's occasional use of cocaine to relieve the tensions of a difficult case; but now, after seeing Holmes suffering from delusions and hysteria, Watson realizes Holmes has become a slave to the drug. His drug-induced madness is so severe that he suspects his harmless old schoolteacher, Professor Moriarty (Laurence Olivier), of being a master criminal.

Fearing for Holmes's well-being, Watson consults Sherlock's older brother, Mycroft (Charles Gray), who suggests his brother be placed in the care of a Viennese doctor named Freud, who has had great success curing drug addicts. Knowing the stubborn Holmes will never agree to see a doctor, Watson cleverly tells him the "evil" Professor Moriarty has fled to Vienna and that it is Holmes's duty to follow

Robert Duvall, Alan Arkin, Nicol Williamson

him. Holmes immediately boards a train for Vienna, and once there he is tricked into going to Freud's house by Watson, who arranged for Moriarty to leave a trail for Sherlock's snoop-hound leading to Freud's doorstep.

Bursting into Freud's living room, Holmes demands Moriarty's surrender, but the professor is nowhere in sight. Instead, the gentle, persuasive Freud (Alan Arkin) introduces himself and gradually calms the detective into such a relaxed state that he admits his desperate need for medical attention. Before retiring upstairs for treatment, Holmes dazzles Freud with a display of his deductive-reasoning skills, recounting the intimate details of Freud's life by simply examining personal effects in the doctor's study. Later, Freud orders Holmes to stop the drug "cold turkey," which makes Holmes's life a hellish nightmare for the next two weeks.

After withdrawal, Holmes recovers somewhat but sinks into a deep depression, refusing to eat even a morsel of food. His outlook changes, however, when another of Freud's drug-addicted patients, Lola Devereaux (Vanessa Redgrave), suddenly disappears. Once again feeling the "thrill of the chase," Holmes insists Freud allow him to solve the case, and the doctor agrees, knowing it would be the best possible therapy. After learning that Lola has been kidnapped by an unscrupulous pasha (Gertan Klauber), who is taking her to his country via a private train, Holmes hijacks a commercial train and with the help of Watson and Freud, catches up to the pasha by operating the train at full speed.

Fully recovered, Holmes boards a pleasure cruiser in preparation for a holiday and is delighted to see Lola Devereaux on the sun deck. Drawn to each other, the two agree to spend their holidays together.

Sherlock Holmes, Sir Arthur Conan Doyle's super-sleuth, was one of the most popular screen characters of the forties. From 1941 to 1946, Universal Pictures produced a series of twelve "modernized" Sherlock mysteries, all starring Basil Rathbone as Holmes and Nigel Bruce as Dr. Watson. The films range from very good to mediocre, but they were all surprisingly effective considering their shoestring budgets; and two of them—*The Scarlet Claw* and *The Pearl of*

Vanessa Redgrave, Robert Duvall, Nicol Williamson, Alan Arkin

Saving Lola from her unpleasant fate, Holmes, Watson, and Freud return to Vienna, where Freud insists on hypnotizing Holmes before pronouncing him cured. Freud hopes to find the source of Holmes's fascination with crime as well as the origin of his bizarre delusion about Moriarty. Placing Holmes in a trance that takes him back to childhood, Freud learns that young Sherlock received a severe psychic shock when he discovered Moriarty in bed with his mother.

Death—are among the most atmospheric "B" mysteries ever produced. All of the films made money, and the series would have no doubt continued if it hadn't been for Rathbone's desire to get away from the part.

Perhaps the series' only real drawback, in retrospect, was its relegation to "B" picture status, and it is unfortunate that none of the films was given large-scale treatment, as one would imagine that a Sherlock Holmes story, with its plush Victorian set-

Robert Duvall, Samantha Eggar

Laurence Olivier

tings and fog-shrouded moors, would be a "natural" for big-budget, Technicolor production. However, Universal, a particularly budget-conscious studio during the forties, reserved this kind of treatment only for its musical extravaganzas such as the 1943 remake of *The Phantom of the Opera*.

Ironically, the best Sherlock Holmes film of the seventies was *The Seven-Per-Cent Solution*, a lavish, opulent, and expensive exercise produced by Universal. *The Seven-Per-Cent Solution* was based on the best-selling novel by Nicholas Meyer, a young screenwriter and Holmes fanatic who had written the book in his spare time. The film, released in 1976, was a substantial hit, containing a brisk screenplay by Meyer and excellent direction by Herbert Ross.

Aside from its large budget and elaborate production, the film was also different from the forties efforts in the way it presented Holmes. While the Rathbone Holmes was always depicted as an infallible crusader who could easily overcome *any* opposition, Nicol Williamson portrayed him as a rather tormented genius, possessed of great deductive powers but also vulnerable and human in a manner that was never seen in the Rathbone films. Williamson broke with tradition completely by acting the part in a naturalistic fashion, exhibiting none of the broad theatrics Rathbone brought to the character. Interestingly, Williamson had done much the same with the part of Hamlet in the sixties, and during this time he dazzled the theatrical world with his unique and unhistrionic approach to the role.

Aside from Williamson's fine performance, *The Seven-Per-Cent Solution* also contains superb portrayals by Alan Arkin, Robert Duvall, and especially Laurence Olivier as the surprisingly meek and timid Professor Moriarty (a far cry from the malevolent Moriartys of George Zucco, Lionel Atwill, and Henry Daniell).

KING KONG

A Paramount Picture; Directed by John Guillermin; Produced by Dino De Laurentiis; Screenplay by Lorenzo Semple, Jr.; Photography by Richard H. Kline; Film editor: Ralph E. Winters; Production design by Mario Chiari and Dale Hennesy; Costumes by Moss Mabry; Music by John Barry; Executive producers: Federico De Laurentiis and Christian Ferry; Assistant directors: Pat Kehoe, Kurt Neumann, and David McGiffert; Choreography by Claude Thompson; Filmed in Panavision and color; Running time: 134 minutes

CAST:
Jack Prescott (JEFF BRIDGES), *Fred Wilson*

Jessica Lange

(CHARLES GRODIN), *Dwan* (JESSICA LANGE), *Bagley* (Réne Auberjonois), *Captain Ross* (John Randolph), *Joe Perko* (Jack O'Halloran), *Boan* (Julius Harris), *Garcia* (Jorge Moreno), *Sunfish* (Dennis Fimple), *Carnahan* (Ed Lauter), *City official* (John Agar), *Chinese cook* (John Lone), *Timmons* (Mario Gallo), *Petrox chairman* (Sid Conrad)

Petrox Oil official Fred Wilson (Charles Grodin) charters a ship to a remote island in the Pacific. He has heard the island has a limitless supply of oil, and intends taking every drop of it back to America. Jack Prescott (Jeff Bridges), a Princeton paleontologist who has stowed away for the voyage, tells Wilson he is actually heading for "Skull Island," which, according to legend, is inhabited by prehistoric monsters. Warning Wilson that he'll find more than just oil on the island, Prescott tells him of the hostile natives who live there, and of their worship of "Kong, the beast that touches Heaven." Dismissing this as nonsense, Wilson continues the voyage. Days later, Wilson and his crew rescue the shipwrecked Dwan (Jessica Lange), a beautiful girl who aspires to be a film star.

Arriving at the island sometime afterward, Jack, Dwan, Wilson, and the crew witness the natives holding a bizarre ritual, in which a tribal virgin is readied for "marriage" to Kong. Seeing Dwan, the chief insists that *she* become Kong's "bride," and, alarmed, Wilson and Prescott hustle her back to the ship. Later, the natives kidnap Dwan, and in an elaborate ceremony she is given over to Kong, a giant gorilla.

Learning of this, Jack, Wilson and the crew follow the monster's tracks into the island's primeval forest,

but most of the men are killed when they provoke Kong by firing at him. Jack and Wilson survive, however, and Jack continues pursuit of the great ape while Wilson sets an ingenious trap for Kong on the beach. Luckily, Jack rescues Dwan, and, noticing that his "bride" has been taken, Kong heads for the shore, where he falls into Wilson's trap.

Taking the beast to New York, Wilson plans to use him in a Petrox commercial campaign, and he persuades Dwan to appear at an outdoor rally. On the night of the rally, Kong is put on rather tasteless display—a huge Petrox gas pump slowly rises to reveal a chained and helpless Kong underneath. Far from happy, Dwan feels pity for Kong, realizing he never tried to harm her. When the press snap flash pictures of Dwan, Kong breaks his bonds and goes on a rampage. Dwan runs away with Jack, and Wilson is killed in the ensuing chaos.

Searching through Manhattan for Dwan, Kong finally abducts her after causing millions of dollars in damage. He takes her to the top of the World Trade Center, and a city official (John Agar) orders that he be shot down by assault helicopters. Jack, however, thinks it's criminal to kill a "rare species of animal," and Dwan has come to regard the beast with affection. Despite this, Kong is brutally machine-gunned after putting Dwan down at a safe distance. Fatally weakened, Kong falls to his death.

It is well known that most remakes of "classic" films turn out disastrously, but this lavish retelling of *King Kong* is certainly an exception to the rule. The 1933 horror-adventure film, which starred Fay Wray, Robert Armstrong, and Bruce Cabot, is one of the

Jessica Lange

legendary films of old Hollywood, and Kong himself, whom Fay Wray once jokingly called "the tallest, darkest leading man in Hollywood," is, perhaps, the most "famous" monster in motion-picture history.

Though the remake, produced by Dino De Laurentiis on a budget of reportedly over $50 million, pretty much follows the basic story line of the original, it is substantially different in several respects. Its Kong is actually a man (makeup wizard Rick Baker) inside a masterfully designed gorilla suit, whereas the first Kong was an animated model. The remake contains no prehistoric beasts lurking around Kong's primeval island, which is probably the most disappointing thing about the picture, and aside from a rather brief tangle with a gigantic rattlesnake, the new Kong is not allowed to indulge in any of the titanic dinosaur battles that made the 1933 film so exciting.

Despite these differences, 1976's *King Kong* opened to fairly favorable reviews, and while it is generally acknowledged that the film doesn't compare with the magnificent original, the remake does manage to evoke more audience sympathy for the monster. The main reason for this is that the unyielding terror of Fay Wray in the first film is here replaced by a strangely compelling rapport between Jessica Lange and her giant captor. Unlike Wray, whose fear of Kong never let up for one second, Lange sort of "gets to know" her captor, and develops genuine affection for him late in the story, which makes his death all the sadder. Also, Kong seemed a much more flexible character in the remake, his wide range of facial expressions an incredible technical achievement.

Jessica Lange

169

1977

Robert Shaw

BLACK SUNDAY

A Paramount Picture; Directed by John Franken-
heimer; Produced by Robert Evans; Screenplay by
Ernest Lehman, Kenneth Ross, and Ivan Moffat;
Based on the novel by Thomas Harris; Photography
by John Alonzo; Film editor: Rom Rolf; Art direc-
tor: Walter Tyler; Makeup by Bob Dawn and Brad
Wilder; Sound by John K. Wilkinson, Gene Canta-
messa, and Howard Beals; Music by John Williams;
Costumes by Ray Summers; Filmed in Panavision;
Color by Movielab; Running time: 145 minutes

CAST:
Major David Kabakov (ROBERT SHAW), *Dahlia
Iyad* (MARTHE KELLER), *Michael Lander*
(BRUCE DERN), *Corley* (FRITZ WEAVER), *Fasil*
(Bekim Fehmiu), *Nageeb* (Victor Campos), *Muzi*
(Michael V. Gazzo), *Fowler* (Walter Brooke), *Farley*
(Tom McFadden), *Col. Riaf* (Walter Gotell), *Pugh*
(William Daniels), *Vickers* (Robert Patten), *Sim-
mons* (Nick Nicolary), *Pearson* (Jack Rader), *TV
director* (John Frankenheimer)

At a remote villa in Lebanon, Fasil (Bekim
Fehmiu) meets with fellow Black September terrorists Nageeb (Victor Campos) and Dahlia (Marthe
Keller) to plot an assault on the United States. To
convince America that supporting Israel is dangerous, the terrorists plan to massacre a large portion of

the crowd at the Super Bowl by attaching to the
underbelly of the Goodyear Blimp an explosive
device capable of unleashing thousands of steel darts.

To make this a very real possibility, the beautiful
Dahlia has made a sexual and psychological slave of
the blimp's pilot, Michael Lander (Bruce Dern), a
disturbed Vietnam veteran. Having no qualms about
slaughtering thousands of people, the deranged
Lander relishes the idea of spectacularly avenging
himself on a country that has "forgotten him."

Recording their plan for an attack "somewhere in
America" on a cassette tape, Dahlia, Fasil, and
Nageeb retire for the night, but are awakened when
Israeli commandos raid the villa. Fasil escapes, but
Nageeb is gunned down by Major David Kabakov
(Robert Shaw), the squadleader who, for some
reason, finds himself unable to pull the trigger on
Dahlia. This proves a mistake, as she heads for
America to carry on with the plan when the comman-
dos depart. Confiscating the terrorists' cassette,
Kabakov hears their assault plans, then flies to
Washington to inform the FBI.

Also arriving in the States, Dahlia visits her contact, a dubious importer named Musi (Michael V.
Gazzo), who gives her a large quantity of plastic explosive. Turning it over to Lander a few weeks later,
Dahlia meets with Fasil, and he tells her that
Kabakov and the FBI have guessed their identities by
repeatedly playing the tape. Dahlia refuses to
postpone the attack, and she and Lander fashion a
bomblike nacelle for the blimp containing enough ex-

171

plosive to fire all the darts into the Super Bowl stands.

Meanwhile, Kabakov and the FBI arrive in town hoping to apprehend Fasil, a cunning and deadly terrorist (it was he who engineered the attack on Israeli athletes at the 1972 Olympics). In an elaborate stakeout, several FBI men wait in the lobby of Fasil's hotel; told by the manager that Fasil has stepped out for a moment, Kabakov stations himself across the street. Within minutes, Fasil returns and guesses something is wrong. Before the feds have a chance to draw their weapons, Fasil produces a short-barreled .357 Magnum and blasts his way out of the lobby. A superb marksman, Fasil kills three FBI agents, two citizens, and a policeman before he is gunned down by Kabakov. Examining Fasil's effects at the hotel, Kabakov learns the site of the assault will be the Super Bowl.

Later, however, Dahlia's plans crumble when Lander tells her he is being replaced by another pilot, Captain Farley (Tom McFadden), on the day of the game. Undaunted, Dahlia poses as a hotel waitress, killing Farley after gaining entrance to his room. This clears the field for Lander, who, on the big day, shows up for duty and jokingly tells the crew that Farley has been incapacitated by a hangover. Fastening the nacelle to the blimp after slaughtering the ground crew in a barrage of machine-gun fire, Dahlia and Lander enter the pilot's cabin and launch the dirigible.

Lander steers the blimp toward the stadium, unaware that Kabakov knows of their plan and is giving pursuit in a jet helicopter. Firing his machine gun into the pilot's cabin after catching up with the

Bruce Dern, Marthe Keller

blimp, Kabakov kills Dahlia and wounds Lander, who nonetheless lights the fuse to detonate the explosive.

Seeing the blimp is still heading for the stadium, Kabakov swings down on a tow line, attempting to hook it to the blimp's tail fin. Before he can do this,

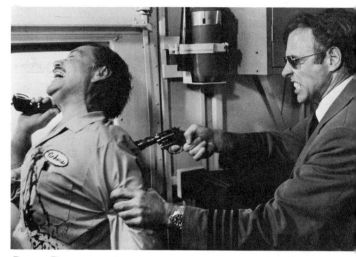

Bruce Dern

however, the blimp blunders into the stadium at a dangerously low altitude, causing a panic. Kabakov finally hooks the blimp to the tow line, however, and the copter tows it out to sea, where the explosion safely occurs.

The decade's many "disaster" films, such as *The Poseidon Adventure, Earthquake, The Towering Inferno,* and the *Airport* sequels, are primarily known for two things—their dazzling special effects and their truly impressive all-star casts. These films were probably the closest thing to old-fashioned "escapist" entertainment that seventies cinema had to offer, and they all reaped tremendous box-office profits as a result. Obviously, their enormous popularity stems from the fact that, for the price of admission, audiences could not only experience the vicarious thrill of watching a spectacular crisis on screen, but could also see many of their favorite movie stars in the process. Though audiences seemed to love them, these films were almost all burdened with rather sophomoric scripts, featuring silly dialogue and story lines that were obviously constructed merely to provide an excuse for the special-effects scenes and which rarely gave the actors a chance to do much of anything with their one-dimensional roles.

John Frankenheimer's 1977 production of *Black Sunday* was an interesting attempt at a "thinking man's" disaster film, and it emerged as a cut above the others because it contained a good, solid story

Robert Shaw

line in addition to all the thrills. Three top writers worked on the screenplay for *Black Sunday*—Ernest Lehman, Kenneth Ross, and Ivan Moffat—and it is by far the best script ever written for a film of this kind. It is both literate and fast-moving, and its subject matter is a great deal more topical than that of most disaster dramas.

While the film lacked the star-studded cast of a *Towering Inferno* or an *Earthquake, Black Sunday* provided its five leading actors—Robert Shaw, Marthe Keller, Bruce Dern, Fritz Weaver, and Bekim Fehmiu—with meaty, three-dimensional roles, and its pulse-pounding finale, in which the Goodyear Blimp soars menacingly into the Super Bowl, is one of the cinema's all-time great action-suspense sequences.

STAR WARS

A 20th Century-Fox Picture; Directed and written by George Lucas; Produced by Gary Kurtz; Photography by Gilbert Taylor; Music by John Williams; Film editors: Paul Hirsch, Marcia Lucas, and

Bruce Dern, Marthe Keller

Richard Chew; Production designer: John Barry; Art direction: Norman Reynolds and Leslie Dilley; Set decoration: Roger Christian; Special photographic effects supervisor: John Dykstra; Titles by Dan Perri; Costumes by John Mollo; Makeup by Stuart

Anthony Daniels, Mark Hamill, Alec Guinness

Freeborn; Chief model maker: Grant McCune; Electronics design: Alvah J. Miller; Animation and rotoscope design: Adam Beckett; Filmed in Technicolor and Panavision; Running time: 119 minutes

CAST:
Luke Skywalker (MARK HAMILL), *Ben (Obi-Wan) Kenobi* (ALEC GUINNESS), *Princess Leia Organa* (CARRIE FISHER), *Grand Moff Tarkin* (PETER

Anthony Daniels, Kenny Baker

CUSHING), *Han Solo* (HARRISON FORD), *C3PO* (ANTHONY DANIELS), *R2-D2* (KENNY BAKER), *Lord Darth Vader* (DAVID PROWSE), *Darth Vader's voice* (JAMES EARL JONES), *Chewbacca* (PETER MAYHEW), *Chief Jawa* (Jack Purvis), *Uncle Owen Lars* (Phil Brown), *Aunt Beru Lars* (Shelagh Fraser), *General Dodonna* (Alex McCrindle), *General Willard* (Eddie Byrne), *Red Leader* (Drewe Henley), *Red Two* (Dennis Lawson), *Red Three* (Garrick Hagon), *Red Four* (Jack Klaff)

Carrie Fisher, Mark Hamill

"A long time ago in a galaxy far, far away," the forces of evil have swept across the universe at the hands of the Imperial Galactic Empire. Aboard a transport ship that has been crippled in a skirmish with the Empire's fighters, good Princess Leia (Carrie Fisher) waits to be apprehended by the Empire's villainous rulers, Grand Moff Tarkin (Peter Cushing) and Lord Darth Vader (David Prowse). Before her capture, however, she steals blueprints to the "Death Star," the Empire's enormous battlestation, and feeds them, along with an S.O.S. plea, into the data system of her small robot companion, R2-D2 (Kenny Baker). The Princess is then taken into custody by Vader's "stormtroopers," and Vader orders that R2 and C3PO (Anthony Daniels), another robot, be abandoned on the remote planet Tatooine.

Roaming around the planet's barren surface, R2 and C3PO are picked up by "jawas" (small gremlin-like scavengers who sell discarded robots for scrap), and are eventually sold to Luke Skywalker (Mark Hamill), a young adventurer. While adjusting R2's inner workings sometime later, Luke accidentally trips one of his switches, and Princess Leia's plea for help materializes via a holograph. In her message, she implores the aid of Obi-Wan Kenobi (Alec Guinness), the last of the Jedi Knights, heroic crusaders from ancient times whose strength and wisdom were linked to "The Force," the strongest power in the universe.

Later, Luke visits Kenobi, who agrees to help rescue the Princess. Accompanied by R2 and C3PO, Kenobi and Luke travel to a distant province hoping to find a pilot brave enough to fly them to the Death Star, where the Princess is being held prisoner. They find such a man in Han Solo (Harrison Ford), a cocky, hotshot mercenary who will fly anywhere in the universe for the right price.

Flying to the Death Star aboard Solo's ship, Luke, Solo, and Solo's large, anthropoid sidekick Chewbacca (Peter Mayhew) eventually free the Princess, while Kenobi seeks out his archenemy Darth Vader, a former Jedi who has misused "The Force" by cultivating its "darker powers."

In one of the Death Star's abandoned hallways, Kenobi and Vader square off with "laser" swords, and unfortunately Kenobi is slain in the duel. His comrades escape safely, however, and later extract the Death Star blueprint data from R2-D2's computer bank. Luckily, it reveals all the inner workings of the battlestation, including the one supremely vulnerable area which, if struck by a missile, would explode the entire operation.

Mark Hamill, Alec Guinness

the Princess. During the attack, however, when most of Luke's men are shot down by Imperial fighters, Solo comes to his aid. Zeroing in on the target area, Luke hits it with one well-placed shot, and the Death Star is destroyed.

At an elaborate celebration sometime afterward, Princess Leia decorates Luke, Solo, and Chewbacca for their bravery.

When, in 1973, George Lucas first conceived the idea for *Star Wars*, he was not setting out to make the biggest "blockbuster" in history. His intention was to make an old-fashioned "escapist" adventure story, set in outer space, glorifying the triumph of good over evil, and filled with colorful heroes and villains from distant galaxies and times. He wanted to make a film that children could enjoy, a kind of latter-day Buck Rogers saga that would return filmgoing to the glorious "event" it no doubt was when such films were popular during Hollywood's

Harrison Ford

A massive attack on the Death Star is planned, and as zero hour approaches Luke and a squad of well-chosen pilots prepare to take off in fighter ships. Solo, however, refuses to go along, insisting he's only interested in getting a financial reward for rescuing

David Prowse, Carrie Fisher

Peter Mayhew, Mark Hamill,
Alec Guinness, Harrison Ford

Harrison Ford, Mark Hamill,
Anthony Daniels

Mark Hamill

177

Golden Age. He originally thought of remaking the Flash Gordon serials of the thirties, but found that not only were the rights to them astronomically expensive, but also that the copyright owners wanted to exercise a great deal of creative control over any remakes.

Deciding to concoct his own space opera, Lucas fashioned a fourteen-page outline, then began approaching the major studios with the idea. United Artists and Universal displayed little interest, no doubt because both studios knew full well that science fiction films (until recently) have traditionally had very limited audience appeal. With the growing success of the just-released *American Graffiti,* however, Lucas was gaining the reputation of being a filmmaker of extraordinary ability, and 20th Century-Fox eventually agreed to back the project in late 1973. Lucas wrote four complete screenplays for *Star Wars* before he was satisfied, but the one he settled on was no doubt the best.

When *Star Wars* was released in May 1977, it grossed back its $9 million production and advertising budget in two months, and went on to become the most successful film in history, outgrossing the previous record-holder, *Jaws.* The film's incredible array of characters, the beautifully designed space vehicles, and the unique "laser-powered" weaponry

Alec Guinness

Alec Guinness, David Prowse

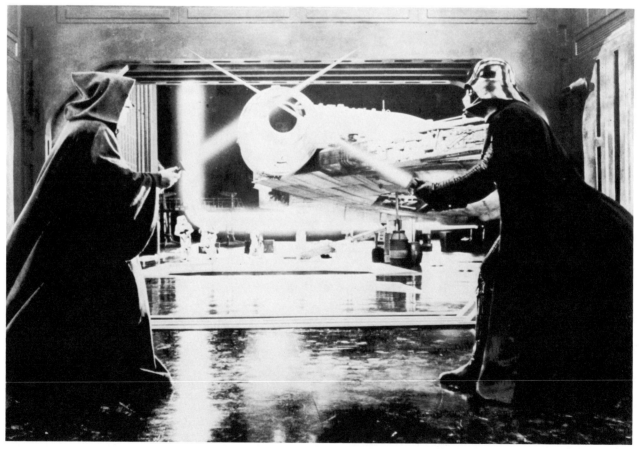

lent themselves especially well to the merchandising of consumer products, and within months of the film's release *Star Wars* bedspreads, lunchboxes, model kits, toys, dolls, and the like were sold by the millions.

More importantly, however, *Star Wars* became exactly what George Lucas had wanted, a cinematic "happening," an "event" that people would want to watch and enjoy over and over again. *Star Wars* is probably the seventies' prime example of unbridled "escapist" entertainment, but this alone does not account for its success.

There are many factors that made *Star Wars* a film that people wanted to see again and again and again (which, during its heyday, meant standing in line for as long as three hours). While its many special-effects scenes of "intergalactic" warfare involving the fighter ships of the Imperial Empire and those of the heroes are among the best of their kind, Lucas made certain that every inch of *Star Wars* (including the less spectacular moments) was designed to keep the audience's imagination stimulated. As such, nearly all the scenes in the film contain something unusual or exciting, making it nearly impossible for an audience to take their eyes off the screen for one second. The chess game between Chewbacca and C3PO aboard Solo's ship is a good example of this, played not with conventional kings, queens, rooks, and pawns, but with tiny animated monsters, who actually do battle for position.

THE TURNING POINT

A 20th Century-Fox Picture; Directed by Herbert Ross; Produced by Herbert Ross and Arthur Laurents; Screenplay by Arthur Laurents; Photography by Robert Surtees; Production designer: Albert Brenner; Costumes by Albert Wolsky; Makeup by Charles Schram; Sound recording by Jerry Jost; Set decorations: Marvin March; Film editor: William Reynolds; Assistant directors: Jack Roe, Tony Bishop, and Peter Burrell; Executive producer: Nora Kaye; Filmed in DeLuxe Color; Running time: 119 minutes

CAST:
Deedee Rogers (SHIRLEY MacLAINE), *Emma Jacklin* (ANNE BANCROFT), *Emilia Rogers* (Leslie Browne), *Yuri* (Mikhail Baryshnikov), *Adelaide* (Martha Scott), *Wayne Rogers* (Tom Skerritt), *Carter* (Marshall Thompson), *Madame Kakharova* (Alexandra Danilova), *Carolyn* (Starr Danias), *Sevilla* (Antoinette Sibley), *Freddie* (Scott Douglas), *Rosie* (Anthony Zerbe), *Arnold* (Daniel Levans), *Michael* (James Mitchell), *Barney* (Donald Petrie), *Ethan* (Phillip Saunders)

Leslie Browne, Mikhail Baryshnikov

During a nationwide tour, the American Ballet Theatre performs in Oklahoma City, where Deedee Rogers (Shirley MacLaine), a former dancer with the company, lives with her husband and three children. Attending the performance, Deedee remembers that, as a dancer, she had always been in competition with her friend Emma Jacklin (Anne Bancroft), now the company's prima ballerina. Deedee forsook her

Mikhail Baryshnikov

Shirley MacLaine, Anne Bancroft, Tom Skerritt, Phillip Saunders

career for marriage, but continues to wonder how far she would have gone as a dancer. After the performance, Deedee introduces Emma to her daughter Emilia (Leslie Browne), an aspiring dancer herself. Invited to audition for the company sometime later, Emilia is accepted and soon leaves for New York to begin training for the fall season.

Meanwhile, Emma learns that she's gradually being phased out of star parts, and realizes that soon she'll be forced to teach. Having forsaken a personal life for her career, Emma starts to envy Deedee, not realizing Deedee would give anything to be in her place.

During training, Emilia falls in love with Yuri (Mikhail Baryshnikov), a handsome dancer with a reputation as a ladies' man. Coaxing Emilia into bed a couple of times, Yuri's roving eye later turns to another girl in the company, which breaks Emilia's heart. Months later, Deedee arrives in New York to attend the fall premiere, and is overcome with pride when Emilia's stunning performance of Duke Ellington's ''Vortex'' brings the house down.

Later that night, however, the envy that Deedee and Emma feel for each other erupts into a violent tussle outside the theatre. Realizing how ridiculous

Anne Bancroft, Leslie Browne

Shirley MacLaine, Anne Bancroft

they look, the two burst out laughing and, knowing that Emilia has a bright future in ballet, they embrace.

Films dealing with ballet have seldom been commercially successful, and only two—Michael Powell's *The Red Shoes* and Herbert Ross's *The Turning Point*—ever managed to find favor with the general public. The reason for this is simple—both were genuinely affecting dramas, blessed with interesting story lines, characters, and situations, and the fact that they also contained beautiful ballet sequences only added to their appeal.

The Turning Point (1977) is an especially seductive entertainment, photographed in luscious color by Robert Surtees, and featuring some brilliant dancing by Mikhail Baryshnikov and Leslie Browne, who also act their parts surprisingly well. Wisely, director

Martha Scott, Anne Bancroft, James Mitchell

Leslie Browne, Shirley MacLaine, Phillip Saunders

181

Herbert Ross made certain that the ballet sequences in *The Turning Point* fit into the framework of the story, and never once do they interfere with the dramatic interludes.

The film also benefits from the excellent acting of Shirley MacLaine and Anne Bancroft in the leading roles. The emotional dilemmas of Deedee, the wife and mother who suddenly regrets having never pursued her dance career, and Emma, the prima ballerina who yearns for a personal life away from the stage, are superbly delineated by the two stars.

CAST:

Lillian Hellman (JANE FONDA), *Julia* (VANESSA REDGRAVE), *Dashiell Hammett* (JASON ROBARDS), *Alan Campbell* (Hal HOLBROOK), *Johann* (Maximilian SCHELL), *Dorothy Parker* (Rosemary Murphy), *Woman passenger* (Dora Doll), *Anne Marie* (Meryl Streep), *Sammy* (John Glover), *Girl passenger* (Elizabeth Mortensen), *Young Lillian* (Susan Jones), *Young Julia* (Lisa Pelikan), *Grandmother* (Cathleen Nesbitt), *Little boy* (Phillip Siegel), *Passport officer* (Gerard Buhr)

Vanessa Redgrave, Jane Fonda

JULIA

A 20th Century-Fox Picture; Directed by Fred Zinnemann; Produced by Richard Roth; Screenplay by Alvin Sargent; Based on the story in the collection *Pentimento* by Lillian Hellman; Photography by Douglas Slocombe; Set decoration: Tessa Davies and Pierre Charron; Production designers: Willy Holt, Gene Callahan, and Carmen Dillon; Makeup by George Frost and Bernardine Anderson; Sound recording by Derek Ball; Sound editor: Leslie Hodgson; Film editors: Walter Murch and Marcel Durham; Filmed in Technicolor; Running time: 117 minutes

The late thirties. Aspiring playwright Lillian Hellman (Jane Fonda) shares a rustic beach house with her lover, mentor, and confidant, mystery writer Dashiell Hammett (Jason Robards). She is in the midst of writing her first play, and after months of work, countless rewrites, and great frustration, she finishes it. It is later produced with great success, and Lillian soon finds herself a wealthy and respected woman of the theatre. Having finally achieved her life's goal, Lillian thinks back to her childhood, and remembers, in particular, the friendship she shared with a girl named Julia.

Julia, the daughter of a wealthy family, was a beautiful and sensitive girl whose intelligence made her a perfect companion for Lillian. She lived in a

Jason Robards

Vanessa Redgrave

huge mansion, which often served as a "playground" for the two girls when Lillian would come for a visit. Lillian remembers how, during her teenage years, Julia became painfully aware of the misfortunes of others and developed a strong social conscience. Feeling somewhat guilty about her own wealth and determined to be of use to the world, Julia went to Vienna to study medicine with Sigmund Freud. Not long afterward, however, she abandoned her studies to join the anti-fascist crusade, and was seriously hurt in a scuffle with fascist youth.

Wanting to see her childhood friend again, Lillian now travels to Vienna, where she finds the mature Julia (Vanessa Redgrave) in a hospital recovering from another encounter with fascists. Happy to be reunited with Lillian, Julia tells her that she'll continue fighting the fascists and Nazis no matter what the cost.

Some time later, as the war in Europe intensifies, Lillian attends a drama festival in Moscow, where one evening she is approached by one of Julia's fellow freedom-fighters, Johann (Maximilian Schell). He informs her that he and Julia are leading members of the underground resistance, a group dedicated to keeping freedom alive in Nazi-torn Europe. Knowing of Lillian's love and respect for Julia, he asks that she perform an unusual and dangerous favor for her friend. He requests that Lillian smuggle $50,000 in resistance money into Berlin, so it can be used to aid the victims of Nazi oppression.

Lillian agrees without hesitation, and is given instructions by Johann—she will board a train for Berlin, and upon her arrival she will give the money to Julia, who will be waiting for her in a small café near the train depot. Successfully carrying out the plan, Lillian returns to America, and is saddened to learn that Julia was murdered by fascist thugs not long after their final meeting.

Lillian Hellman, one of America's most respected playwrights, compiled a collection of autobiographical essays entitled *Pentimento: A Book of Portraits* in 1973. Published by Little, Brown and Company, the book became a huge success, and remained on the *New York Times Best-Seller List* for four months. One of the most memorable stories in the book was "Julia," the gentle, moving account of how a childhood friend of Miss Hellman's, a girl named Julia, fought courageously against fascist and Nazi oppression, and how Miss Hellman herself was allowed to aid in the cause by smuggling $50,000 in resistance money over the Berlin border.

The story, which was both suspenseful and inspiring, was a natural for screen treatment, and in 1977 it was the subject of a major motion picture fea-

Jane Fonda, Maximilian Schell

Jane Fonda, Vanessa Redgrave

turing Jane Fonda and Vanessa Redgrave in the lead roles under the direction of Fred Zinnemann. Because the story was a remembrance, the film version was narrated by the solitary figure of Lillian Hellman (Fonda) as she might appear today, quietly fishing on a serene lake at Martha's Vineyard.

Julia emerged as a flawlessly acted film, containing sensitive portrayals from Fonda, Redgrave, Robards, and especially Maximilian Schell as Johann, the quietly dignified victim of oppression. The young actresses who play Julia and Lillian in their youth are also excellent, and their believability is enhanced by their extraordinary resemblances to Fonda and Redgrave.

Aside from the acting, *Julia's* major strength is, of course, the way it depicts the deep friendship of the two characters, going from childhood to their adult lives, when Lillian's admiration of Julia becomes increasingly profound.

When they meet for the last time in the small Berlin café, it is rather touching. Lillian has become wealthy, famous, and respected; while the years of freedom fighting have been less than kind to Julia, leaving her with only one leg and forcing her to abandon her child. During this particular scene, Fonda is excellent, as she looks at Julia and weeps, then rages to herself against life's unfairness, bitterly asking, "Why does it have to be like this?"

ANNIE HALL

A United Artists Release; Directed by Woody Allen; Produced by Charles H. Joffe; Screenplay by Woody Allen and Marshall Brickman; Photography by Gordon Willis; Art direction by Mel Bourne; Costumes by Ruth Morley; Assistant directors: Fred Blankfein and Fred T. Gallo; Film editor: Ralph Rosenblum;

Hairstyles: Romaine Green; Casting by Juliet Taylor; Makeup by Fern Buchner; Set decorations by Robert Drumheller and Justin Scoppa, Jr.; Filmed in DeLuxe Color; Running time: 93 minutes

CAST:
Alvy Singer (WOODY ALLEN), *Annie Hall* (DIANE KEATON), *Allison* (Carol Kane), *Rob* (Tony Roberts), *Pam* (Shelley Duvall), *Momma Hall* (Colleen Dewhurst), *Robin* (Janet Margolin), *Duane* (Christopher Walken), *Dad Hall* (Donald Symington), *Alvy's father* (Mordecai Lawner), *Alvy's mother* (Joan Newman), *Alvy's uncle* (Martin Rosenblatt), *Alvy's aunt* (Ruth Volner), *Aunt Tessie* (Rashel Novikoff), *Little Alvy* (Jonathan Munk), *Tony Lacey* (Paul Simon), *Himself* (Marshall McLuhan)

Woody Allen, Tony Roberts, Diane Keaton

New York. After two unhappy marriages, hotshot comedy writer Alvy Singer (Woody Allen) meets Annie Hall (Diane Keaton), a shy midwesterner who wants to be a singing star. Enormously insecure, Alvy believes life is divided between the "miserable and the horrible," but his wonderful rapport with Annie leads him to believe there may be hope for him

Woody Allen

yet. Though they do not marry, they have a long, satisfying relationship, during which Alvy encourages her to work on and perfect her singing. All goes well until Annie introduces Alvy to her conservative family in Kansas. During a family dinner, it becomes clear that Annie's mother (Colleen Dewhurst) and father (Donald Symington) don't approve of Alvy.

Returning to New York, Alvy and Annie decide to move in together, but soon Alvy's insecurities get the better of him, and he starts wondering why Annie always needs marijuana before they make love. ("Why don't you take sodium pentothal?" he says. "Then you could sleep through the whole thing!") When the relationship finally crumbles, Annie moves out, and Alvy begins dating Pam (Shelley Duvall), a writer for *Rolling Stone*, whose far-out observations cause Alvy to wince.

Later, Alvy gets a middle-of-the-night phone call from Annie, who says she desperately needs his help. Arriving at Annie's, Alvy learns she simply wants him to kill a large spider in her bathroom. Alvy thinks this is ridiculous until he sees the spider (which, in Alvy's words, is "the size of a Buick"). Afterward, however, Annie tearfully admits she has missed Alvy, and they reconcile.

Meanwhile, Annie's singing continues to improve, and one evening she is allowed to perform solo at a posh nightclub. Her beautiful, bluesy rendition of "Seems Like Old Times" catches the attention of record impresario Tony Lacey (Paul Simon), who invites her to work with him at his home in the Hollywood Hills. Mesmerized by such an incredible oppor-

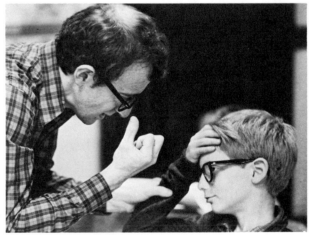

Woody Allen, Jonathan Munk

tunity, Annie goes to Hollywood, leaving poor Alvy out in the cold.

Realizing Annie's departure has made his life finally change from "miserable" to "horrible," Alvy flies to Los Angeles and begs Annie to marry him, but she politely refuses. Alvy reacts philosophically, comparing life to the old joke about the man who refused

to commit his brother (who thought he was a chicken) because the fellow "needed the eggs." Alvy concludes that people endure the crazy heartache of relationships because "most of us need the eggs."

The films of Woody Allen have always been enormously popular with audiences. They are not only exceptional screen comedies, but they also examine the silly foibles of mankind in a manner similar to more serious films. Because of their hilarity, however, they remain far more entertaining than most films dealing with the problems of man. Woody Allen's screen persona, the short, neurotic, sensitive soul seeking love, beauty, and truth in a crazy world, became as much of a hero to seventies audiences as the characters played by Jack Nicholson and Clint Eastwood, and

Woody Allen, Diane Keaton

Allen's legions of fans never object to his comedies' also making serious statements about politics, sex, the absurdities of love, the future, and life in general.

Annie Hall, a love story involving a neurotic comedy writer and a shy girl from Kansas with singing ambitions, represents the peak of Allen's skills as a filmmaker, and he obviously lavished great care on it, no doubt because its story line was heavily autobiographical. Allen's enthusiasm for the project paid off handsomely, and it was the first of his films to win the Academy Award as the year's Best Picture, in addition to all the other major Oscars except Best Actor. For all its comedy, the romance between Alvy and Annie is both realistic and touching, and their

185

Woody Allen

painful on-again/off-again relationship was greatly identified with by audiences.

Typical of Allen, *Annie Hall* also explores in humorous-serious fashion the often bizarre nature of people, particularly when Alvy goes to Kansas to meet Annie's oddball family. Her mother, father, and grandmother are the sternest puritans imaginable, who obviously have no use for a "crazy writer from New York." Similarly, Annie's brother Duane (Christopher Walken, in a brilliant bit) is shown to be a strange young man who, while sitting in his darkened room, tells Alvy that he has fantasies about someday crashing his car into oncoming traffic. It is a tribute to Allen's conceptual skill that, for this eerie little exchange, he seemed to make Duane's appearance slightly suggestive of the Dick Hickock character in *In Cold Blood*.

THE SENTINEL

A Universal Picture; Directed by Michael Winner; Produced by Michael Winner and Jeffrey Konvitz; Screenplay by Michael Winner and Jeffrey Konvitz; Based on the novel by Jeffrey Konvitz; Photography by Dick Kratina; Music by Gil Melle; Film editors: Bernard Gribble and Terence Rawlings; Production designer: Philip Rosenberg; Set decorations: Ed Stewart; Sound by Ted Mason, Les Lazarowitz, and Hugh Train; Special visual effects by Albert Whitlock; Costumes by Peggy Farrell; Special make-up: Dick Smith and Bob Laden; Hairstyles by Bill Farley; Filmed in Technicolor; Running time: 93 minutes

CAST:
Michael Lerman (CHRIS SARANDON), *Alison Parker* (CRISTINA RAINES), *Charles Chazen* (BURGESS MEREDITH), *Monsignor Franchino* (ARTHUR KENNEDY), *Robed figure* (JOSE FERRER), *Miss Logan* (AVA GARDNER), *Prof. Ruzinsky* (MARTIN BALSAM), *Father Halliran* (JOHN CARRADINE), *Detective Gatz* (ELI WALLACH), *Gerde* (SYLVIA MILES), *Rizzo* (CHRISTOPHER WALKEN), *Jennifer* (Deborah Raffin), *Sandra* (Beverly D'Angelo), *Alison's father* (Fred Stuthman), *Brenner* (Hank Garrett), *Perry* (William Hickey), *Priest* (Reid Shelton)

Manhattan. Alison Parker (Cristina Raines), a top model, lives in a fashionable apartment with her lawyer-finance Michael Lerman (Chris Sarandon). Feeling she needs to be alone for a while, Alison moves into a Brooklyn Heights brownstone where, oddly, an aged, blind priest—Father Halliran (John Carradine)—keeps a tireless vigil at the top-floor window. Alison's fellow tenants include two lesbians, Gerde (Sylvia Miles) and Sandra (Beverly D'Angelo), as well as Charles Chazen (Burgess Meredith), a nosy eccentric.

Later, Chazen invites Alison to a birthday party for his pet cat, and there she meets her other neighbors, all rather bizarre people. That night, Alison has a severe bout of insomnia, made worse by weird sounds coming from the top floor. She complains to the rental agent, Miss Logan (Ava Gardner), about the "noisy neighbors," but Miss Logan insists that she and Father Halliran are the only tenants in the building, proving it by showing Allison the other apartments are empty.

Several nights later, Alison is awakened by the noises again and, determined to find the cause arms herself with a butcher knife and ascends the stairs. On the top floor, Alison is horrified when the rotting corpse of her recently deceased father (a cancer victim) leaps at her from the shadows. Stabbing it

repeatedly, Alison runs out of the building, and later tells Michael about the strange goings-on.

Trying in vain to see Father Halliran, Michael visits Monsignor Franchino (Arthur Kennedy), head of the "Brotherhood of Protectors," who own the brownstone. When told of Alison's experiences, Franchino is evasive, but Michael sneaks into his office after hours, unearthing a list of names dating back through the centuries and ending with Halliran who, according to the document, will soon die and be "replaced" by Alison, who has been chosen as the next "sentinel."

Michael then goes to the brownstone and uncovers a wall plaque in its entry hall stating the building is the "doorway to Hell," and he realizes the "Brotherhood" has been keeping a sentinel at the house to protect the world from demonic invasion. Later, Alison returns to find Michael horribly slain. Running to the top floor, Alison is confronted by Chazen (who is no doubt the Devil) and her neighbors (who are all the "ghosts" of executed criminals) as well as the sickeningly deformed "armies of Hell." To prevent Alison from becoming the new sentinel, they converge on her and try to drive her mad with their hideousness. Father Halliran, however, fends them

Cristina Raines

Cristina Raines, Ava Gardner

Burgess Meredith

Cristina Raines

off with a crucifix, then dies of a heart attack. Weeks later, Alison, now a nun, begins her vigil.

The Exorcist (1971) and *The Omen* (1976) turned out to be the most successful horror films in history, and they grossed enormous sums for their respective studios, Warner Bros. and 20th Century-Fox. In 1977, Universal, which had been *the* horror movie studio throughout the thirties and forties, produced *The Sentinel,* a slick "formula" horror film dealing, once again, with demonic invasion and obviously intended to attract the same audience that had made *The Exorcist* and *The Omen* such blockbusters.

Written by director Michael Winner and a young producer named Jeffrey Konvitz, *The Sentinel* combined certain plot elements of *The Exorcist* with those of another fine shocker, *Rosemary's Baby* (1967), and was an extremely effective little thriller despite its tendency to be a bit *too* gruesome. This was an all-out "spook show," lacking the religious and political overtones of the earlier entries, and purely intended to scare audiences with as many fright devices as it could cram into its brief 93-minute running time.

The Sentinel never came close to the success of its predecessors, but it did contain some powerful horror scenes that assure it a place in the history of its genre. Particularly frightening are Alison's struggle with the ghoulish apparition of her dead father; the two lesbians, Gerde and Sandra, devouring the corpse of Alison's fiancé; and, of course, the onslaught of the hideous "armies of Hell" at the conclusion. The last is undoubtedly one of the most terrifying interludes in seventies cinema; interestingly, many people left the theater thinking they'd just seen the greatest monster makeups in history, as the "armies of Hell" were, perhaps, the most horrible creatures ever witnessed on screen. Some time after *The Sentinel*'s release, however, Winner made it known that he used people with actual deformities (from sideshows and hospitals), which may have prevented the film from becoming more successful.

THE SPY WHO LOVED ME

A United Artists Picture; An Eon Production; Directed by Lewis Gilbert; Produced by Albert R. Broccoli; Screenplay by Christopher Wood and Richard Maibaum; Based on the novel by Ian Fleming; Photography by Claude Renoir; Associate producer: William P. Cartlidge; Special photographic effects by Alan Maley; Film editor: John Glen; Production designer: Ken Adam; Music by Marvin Hamlisch; "James Bond Theme" by Monty Norman; Song: "Nobody Does It Better," written by

Marvin Hamlisch and Carole Bayer Sager and performed by Carly Simon; Filmed in Eastmancolor and Panavision; Running time: 125 minutes

CAST:
James Bond (ROGER MOORE), *Anya* (Barbara Bach), *Stromberg* (Curt Jurgens), *Jaws* (Richard Kiel), *Naomi* (Caroline Munro), *"M"* (Bernard Lee), *Minister of Defense* (Geoffrey Keen), *Miss Moneypenny* (Lois Maxwell), *Capt. Benson* (George Baker), *Sergei* (Michael Billington), *"Q"* Desmond Llewelyn), *Felicca* (Olga Bisera), *Sheikh Hosein (*Edward de Souza), *Gen. Gogol* (Walter Gotell), *Capt. of the* Liparus (Sydney Tafler), *Log-cabin girl* (Sue Vanner), *Fekkesh* (Nadim Sawalha), *Adm. Hargreaves* (Robert Brown), *Sandor* (Milton Reid), *Barman* (Albert Moses)

Barbara Bach, Roger Moore

James Bond (Roger Moore) investigates the disappearance of two nuclear submarines—one British, the other Soviet. Joining forces with Major Anya Amasova (Barbara Bach), a gorgeous agent from the Soviet Union, Bond discovers the subs were "kidnaped" by Stromberg (Curt Jurgens), a wealthy shipping magnate who wants to destroy the world so he can build a new one under the sea.

Stationed in a huge underwater fortress, Stromberg uses a gigantic tanker, the *Liparus,* to abduct nuclear submarines so he can gain access to their missiles. Realizing Bond has learned of his plan, Stromberg dispatches his henchman Jaws (Richard Kiel), an indestructible seven-foot giant with steel teeth. Jaws pursues Bond over half the globe, but the clever Bond outfoxes him at every turn.

Determined to have a showdown with Stromberg, Bond boards a British sub, which is acting as a decoy for the *Liparus*. After the huge tanker "swallows" the sub, Bond is taken prisoner, and learns that Stromberg is preparing to launch two nuclear missiles as a prelude to global destruction.

Later, Bond prevents the missiles from striking their targets, and kills Stromberg in a dramatic shoot-out.

Following his appearance in 1967's *You Only Live Twice,* Sean Connery officially announced his retirement from the James Bond series, claiming that he yearned to play more serious roles and that he felt creatively stifled by his identification with Ian Fleming's superspy. No amount of money could have persuaded Connery to appear in the next Bond adventure, *On Her Majesty's Secret Service,* and the role was subsequently given to George Lazenby, a tall, good-looking male model who suited the part physically but whose experience as an actor was extremely limited.

Roger Moore, Milton Reid

Roger Moore, Richard Kiel

Barbara Bach, Roger Moore

Though *On Her Majesty's Secret Service* (which was released in 1969) contained some of the finest, most exciting action sequences of any Bond feature, the critics were generally unkind to Lazenby, who turned in a competent performance but lacked the sensual magnetism so essential to the role.

Some time after *On Her Majesty's Secret Service*, Connery was lured back to play Bond in 1971's *Diamonds Are Forever*, which, despite his presence and the lavish production values, emerged as the

weakest in the series. Connery's lacklustre, pedestrian performance made it painfully obvious that he was all but fed up with the character and that a replacement who could do the part justice was badly needed if the series was to continue.

Since the Bond adventures were and still are among the most successful series of films in history, their producer, Albert R. Broccoli, had every intention of continuing to make them, and following *Diamonds* he began an arduous search for a new

190

James Bond. Since one of Connery's reasons for abandoning the character was his belief that he was getting too old to play it, it is somewhat ironic that the actor Broccoli eventually signed was Roger Moore, who is older than Connery by several years. Though he lacked the brutish, physical intensity Connery brought to the role, Moore imbued his James Bond with a certain gentlemanly sophistication and dry sense of humor, and of his four (to date) outings as Bond—*Live and Let Die* (1973), *The Man With the Golden Gun* (1974), *The Spy Who Loved Me* (1977), and *Moonraker* (1979)—*The Spy Who Loved Me* is by far the best and the most entertaining.

It could be argued that this film is the most visually striking of all the Bonds (thanks to the lush photography of Claude Renoir) and that it places the character in some of his most exciting situations. *The Spy Who Loved Me* begins strongly with a breathtaking ski chase—pursued by a group of enemy spies armed with machine guns, Bond is forced to ski off a cliffside into a spectacular, seemingly eternal freefall, finally opening a concealed parachute about halfway down. This stunt, certainly one of the most incredible in film history, was actually performed by Rick Sylvester.

CLOSE ENCOUNTERS OF THE THIRD KIND

Director Steven Spielberg with composer John Williams

A Columbia Picture; Directed and written by Steven Spielberg; Produced by Julia Phillips and Michael Phillips; Photography by Vilmos Zsigmond; Production designed by Joe Alves; Film editor: Michael Kahn; Visual effects concepts by Steven Spielberg; Special photographic effects by Douglas Trumbull; Music by John Williams; Art direction: Dan Lomino; Set decoration: Phil Abramson; Associate producer: Clark Paylow; Photography on special sequence in India: Douglas Slocombe; Dolby sound supervisor: Steve Katz; Special effects consultant: Roy Arbogast; Filmed in color; Running time: 135 minutes

Richard Dreyfuss

CAST:

Roy Neary (RICHARD DREYFUSS), *Claude Lacombe* (FRANÇOIS TRUFFAUT), *Jillian Guiler* (Melinda Dillon), *Ronnie Neary* (Teri Garr), *David Laughlin* (Bob Balaban), *Robert* (Lance Hendriksen), *Barry Guiler* (Cary Guffey), *Wild Bill* (Warren Kimmerling), *Jean-Claude* (Phillip Dodds), *Farmer* (Robert Blossom), *Brad Neary* (Shawn Bishop), *Sylvia Neary* (Adrienne Campbell), *Toby Neary* (Justin Dreyfuss), *Maj. Benchley* (George Dicenzo), *M.P.* (Carl Weathers), *Highway patrolman* (Roger Ernest), *Larry Butler* (Josef Sommer), *Ike* (Gene Dynarski), *Team leader* (Merrill Connally), *Hawker* (Gene Rader), *ARP musician* (Phil Dodds), *ARP project member* (F. J. O'Neil)

When Muncie, Indiana, is hit by a massive power blackout, a team of linemen is dispatched to investigate. One of them, Roy Neary (Richard Dreyfuss), has a mind-boggling encounter with a large

191

spacecraft at a deserted railroad crossing. After the giant ship examines Neary's truck by bathing it in an intense, scorching floodlight, Neary speeds off into the hills, where he meets a group of people who've had a similar experience. Among them are Jillian Guiler (Melinda Dillon) and her young son Barry (Cary Guffey) who, for some reason, has a playful urge to follow the alien vessel. After seeing a squad of smaller UFO's speeding through the night, Neary returns home, completely obsessed by what happened. Oddly, the image of a huge mountain begins to dominate his thoughts, and he spends almost every waking hour drawing and sculpting models of it.

Later, the alien ships converge on Jillian's house, and little Barry is snatched aboard before they speed away. Concerned over Barry's safety, Jillian reports what happened to the authorities, but her story is met with great skepticism. Feeling she can trust Neary, she tells him of Barry's abduction and reveals that she, too, has lately been obsessed by the image of a mountain.

Finally recognizing Wyoming's Devil's Tower as the image in their minds, Neary and Jillian drive to Wyoming but find that the area surrounding the tower has been mysteriously placed off-limits by the military. Although ordered by military police to leave the area, Neary and Jillian try to sneak through via a back road but are apprehended and taken into custody.

At a secret military installation nearby, they are questioned by Claude Lacombe (François Truffaut), esteemed UFO researcher and government consultant on such matters. He asks Neary about his recent "close encounter" in Muncie, and about his recurring mental image of Devil's Tower. What Lacombe doesn't tell Neary is that Devil's Tower is a secret landing site for UFO's and that the aliens have been in friendly communication with Lacombe and his associates for years.

After their interrogation, Neary and Jillian are ordered to return home, but, determined to learn the truth, they escape and climb the tower. Reaching the top around nightfall, they behold an incredible vision—several small UFO's converge on a large runway and communicate with Lacombe and his staff via musical sound waves. Following this, a gigantic "mother ship" descends, releasing Barry along with dozens of other people who had been taken aboard. As Jillian embraces Barry, Neary slowly makes his way to the landing site, where he stands awestruck next to Lacombe. A small alien descends the ship's passenger ramp, giving a message of love and goodwill to Lacombe via sign language. Neary is then sworn to secrecy and invited to go along with the aliens on an expedition into space.

The UFO film, a staple of the American cinema since Christian Nyby's 1951 "classic" *The Thing*,

Richard Dreyfuss, Bob Balaban, François Truffaut

Melinda Dillon

Richard Dreyfuss

finally reached its apex in this multimillion-dollar blockbuster, written and directed by Steven Spielberg. *Close Encounters of the Third Kind* remains the most popular and successful film in the history of its genre, and though UFO "classics" such as *The Day the Earth Stood Still* (1951), *War of the Worlds* (1953), and *Earth Versus the Flying Saucers* (1956) continue to have a devoted following among hard-core movie buffs, none of them ever managed to gain such wide acceptance with the general public.

While *Close Encounters of the Third Kind* contains all the thought-provoking philosophy inherent in this kind of film, it was also produced on a spectacular scale. Unlike its predecessors, it had the advantage of an enormous budget and lavish production values, and as such its special effects, settings, photography, music, and sound are among the most striking ever conceived. Executed by Douglas Trumbull and his staff, its visual effects are stunning, and their wide-screen/Dolby sound reproduction gives them an awesome quality most other films of the genre can't match.

Director Steven Spielberg had the project in mind for several years; even before *Jaws* was completed, he and producers Julia and Michael Phillips approached Columbia with the idea. Spielberg is to be commended for his deft engineering of the mammoth film, and he no doubt realized that he was depicting what would, in reality, be one of the most wondrous and important events in the history of humans. As such, the director cleverly imbued even the simplest scenes with an extraordinary "magical" quality through the skillful use of camera angles, lighting, and texture. Even his early shot of suburban Muncie at night has a mystical look to it, and the metallic blue-gray of the streets and buildings, offset by the shimmer of a million tiny electric lights, gives it the look of a "dream city" of the future.

As another unique touch, all the UFO appearances in the film are preceded by a great upheaval of the elements—eerie, unnatural cloud formations appear in the sky before each visitation. The UFO's themselves are superbly designed, from the ship that Neary first encounters at the railroad crossing (a white space cruiser resembling similar vehicles in *2001* and *Silent Running*) to the smaller pods which glide through the sky emitting beams of multicolored light. Most fascinating of all, however, is the titanic "mother ship" which appears at the climax; this emerged as the most popular element in the film (many viewers saw *Close Encounters* three and four times just to get another look at it).

Interestingly, Spielberg first envisioned the character of Roy Neary as a middle-aged man, and thought Jack Nicholson ideal for the role. Nicholson was bound by other commitments, however, and Richard Dreyfuss, who had appeared in Spielberg's *Jaws*, eventually talked the director into giving him the part. The touching finale of *Close Encounters of the Third Kind*, in which the tiny alien enacts his silent communion with Lacombe, added enormously to making the picture one of the decade's most positive and uplifting.

SATURDAY NIGHT FEVER

A Paramount Picture; Directed by John Badham; Produced by Robert Stigwood; Screenplay by Norman Wexler; Based on a story by Nik Cohn; Photography by Ralf D. Bode; Film editor: David Rawlins; Set decorations: George Detitta; Production designer: Charles Bailey; Costumes by Patrizia von Brandenstein; Dance consultant: Jo-Jo Smith; Choreography by Lester Wilson; Makeup by Max

193

Karen Gorney, John Travolta

Henriquez; Technical consultant: James Gambina; Sound recording by Les Lazarowitz; Color by Movielab; Running time: 118 minutes

CAST:
Tony Manero (JOHN TRAVOLTA), *Stephanie* (Karen Lynn Gorney), *Joey* (Joseph Cali), *Bobby C.* (Barry Miller), *Double J* (Paul Pape), *Annette* (Donna Pescow), *Flo* (Julie Bovasso), *Gus* (Bruce Ornstein), *Frank Manero, Jr.* (Martin Shakar), *Frank Manero, Sr.* (Val Bisoglio), *Grandmother* (Nina Hansen), *D.J.* (Monti Rock III), *Linda* (Lisa Peluso), *Fusco* (Sam J. Coppola), *Doreen* (Denny Dillon), *Pete* (Bert Michaels), *Becker* (Robert Weil)

Nineteen-year-old Tony Manero (John Travolta), a paint-store clerk in Brooklyn, is the disco king at "2001 Odyssey," a popular night spot. Though Tony is one of the finest dancers around, his family disapproves of his life-style, and his parents often bemoaningly compare him to his brother Frank (Martin Shakar), a serious young man preparing for the priesthood.

At the Odyssey one Saturday night, Tony meets fellow Brooklynite Stephanie (Karen Lynn Gorney), who is also a fine dancer, and he persuades her to be his partner for an upcoming dance contest. A few years older than Tony, Stephanie is an ambitious public-relations secretary determined to leave Brooklyn and move to Manhattan. Although she argues with Tony over his lack of ambition, the two are superb on the dance floor, and they begin practicing daily for the contest. Meanwhile, Tony dumps his sometimes girlfriend Annette (Donna Pescow) and learns that his best friend Bobby C. (Barry Miller) has "gotten into trouble" with a girl.

On the night of the dance contest, Tony and Stephanie perform well but are outclassed by a young Puerto Rican couple. Due to racial prejudice, however, Tony and Stephanie are awarded first prize; realizing they don't deserve it, Tony gives the trophy to the Puerto Ricans. Later, Tony makes a crude pass at Stephanie, and she runs away from him. Despairing, Tony accompanies Annette, Bobby C., and three other friends to the Verrazano Bridge, where Annette submits to Tony's buddies in an effort to make him jealous. The incident turns ugly, however, when Annette begins crying and Bobby is reminded of his predicament. Suddenly feeling that life is closing in on him, Bobby begins playing daredevil on one of the bridge cables and, losing his balance, falls to his death. Shaken, Tony goes to Stephanie's apartment, where he apologizes for his bad behavior and agrees to be her friend.

John Travolta, Karen Gorney

John Travolta

Some of the cinema's most realistic and compelling dramas can be found among the films of the seventies. Because of the relaxed censorship laws, filmmakers, writers, and actors had almost unlimited freedom to explore the human condition in ways that would have been unthinkable during the forties, fifties, and sixties. As a result of this, the leading actors of the decade were provided with roles of extraordinary dimension and depth, ones which allowed the performers to leave impressions on the minds of audiences that won't be easily forgotten. Though the decade's standout performances by actors in serious dramatic roles were many, a few of them come to mind as being close to perfection. George C. Scott in *Patton,* Oliver Reed in *Women in Love,* Jack Nicholson in *Five Easy Pieces,* Malcolm McDowell in *A Clockwork Orange,* Marlon Brando in *The Godfather,* Laurence Olivier in *Sleuth,* Al Pacino in *The Godfather, Part II,* Donald Sutherland in *The Day of the Locust,* Robert De Niro in *Taxi Driver,* Peter Finch in *Network,* and Christopher Walken and John Savage in *The Deer Hunter* are among the most unforgettable pieces of acting ever recorded on film. Despite this, however, the single film performance of the seventies that seemed to have the greatest impact on audiences was John Travolta's in *Saturday Night Fever.*

John Travolta, Karen Gorney

John Travolta

A simple drama concerning a young paint-store clerk who moonlights as a disco king, the film was directed with style and flair by John Badham; but *Saturday Night Fever*'s overwhelming success was chiefly due to the public's fascination with Travolta's flashy, sexy portrayal of Tony Manero. It ranks as one of the few instances in movie history in which an actor became a kind of cult figure based on a single film role, and a rather lightly written one at that.

Though his popular Vinnie Barbarino characterization on television's "Welcome Back, Kotter" had established him as an idol among the teenaged set, Travolta's screen credits prior to *Saturday Night Fever* were rather skimpy. Aside from a bit part in 1975's *The Devil's Rain,* his only appearance on the big screen was as the villainous Billy Nolan in Brian De Palma's *Carrie.* Though his performance in the film was an energetic study of adolescent menace, it did not reveal any kind of potential for movie superstardom. With *Saturday Night Fever,* however, Travolta simply found the one role that *ideally* suited

197

his talents, and this, combined with the actor's natural charisma, is probably why *Saturday Night Fever* skyrocketed him to front-ranking stardom.

While Travolta acted the part of Tony with skill, the real dazzle admittedly happened when he was featured in his many disco dance routines, superbly choreographed by Lester Wilson and revealing that, properly done, a disco dance could, indeed, be a beautiful thing to watch. Travolta's brilliant solo dance to the tune "You Should Be Dancin' " emerged as the standout number of the film, and it was enhanced enormously by Ralf D. Bode's mobile camerawork and the colorful, electronic glitter of the disco setting. The soundtrack LP for *Saturday Night Fever,* performed by the Bee Gees and other pop music stars, also became a huge hit, and to date it has sold a staggering twenty-seven million copies.

THE GAUNTLET

Clint Eastwood

A Warner Bros. Presentation of a Malpaso Company Film; Directed by Clint Eastwood; Produced by Robert Daley; Screenplay by Michael Butler and Dennis Shryack; Photography by Rexford Metz; Set decorations: Ira Bates; Film editors: Ferris Webster and Joel Cox; Music by Jerry Fielding; Costumes by Glenn Wright; Makeup by Don Schoenfeld; Sound recording by Bert Hallberg; Special effects by Chuck Gaspar; Associate producer: Fritz Manes; Assistant directors: Al Silvani, Lynn Morgan, Richard

Hashimoto, and Peter Bergquist; Filmed in Panavision and DeLuxe Color; Running time: 109 minutes

CAST:
Ben Shockley (CLINT EASTWOOD), *Gus Mally* (Sondra LOCKE), *Josephson* (Pat Hingle), *Blakelock* (William Prince), *Constable* (Bill McKinney), *Feyderspiel* (Michael Cavanaugh), *Bookie* (Douglas McGrath), *Matron* (Mara Corday), *Waitress* (Carole Cook), *Desk Sergeant* (Jeff Morris), *Bikers* (Dan Vadis, Roy Jenson, Samantha Doane), *Bus driver* (Carver Barnes), *Paramedic* (Robert Barrett), *Lieutenant* (Teddy Bear)

Ben Shockley (Clint Eastwood), a washed-up, hard-drinking Phoenix police officer, is ordered to escort a trial witness back from a Las Vegas jail. The order is issued by Commissioner Blakelock (William Prince), who tells Ben that the prisoner, Gus Mally, is a routine witness in an unimportant trial.

In Vegas, Ben is surprised when Gus Mally turns out to be a woman (Sondra Locke). A highly paid prostitute, she tells Ben that someone is going to try and prevent their return to Phoenix, and that the Vegas odds-makers have given fifty-to-one on a "horse" called "Mally-No-Show." Ben checks this out and finds it's true but dismisses it as coincidence.

Ambushed on their way to the airport, however, the two are forced to hide out at Mally's house, from which Ben telephones Blakelock for help. Soon afterward, an army of police pull up and for some reason order Mally and Ben to "surrender." Incredibly, the officers then open fire on the house, forcing Mally and Shockley to escape via an underground passage. Realizing it's Blakelock who's trying to stop them, Ben and Mally hijack a police car, then head for Phoenix. Along the way, they lock horns with three vicious motorcyclists and are pursued by snipers in a high-speed helicopter.

Miraculously overcoming the obstacles, Mally and Ben take refuge in a small hotel, where Mally confesses she once serviced Blakelock, whose sexual tastes were grotesquely perverse. It becomes obvious that this is why Blakelock is out to stop them; and Ben also realizes Blakelock gave him the task in the first place because the Commissioner was certain of Shockley's inability to carry it out. This angers Ben, who determines to deliver Mally no matter what the cost.

The next day, Ben and Mally hijack a bus and surround the driver's seat with pig iron to protect against any armed attacks. Ben then phones Blakelock and announces his intent to arrive in Phoenix the following day. In an effort to prevent this, Blakelock orders the streets cleared, then places a thousand patrolmen in the downtown area, telling them to stop the bus as soon as it's in range. As the

Clint Eastwood

bus rumbles into town, the police unleash an endless barrage of gunfire. Incredibly, the bus moves steadily onward, finally coming to a crashing halt on the steps of City Hall. Ben and Mally emerge somehow unharmed, and when the officers see it is Ben, one of their own men, they refuse to take further action. However, Blakelock's mind snaps under the threat of scandal, and he shoots Ben. Mally then grabs Ben's .357 Magnum and kills the Commissioner, after which Ben rises with only a minor wound. Their incredible odyssey has made them fall in love, and since Mally puts her last $5,000 on ''Mally-No-Show,'' she and Ben will have money enough to build a new life.

The third Dirty Harry film, *The Enforcer*, was little more than a slick, ''packaged'' entertainment, lacking the style of the original and the high-powered action of the first sequel. Despite this, the film was a huge moneymaker, outgrossing both of Eastwood's previous pictures, *The Eiger Sanction* (1975) and *The Outlaw Josey Wales* (1976). For his next film, Eastwood chose another police drama, *The Gauntlet*, in which he would play a slightly less-than-heroic plain-clothes officer, Ben Shockley. Eastwood was intrigued by the challenging, offbeat role, for though Shockley was a tough, cynical, Magnum-carrying cop like Dirty Harry, he was also a drunk and a bit of a washout.

Released in 1977, *The Gauntlet* emerged as an entertaining combination of suspense drama,

Clint Eastwood, Sondra Locke

romance, and *Magnum Force*-style "shoot-'em-up," pitting Eastwood against a dastardly, perverted villain (played to the hilt by William Prince) and teaming him romantically with his lovely young co-star from *Josey Wales,* Sondra Locke. Once again, audiences loved the film, while the critics shook their heads in disbelief, commenting that *The Gauntlet*'s plot was truly absurd and that the climax in which the Phoenix police bombard the bus with a million rounds of ammunition was laughably implausible. Admittedly, the picture does suffer from a certain

"overkill" during its final action sequence, and the "fairy tale" ending (Mally's hefty bet on the "No-Show" horse allowing her and Ben to live "happily ever after") is a little contrived, but the film's success proved that audiences were more than willing to suspend their disbelief.

Ben Shockley turned out to be Eastwood's last "action role" of the decade, and he followed it with two radically different kinds of outings, *Every Which Way but Loose* (1978), a nutty comedy; and *Escape from Alcatraz* (1979), a brooding prison drama.

The Gauntlet is of particular interest to the actor's fans because it gives Eastwood one of the rare monologues of his career when, toward the end of the film, Ben tells Mally about his life with a mixture of nostalgia and sorrow. Because his characters have usually been men of few words, seeing Eastwood deliver a long, dramatic soliloquy is fascinating.

Clint Eastwood, Sondra Locke

Michael Cavanaugh, Clint Eastwood, Sondra Locke

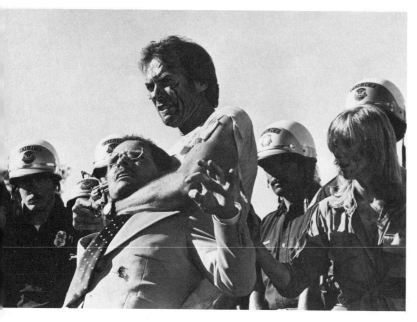

THE GOODBYE GIRL

A Columbia-Warners Release; Directed by Herbert Ross; Produced by Ray Stark; Screenplay by Neil Simon; Photography by David M. Walsh; Production designer: Albert Brenner; Set decorations by Jerry Wunderlich; Sound recording by Jerry Jost and James Sabat; Makeup by Alan Whitney Snyder; Film editor: John F. Burnett; Special effects by Albert Griswold; Costumes by Ann Roth; Music by David Grusin; Song: "The Goodbye Girl," written and performed by David Gates; Filmed in Metrocolor; Running time: 110 minutes

CAST:
Elliott Garfield (RICHARD DREYFUSS), *Paula McFadden* (MARSHA MASON), *Lucy McFadden* (Quinn Cummings), *Mark Morgenweiss* (Paul Benedict), *Donna Douglas* (Barbara Rhodes), *Mrs. Crosby* (Theresa Merritt), *Ronnie* (Michael Shawn), *Rhonda Fontana* (Patricia Pearcy), *Assistant choreographer* (Gene Castle), *Dance instructor* (Daniel Levans)

Richard Dreyfuss, Marsha Mason

New York. Suddenly abandoned by the actor she'd been living with for several years, former Broadway dancer Paula McFadden (Marsha Mason) vows never to love again. On a wet and stormy evening some time later, Elliott Garfield (Richard Dreyfuss), a young actor friend of her former lover, arrives at Paula's apartment, explaining that her "ex" invited him to stay at the place until he was able to find steady work on the New York stage. Although Paula refuses to let him in, Elliott informs her he has a perfect legal right, having made a rental deposit on the place several months earlier. When Elliott offers to share the rent with her, Paula reluctantly agrees to let him stay.

Later, Elliott lands the lead in an off-off-Broadway production of *Richard III*, but soon clashes with the director, who tells him to play Richard as a swishy homosexual. Meanwhile, Paula and her daughter Lucy (Quinn Cummings) begin warming up to the likable Elliott, but Paula keeps her feelings in check, not wanting to be hurt again. On the opening night of the play, Paula and Lucy attend, and Elliott performs brilliantly, but the critics blast "his" bizarre interpretation of Richard, and Elliott is heartbroken. Deeply depressed, he is comforted by Paula, and the two fall in love.

However, Paula becomes worried when, a week later, Elliott accepts a film role requiring him to go on location for eight weeks. Although Elliott assures her he'll be back, Paula thinks it's another kiss-off, and after Elliott leaves she and Lucy become depressed, thinking they've been abandoned once

Marsha Mason, Richard Dreyfuss

Richard Dreyfuss

trayal of Elliott Garfield. In addition, Dave Gates's song, "The Goodbye Girl," which perfectly captured the film's poignantly romantic mood, became one of the more popular records of 1977.

All things considered, *The Goodbye Girl* could hardly miss being a fine film, since it was the collaborative effort of several major talents in the industry. Its producer was the veteran Ray Stark, whose previous credits included films like *Lolita* (1962) and *Funny Girl* (1967). And its director was Herbert Ross, the man responsible for *Play It Again, Sam* (1972) and *The Turning Point* (1977). It was written by Neil Simon, and it cast the immensely popular Richard Dreyfuss in the leading role. Interestingly, with his appearance in *The Goodbye Girl*, Dreyfuss became the highest-grossing screen actor of the decade, which isn't surprising, since his two previous films were *Jaws* and *Close Encounters of the Third Kind*.

again. It then begins to rain and the phone rings—it turns out to be Elliott who, to ease Paula's mind, invites her to go along with him.

The phenomenal success of *Love Story* proved that sentimental screen romances were still bankable in the seventies. Not surprisingly, the remainder of the decade saw the production of many similar films, most of which triumphed because their idealism was a welcome change of pace from the cynical reality of most seventies cinema.

One of the decade's best all-around romantic films was Herbert Ross's *The Goodbye Girl*, a warm, sentimental comedy-drama that struck a truly responsive chord in audiences and became one of the year's biggest hits. The film featured delightful performances by Richard Dreyfuss, Marsha Mason, and Quinn Cummings; and Dreyfuss beat some fierce competition to win the year's Best Actor Oscar for his por-

Quinn Cummings, Richard Dreyfuss

Richard Dreyfuss, Marsha Mason

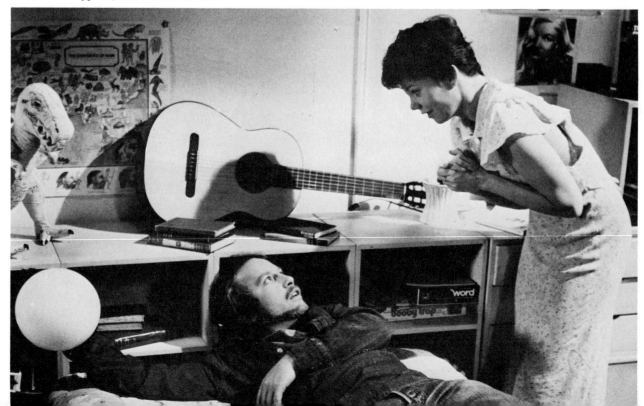

1978

COMA

Rip Torn, Genevieve Bujold

An MGM Picture; Directed by Michael Crichton; Produced by Martin Erlichman; Screenplay by Michael Crichton; Based on the novel by Robin Cook; Photography by Victor J. Kemper; Film editor: David Bretherton; Set decorations: Rick Simpson; Production designer: Albert Brenner; Music by Jerry Goldsmith; Sound recording: Bill Griffith, William McCaughey, Michael J. Kohut, and Aaron Rochin; Makeup by Don Schoenfeld; Special effects by Joe Day and Ernie Smith; Costumes by Eddie Marks and Yvonne Kubis; Filmed in Metrocolor; Running time: 112 minutes

CAST:

Dr. Susan Wheeler (GENEVIEVE BUJOLD), *Dr. Mark Bellows* (MICHAEL DOUGLAS), *Mrs. Emerson* (ELIZABETH ASHLEY), *Dr. George A. Harris* (RICHARD WIDMARK), *Dr. George* (RIP TORN), *Nancy Greenly* (Lois Chiles), *Dr. Morelind* (Harry Rhodes), *Kelly* (Frank Downing), *Computer technician* (Gary Barton), *Jim* (Richard Doyle), *Dr. Marcus* (Alan Haufrect), *Vince* (Lance Le Gault), *Chief resident* (Michael MacRae), *Sean Murphy* (Tom

Selleck), *Dr. Goodman* (Charles Siebert), *Lab technician* (William Wintersole), *1st doctor* (Ernest Anderson), *2nd doctor* (Harry Basch), *3rd doctor* (Maury Cooper), *Dance instructor* (Joni Palmer), *Diane* (Joanna Kerns), *Sally* (Kay Cole), *Woman in elevator* (Sarina C. Grant)

Boston Memorial Hospital. Surgical resident Dr. Susan Wheeler (Genevieve Bujold) is disturbed when her friend Nancy Greenly (Lois Chiles) emerges from routine surgery in a deep coma. Learning that many similar cases have occurred over the past year, Susan demands to see the files on coma patients, but the chief anaesthetist, Dr. George (Rip Torn), refuses to release them. Dr. Mark Bellows (Michael Douglas), Susan's fiancé, insists she's overreacting to the situation because of Nancy, but the next day another healthy patient suffers the same fate.

That night, Susan breaks into Dr. George's office to examine the files, which reveal all the year's coma cases originated in operating room 8, and were later transferred to the Jefferson Institute. Suspecting foul play, Susan is later approached by Kelly (Frank Downing), a maintenance man, who asks to meet with her in the hospital generator room after hours, promising to reveal the hospital's terrible secret at

Michael Crichton

Genevieve Bujold

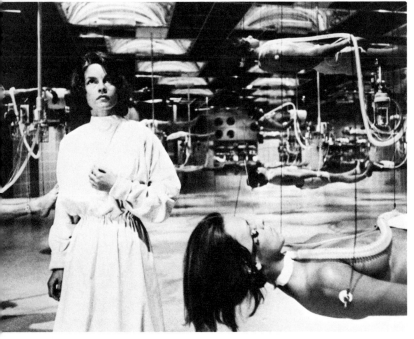

Genevieve Bujold

that time. Before this can happen, however, Kelly is electrocuted by a mysterious killer, who then pursues Susan through the hospital. Evading her assailant, Susan searches the generator room and finds a small electrical device which, when activated, feeds carbon monoxide into the anaesthesia tanks in O.R. 8. She tells Mark about this but he doesn't believe her.

Determined to learn the truth, Susan visits the Jefferson Institute, located on a remote hillside and tended only by Nurse Emerson (Elizabeth Ashley) and her staff. By chance, Emerson is leading a group of doctors on a tour of the place, so Susan easily

Genevieve Bujold

Richard Widmark, Genevieve Bujold

Michael Douglas

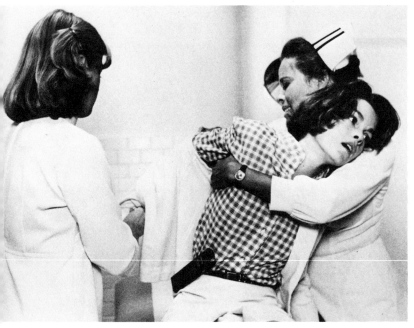

206

gains entrance. After Emerson shows the doctors a large "life-support" chamber in which the coma victims are being kept alive indefinitely, the tour concludes. While the others depart, Susan sneaks into an off-limits area, where she learns that the coma patients' organs are actually being auctioned for transplants around the world. She also finds out that a "Dr. George" is head of the operation, and naturally suspects the anaesthetist.

Returning to Boston Memorial, Susan tells her superior, Dr. Harris (Richard Widmark), what she has discovered. However, Harris (whose first name is George) turns out to be the real culprit, and he slips Susan a drug that simulates appendicitis. Preparing her for surgery, Harris insists on O.R. 8, which makes Mark suspicious. Running to the generator room, Mark destroys the carbon-monoxide device before Harris has a chance to activate it. Mark saves Susan's life, and Harris is arrested.

Coma, a slick, enjoyable thriller in the Alfred Hitchcock mold, was released by MGM in early 1978, and did exceptional business at the box office. It was based on the best-selling suspense novel by Robin Cook, a prominent ophthalmologist who wrote the book in his spare time, and was written for the screen and directed by Michael Crichton who, considering his background, was a most appropriate choice for the job.

Like Cook, Crichton is a medical doctor with several best-selling novels to his credit—*The Andromeda Strain, The Terminal Man, The Great Train Robbery*, and others—and he also managed to establish himself, with a superb science fiction opus, *Westworld* (1973), as a movie director of definite skill. The directing bug first hit Crichton in 1971, when he was on the Universal lot to observe the filming of *The Andromeda Strain*. Watching veteran director Robert Wise at work, Crichton became completely fascinated with the process of moviemaking, and not long afterward he was allowed to direct *Westworld*, which became highly successful.

When, in 1977, MGM bought the motion picture rights to *Coma*, they immediately hired Crichton to direct, realizing that, of all the young filmmakers currently on the scene, he was, perhaps, the best qualified to helm a thriller with a hospital setting. MGM's decision proved to be a good one, and, though it was only his second feature, Crichton fashioned *Coma* into an excellent, gripping mystery film. He drew excellent performances from Genevieve Bujold, Michael Douglas, Elizabeth Ashley, Richard Widmark, and Rip Torn, and he succeeded in giving the film an appropriately eerie and menacing atmosphere. Crichton's film was aided considerably by the splendid music score of veteran composer Jerry Goldsmith, and its metallic, discordant string movements faintly remind the viewer of the "classic" Hitchcock scores of Bernard Herrmann.

JAWS II

A Universal Picture; Directed by Jeannot Szwarc; Produced by Richard D. Zanuck and David Brown; Screenplay by Carl Gottlieb and Howard Sackler; Based on characters created by Peter Benchley; Photography by Michael Butler; Film editor: Neil Travis; Music by John Williams; Production designer and associate producer: Joe Alves; Art direction: Gene Johnson and Stu Campbell; Sound by Jim Alexander; Set decorations: Philip Abramson; Technical adviser; Manfred Zendar; Costumes: Bill Jobe; Makeup by Ron Snyder, Dick Sharp, and Bob Jiras; Filmed in Panavision and Technicolor; Running time: 122 minutes

CAST:
Brody (ROY SCHEIDER), *Ellen Brody* (LORRAINE GARY), *Mayor* (MURRAY HAMILTON), *Peterson* (Joseph Mascolo), *Hendricks* (Jeffrey Kramer), *Tina* (Ann Dusenberry), *Mike* (Mark Gruner), *Dr. Elkins* (Collin Wilcox), *Andrews* (Barry Coe), *Jackie* (Donna Wilkes), *Andy* (Gary Springer), *Ed* (Gary Dubin), *Timmy* (G. Thomas Dunlop), *Polo* (John Dukakis), *Larry* (David Elliott), *Sean* (Marc Gilpin), *Brooke* (Gigi Vorgan), *Patrick* (Ben Marley), *Doug* (Keith Gordon), *Helicopter pilot* (Jerry M. Baxter)

The shark terror that rocked Amity Island is in the past, and the resort has again become a bustling tourist spot. However, the strange disappearance of two scuba divers and a water skier causes Chief Brody (Roy Scheider) great concern. The personal effects of the divers are washed ashore and examined, and a processed photo from their camera reveals what Brody insists is a shark fin. The mayor (Murray Hamilton) dismisses Brody's fears as mere paranoia, resulting from the chief's harrowing experience four years earlier.

Despite this, Brody perches atop the shark observation tower the following day and spots a suspicious shadow in the water. Drawing his gun, Brody screams at tourists to clear the area, but as it turns out the shadow is merely a large school of fish, and Brody is fired for causing a panic.

Meanwhile, two teenagers, Tina (Ann Dusenberry) and Ed (Gary Dubin), sail to a secluded spot when, abruptly, their boat lifts out of the water, tossing Ed overboard. Tina watches with horror as her boyfriend is attacked by a monstrous shark. Later,

Brody finds the hysterical Tina and realizes he's been right all along—another "Great White" is terrorizing Amity.

Learning his two sons have gone on a boating picnic with friends, Brody orders a search of the area, and a rescue helicopter is dispatched. Spotting the youngsters adrift on their small boats, the pilot lowers the copter to tow the kids to safety. Suddenly, however, the shark rises from the sea, dragging the helicopter under. When the pilot fails to report back, Brody commandeers a small cruiser in an effort to find the kids himself. Meanwhile, the shark begins stalking the kids, who remain helplessly stranded.

Jeannie Coulter

Finally, Brody arrives on the scene and, remembering that sharks are drawn to clanging noises, pounds on a metal power cable floating in the water. The giant shark rushes toward Brody and, at the last instant, bites into the cable, electrocuting itself.

A sequel to *Jaws* was inevitable. It was one of history's most profitable and entertaining films, and its studio, Universal, would have been foolish not to try and duplicate its success with a follow-up. It came as no surprise, therefore, when Universal announced its intention to make a *Jaws II*. Richard D. Zanuck and David Brown were again teamed to produce, and the studio rehired Roy Scheider, Lorraine Gary, and Murray Hamilton to repeat their popular roles from the first *Jaws*. The writers of the sequel, Carl Gottlieb and Howard Sackler, were instructed to take an entirely fresh approach in their script, and the studio stipulated that, above all, they did not want a replay of the earlier picture.

To comply with Universal's wish, Gottlieb and Sackler fashioned a rather lengthy screenplay in which the Great White shark returned to terrorize a group of adventuresome teenagers vacationing at the Amity resort. Confident of another success, Universal lavished *Jaws II* with a huge budget (a reported $22 million) and an extensive publicity campaign that was, once again, heralded by a catchy slogan—"Just when you thought it was safe to go back in the water."

However, the finished film, released in 1978, never came close to the quality of the Spielberg original, and though it did well at the box office, it remains a rather stilted motion picture. Most of *Jaws II* simply does not work. The only time it really comes to life is when Scheider, Gary, and Hamilton are on screen, and—sad to say—the rest is pretty dreadful.

The shooting of *Jaws II* had been plagued by problems from the very beginning, which perhaps accounts somewhat for the picture's weaknesses. Filming of *Jaws II* began in June 1977 and ran smoothly until, one month later, the entire production was halted by a major dispute between director John Hancock and producers Zanuck and Brown. Supposedly, Hancock was making a straight "horror film" of *Jaws II* and clashed with the producers over

this approach. Unable to convince Hancock that the film was supposed to be an *adventure* story, Zanuck and Brown fired him, and hired a young television director named Jeannot Szwarc to finish the picture.

Szwarc had few theatrical films to his credit, but he had extensive experience in television, and was especially adept at working under pressure. Though he managed to somehow pull the whole thing together on schedule, *Jaws II* lacks power and conviction, and, oddly, the major weakness turned out to be the shark, seen too readily and often to be really terrifying (the constant reappearances of the beast actually provoked *laughter* from some audiences).

Indeed, the film's one great moment of terror doesn't even involve the shark; it occurs when Brody wades into the surf to investigate a floating timber, only to be horrified when the petrified corpse of a shark victim suddenly rises from the water.

Despite its faults, the performances in *Jaws II* are generally good, especially that of Roy Scheider, who didn't want to make the film and did so only to fulfill his contract.

COMING HOME

A United Artists Picture; Directed by Hal Ashby; Produced by Jerome Hellman; Screenplay by Waldo Salt and Robert C. Jones; Story by Nancy Dowd; Photography by Haskell Wexler; Production designer: Michael Haller; Film editor: Don Zimmerman; Set decorations: George Gaines; Costumes by Ann Roth; Makeup by Garry Liddiard; Associate producer: Bruce Gilbert; Assistant directors: Charles A. Myers and James Bloom; Sound recording: Jeff Wexler; Filmed in DeLuxe Color; Running time: 128 minutes

hospital, where she meets Luke Martin (Jon Voight), a paraplegic consumed by bitterness. She also meets and befriends Vi Munson (Penelope Milford), whose brother Billy (Robert Carradine), recently back from the war, is being treated at the hospital for severe depression.

Over the next few weeks, Luke and Sally discover they went to the same high school, and some time later they become friends. Sensing her friendship has eased Luke's bitterness, she invites him to dinner, and he confesses: "I spend most of my time thinking about making love with you." Though tempted to confess similar feelings of her own, Sally decides to remain faithful to Bob. Weeks later, she journeys to

Bruce Dern, Jane Fonda

CAST:

Sally Hyde (JANE FONDA), *Luke Martin* (JON VOIGHT), *Captain Bob Hyde* (BRUCE DERN), *Vi Munson* (Penelope Milford), *Billy Munson* (Robert Carradine), *Pee Wee* (Charles Cyphers), *Fleta Wilson* (Mary Jackson), *Sgt. Dink Mobley* (Robert Ginty), *Nurse De Groot* (Tresa Hughes), *Virgil* (Willie Tyler), *Tim* (David Glennon), *Corrine* (Olivia Cole)

1968. At a Los Angeles military base, Marine Captain Bob Hyde (Bruce Dern) ships to Vietnam for active duty. Following his departure, his wife Sally (Jane Fonda) begins volunteer work at a veterans'

Hong Kong, where her husband is on furlough, but finds that his recent war experience has left him moody and withdrawn.

Returning to the States, Sally learns that Vi's brother has committed suicide, and that Luke has been released. The next night, Luke chains himself to the gates of a marine recruiting station to protest the war, and succeeds in getting the attention of the media. Seeing the event on a television news program, Sally goes to Luke, giving him moral support during the ordeal and taking him home afterward. That same night, the two make love, and begin a beautiful relationship that lasts for several months. However, their activities are watched by the FBI,

Jane Fonda, Jon Voight

Jon Voight, Jane Fonda

Bruce Dern, Jon Voight

211

Robert Carradine, Jon Voight

Bruce Dern, Jane Fonda

who snap photos of the couple embracing on a beach.

When Bob returns home, he no longer seems to have any interest in Sally, and prefers drinking beer and swapping stories with other veterans. Meanwhile, the FBI tells Bob about Luke and Sally, and, already somewhat unbalanced, he goes berserk and threatens Sally with his assault rifle. Luckily, however, Luke arrives and manages to calm Bob down. The story ends with Luke relating his war experience to a large group of high school students.

Though certainly a topic worth examining, the Vietnam War remained virtually unexplored by the decade's filmmakers until 1978, when two superb motion pictures dealing with the subject were released almost back to back. The films—Hal Ashby's *Coming Home* and Michael Cimino's *The Deer Hunter*—were both enormously profitable and, somewhat ironically, were the two biggest winners in the 1978 Oscar race. The films were extremely different from one another—*Coming Home* was a rather personal, intimate drama, while *The Deer Hunter* was a sprawling, three-hour epic, featuring a huge cast, extensive location shooting, and some of the strongest depictions of the "horrors of war" ever presented. Despite their differences, however, both shared the same central theme—how the lives of ordinary Americans were affected by Vietnam—and this, more than anything else, is what made them so popular with audiences.

Coming Home, released a few months earlier than *The Deer Hunter,* was primarily about the painful readjustment of a paraplegic veteran—Luke Martin—to civilian life, and the story followed him through his gradual transition from an embittered shell to an energetic spokesman for the anti-war movement. The film won Best Actor and Actress honors for Voight and Fonda, and the remarkable chemistry the stars generated in their roles made the relationship between Luke and Sally one of the most compelling in a seventies film. In addition to the fine acting of Voight and Fonda, Bruce Dern's haunting portrait of a gung-ho marine shattered by actual combat experience was also splendid.

HEAVEN CAN WAIT

A Paramount Picture; Directed by Warren Beatty and Buck Henry; Produced by Warren Beatty; Screenplay by Warren Beatty and Elaine May; Based on the play by Harry Segall; Photography by William A. Fraker; Production designer: Paul Sylbert; Film editors: Robert C. Jones and Don Zimmerman; Set

decorations: George Gaines; Special effects by Robert MacDonald; Music by Dave Grusin; Sound recording by Tommy Overton; Makeup by Lee Harmon; Color by Movielab; Running time: 101 minutes

CAST:
Joe Pendleton (WARREN BEATTY), *Betty Logan* (JULIE CHRISTIE), *Mr. Jordan* (JAMES MASON), *Tony Abbott* (CHARLES GRODIN), *Max Corkle* (JACK WARDEN), *Julie Farnsworth* (DYAN CANNON), *The escort* (BUCK HENRY), *Sisk* (Joseph Maher), *Krim* (Vincent Gardenia), *Bentley* (Hamilton Camp), *Everett* (Arthur Malet), *Peters* (Larry Block), *Conway* (Frank Campanella), *Head coach* (Dolph Sweet)

Joe Pendleton (Warren Beatty), star quarterback for the Los Angeles Rams, has a traffic accident while training for the Super Bowl. Seconds later, he awakens to find himself being led to a heavenly "way station" by a mild-mannered "escort" (Buck Henry). Realizing what has happened, Joe insists he's not ready to die and that the accident wasn't serious enough to cause a fatal injury.

Arriving at the station, Joe reveals his predicament to archangel Mr. Jordan (James Mason) who, after

Warren Beatty

214

hearing Joe's story, realizes the escort mistakenly assumed Joe's accident would be fatal. Learning that Joe isn't really "due" for another forty years, Mr. Jordan accompanies him back to earth, where they discover that Joe's body has been cremated. To compensate for the escort's mistake, Mr. Jordan agrees to help Joe find another body.

After a great deal of searching, Joe chooses that of millionaire-industrialist Leo Farnsworth, who has just been murdered by his wife Julia (Dyan Cannon) and secretary Tony (Charles Grodin). Assuming Farnsworth's body seconds after the millionaire's death, Joe/Farnsworth surprises Julia and Tony by suddenly bounding into his study, full of life and vitality and eager to get on with the day's business. After Julia and Tony excuse themselves to get over the shock, "Farnsworth" is visited by a young woman named Betty Logan (Julie Christie) who is protesting an environmentally hazardous refinery "Farnsworth" is building near her village. Complying with her wishes and agreeing with her protest, Joe halts construction on the refinery, and later he and Betty fall in love.

James Mason

James Mason, Warren Beatty, Buck Henry

Still determined to take his place in the Super Bowl, Joe buys the Rams, then hires his old coach, Max Corkle (Jack Warden), to get him into shape. During training, Joe reveals his true identity to the stunned Corkle, but weeks before the game "Farnsworth" is again murdered by Julia and Tony. Joe's spirit returns to Heaven, where he tells Mr. Jordan he just has to play in the Super Bowl, no matter what.

On the night of the game, the Rams' quarterback Tom Jarrett is fatally stricken, and Jordan allows Joe

Warren Beatty

Warren Beatty, Buck Henry

James Mason, Warren Beatty

Julie Christie, Warren Beatty

Warren Beatty

to take over his body. After leading the Rams to a spectacular victory, Joe/Jarrett is told by Mr. Jordan that he will now be Tom Jarrett forever, with no recollection of his former self. After the game, Jarrett runs into Betty outside the stadium, and they are mysteriously drawn to each other.

Heaven Can Wait was an entertaining modernization of the forties "classic" *Here Comes Mr. Jordan,* with Warren Beatty and James Mason assuming the roles originally played by Robert Montgomery and Claude Rains. Though it follows the same basic plot formula as the earlier picture, *Heaven Can Wait* is not a remake in the true sense of the word, as many of its characters and situations are wholly new inventions, not taken from the forties effort.

Warren Beatty produced, codirected, cowrote, and starred in the picture, and his breezy portrayal of football idol Joe Pendleton was an enjoyable change of pace for the actor, obviously seeking to break away from the sexy stereotype of roles such as George in *Shampoo.* Beatty made Joe Pendleton a completely "wholesome" hero, an easygoing "nice guy" and likable innocent who did not display any of the aggressive sexuality of some of Beatty's earlier screen characters. Beatty portrayed Pendleton as a man of honor and a bit of a romantic idealist, a far cry from the manipulative "sex machine" Beatty had played in many other films.

All the elements seemed to come together nicely, and *Heaven Can Wait* became a major box-office success. Though its resemblance to *Here Comes Mr. Jordan* was merely superficial, *Heaven Can Wait* retained some small details from the earlier film, such as making the athlete-protagonist a musician (Montgomery was a boxer who played the saxophone, while Beatty was a football player who was never without his bass clarinet).

Shortly after the film's release, the display poster from *Heaven Can Wait,* featuring a sweat-suited Warren Beatty sporting a pair of angel wings, was marketed commercially (a là the Farrah Fawcett and Cheryl Tiegs posters) with great success.

THE FURY

A 20th Century-Fox Picture; Directed by Brian De Palma; Produced by Frank Yablans; Screenplay by John Farris; Based on his novel; Photography by Richard H. Kline; Film editor: Paul Hirsch; Production designer: Billy Malley; Set decorations: Audrey Blasdel-Goddard; Special effects by A. D. Flowers; Music by John Williams; Costumes by Theoni V. Aldredge; Makeup by William Tuttle; Special makeup effects by Rick Baker; Sound recording by Hal Etherington; Filmed in DeLuxe Color; Running time: 118 minutes

CAST:
Peter Sandza (KIRK DOUGLAS), *Childress* (JOHN CASSAVETES), *Hester* (CARRIE SNODGRASS), *Gillian Bellaver* (AMY IRVING), *Robin Sandza* (ANDREW STEVENS), *Dr. Susan Charles* (FIONA LEWIS), *Dr. Jim McKeever* (CHARLES DURNING), *Dr. Ellen Lindstrom* (Carol Rossen), *Katharine Bellaver* (Joyce Easton), *Raymond Dunwoodie* (William Finley), *Vivian Knuckells* (Jane Lambert), *Blackfish* (Sam Laws), *LaRue* (Melody Thomas), *Cheryl* (Hilary Thompson), *Lander* (Patrick Billingsley), *DeMasi* (Jack Callahan), *Bob* (Dennis Franz), *Marty* (Michael O'Dwyer), *Dr. Ives* (Felix Shuman)

Robin Sandza (Andrew Stevens), a young man gifted with profound telekinetic abilities, vacations at a Mediterranean resort with his father Peter (Kirk Douglas), a high-ranking secret agent, and the latter's associate Childress (John Cassavetes), head of a government agency investigating psychic phenomena. The resort is suddenly raided by terrorists, and when Peter appears to be killed in the skirmish Childress takes Robin under his wing.

As it turns out, Childress doesn't work for the government at all, and is really a treacherous, evil man planning to use those gifted with psychic powers for his own profit. He staged the terrorist attack for the sole purpose of eliminating Peter, so he'd be free to experiment on Robin. Peter, who luckily survived the incident, learns of Childress's treachery and travels back to America, where he hires psychic Raymond Dunwoodie (William Finley) to track down Robin.

After a great deal of searching, Dunwoodie tells Peter that he gets strong telepathic "vibes" from Gillian Bellaver (Amy Irving), a telekinetic schoolgirl currently under observation at the Paragon Institute for Psychic Research, which, Peter later learns, is really a front for Childress's operation. At Paragon, Gillian has lately been receiving psychic "S.O.S." messages from Robin, most of which are telepathic images of his current surroundings.

At his secret headquarters somewhere in the country, Childress begins building Robin's power into a deadly destructive force, hoping to later auction the young man as a secret weapon. His increasing powers, however, begin to warp Robin's mind, and he gradually becomes psychotic.

Later, Peter smuggles Gillian out of Paragon, and they make a long bus journey to Childress's underground installation. Now a deadly telekinetic dynamo as a result of Childress's treatments, Robin

Amy Irving, Charles Durning

Kirk Douglas

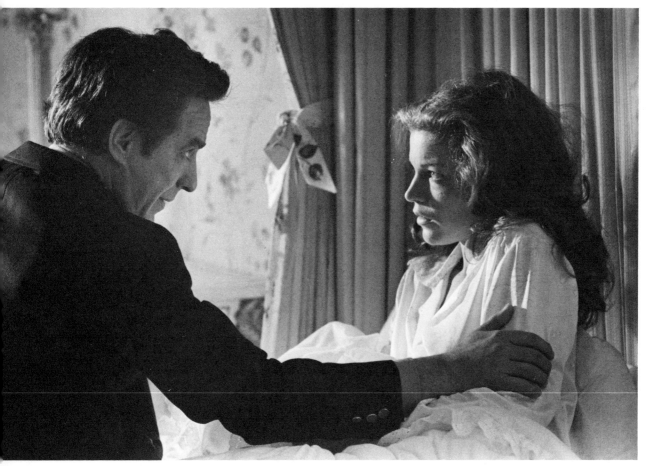

218

turns on his lover Dr. Susan Charles (Fiona Lewis) when she betrays him with another man, and he uses his powers to gruesomely slay her. Peter and Gillian arrive at the hideout sometime after dark and watch in horror as the psychotic Robin accidentally falls to his death from the roof of Childress's mansion. Grief-stricken, Peter commits suicide.

Now hoping to use Gillian as Robin's successor, Childress takes her into his care, but sometime afterward she turns on him, using her growing powers to literally blow him to pieces.

Carrie, released in 1976, was its director Brian De Palma's first major success at the box office. Though the film did extremely well by industry standards,

John Cassavetes, Andrew Stevens

coming close to the $40-million mark, De Palma later revealed that he believed *Carrie* could have easily been a blockbuster in the tradition of *The Exorcist* and *The Omen* if it had been sold properly. The director felt that the studio had made a mistake by marketing *Carrie* as a mere "escapist" chiller rather than as the serious horror film it was. He also speculated that *Carrie* was perhaps prevented from achieving blockbuster status because its cast lacked a major star name, such as Ellen Burstyn in *The Exorcist* or Gregory Peck in *The Omen.*

For his next film, De Palma again returned to the subject of telekinetic children, only this time he also hired a solid Hollywood name to head the cast. *The Fury* (1978) is generally acknowledged as the most elaborate showcase for the talents of Brian De Palma to date, and it contains more bizarre effects than all his earlier films combined.

Kirk Douglas, Amy Irving

Kirk Douglas

The film, a contemporary spy thriller with horrific, supernatural overtones, featured an especially enjoyable performance by veteran star Kirk Douglas in the flashy role of a top secret agent whose telekinetic son is suddenly kidnapped by a ruthless associate. Douglas's energetic portrayal of Peter Sandza dominates the film, and his presence no doubt helped *The Fury* achieve even greater box-office success than *Carrie.*

Douglas was given excellent support by Andrew Stevens and Amy Irving, perfectly cast as the two young psychics, and their roles frequently called upon them to simulate the output of enormous telekinetic energy, which was no easy task. Andrew Stevens's look of intense concentration during his feats was greatly aided by the cosmetic application of pulsating forehead veins by master makeup artist William Tuttle. Whenever Stevens performed one of his psychic stunts, the actor simply squeezed a compression ball in his pants pocket, and the veins, connected to the ball via a tiny air tube, would pulsate "on cue."

Kirk Douglas

Obviously attempting to outdo himself, De Palma imbued *The Fury* with some truly startling effects, most notably Stevens's grisly destruction of Fiona Lewis (raising her into the air, then spinning her at great speed until her body actually breaks apart), and of course Amy Irving's spectacular "exploding" of John Cassavetes at the conclusion. Both these stunts were frighteningly believable, thanks to the realistic dummies created by special makeup wizard Rick Baker.

AN UNMARRIED WOMAN

A 20th Century-Fox Picture; Directed by Paul Mazursky; Produced by Paul Mazursky and Tony Ray; Screenplay by Paul Mazursky; Photography by Arthur Ornitz; Film editor: Stuart H. Pappé; Production designer: Pato Guzman; Set decorations: Edward Stewart; Music by Bill Conti; Costumes by Albert Wolsky; Makeup by Mike Maggi; Sound recording by Dennis Maitland; Filmed in Color by Movielab; Running time: 124 minutes

CAST:
Erica Benton (JILL CLAYBURGH), *Saul Kaplan* (Alan Bates), *Martin Benton* (Michael Murphy), *Charlie* (Cliff Gorman), *Patti* (Lisa Lucas), *Tanya* (Penelope Russianoff), *Sue* (Pat Quinn), *Elaine* (Kelly Bishop), *Jeannette* (Linda Miller), *Bob* (Andrew Duncan), *Dr. Jacobs* (Daniel Seltzer), *Phil* (Matthew

220

Jill Clayburgh, Michael Murphy

Arkin), *Jean* (Novella Nelson), *Edward* (Raymond J. Barry), *Herb* (Ivan Karp), *Fred* (Michael Tucker)

Erica Benton (Jill Clayburgh), who works at a fashionable Manhattan art gallery, is shattered when her husband Martin (Michael Murphy) suddenly informs her that he's in love with a younger woman and wants a divorce. When Martin moves out of their apartment several days later, she shuts herself off from the world for seven weeks, refusing to see anyone. Not knowing where to turn, Erica places herself under the care of a therapist, Tanya (Penelope Russianoff), who tells her that, for her own well-being, she must leave the past behind and reenter the "mainstream of life."

Following Tanya's advice, Erica visits a small bar in the Village, where she runs into Charlie (Cliff Gorman), an aggressive, chauvinistic artist who's been trying to get her into bed ever since he's known her. Feeling the need to ease her depression and wanting the company of a man for the first time in weeks, Erica allows Charlie to take her home for the night. Not really interested in forming a deeper relationship with the arrogant Charlie, however, she refuses to see him again.

In an effort to revitalize her social life, Erica attends an exhibition of works by English artist Saul Kaplan (Alan Bates). Meeting Kaplan, Erica is smitten by his gentleness and sensitivity. They make love at his studio later that night and subsequently begin an ongoing relationship, which angers Charlie. Later, Erica introduces Saul to her bright, strong-willed daughter Patti (Lisa Lucas). At first Patti resents Saul, but soon the artist's warm and likable nature wins her over.

Sometime afterward, Martin begs Erica to take him back, explaining that his young woman has left him for somebody else. Erica refuses, however, telling Martin that she has actually grown to relish her freedom and independence. Later, Erica secures a higher-paying job, allowing her and Patti to move to a new apartment; and her beautiful, "open" relationship with Saul continues to flourish.

The "women's pictures" of the seventies were a far cry from those of past decades. Throughout the thirties, forties, and fifties, the very term "women's picture" seemed synonymous with gushy soap operas depicting women as emotionally helpless creatures whose entire lives revolved around finding the ideal man and having a family.

The seventies saw the production of three splendid films dealing with the problems of women—*Diary of a Mad Housewife* (1970), *Alice Doesn't Live Here Anymore* (1975), and *An Unmarried Woman* (1978). These were tough, no-nonsense dramas, showing

Michael Murphy, Jill Clayburgh

221

Andrew Duncan, Jill Clayburgh

Jill Clayburgh

Jill Clayburgh

what it is like to be a woman in a male-dominated world and obviously seeking to destroy the romantic fantasy created by the earlier pictures. In each of them, the protagonists were shown to be intelligent, self-sufficient women trying to survive in a world ruled by men, and all were placed in the situation of having to seek identities of their own away from their husbands. These films told their stories from a woman's point of view, and curiously they all raised some serious questions about the validity of marriage.

An Unmarried Woman, written and directed by Paul Mazursky and starring Jill Clayburgh, is perhaps the most satisfying of the three, and it seemed to have far more appeal to audiences than the other two. Jill Clayburgh as the title character delivered one of the decade's best and most insightful performances by an actress, and Alan Bates and Cliff Gorman were also excellent as the men in her life.

Though *An Unmarried Woman* is chiefly noted for the wonderful acting by the cast, Paul Mazursky's finely paced direction and the jaunty, offbeat, jazz-oriented music score by Bill Conti also contributed to the film's quality.

Jill Clayburgh, Lisa Lucas

Alan Bates, Jill Clayburgh

Don Stroud, Gary Busey, Charles Martin Smith

THE BUDDY HOLLY STORY

An Entertainment Release; Directed by Steve Rash; Produced by Freddy Bauer; Screenplay by Robert Gittler; Story by Alan Swyer; Based on the book by John Coldrosen; Photography by Steven Larner; Film editor: David Blewitt; Production designer: Joel Schiller; Set decoration: Tom Roysden; Special effects: Robbie Knott; Costumes by Michael Butler, Thalia Phillips, and Warren Flores; Choreography by Maggie Rash; Makeup by Marvin Westmore and Doris Alexander; Sound recording by Willie Burton; Filmed in color; Running time: 114 minutes

CAST:

Buddy Holly (GARY BUSEY), *Jesse Clarence* (Don Stroud), *Ray Bob Simmons* (Charles Martin Smith), *Ross Turner* (Conrad Janis), *Riley Randolph* (William Jordan), *Maria Elena Santiago* (Maria Richwine), *Cindy Lou* (Amy Johnston), *Sol Gittler* (Dick O'Neil), *"Madman Mancuso"* (Fred Travalena), *Mrs. Holly* (Neva Patterson), *Mr. Holly* (Arch Johnson) *T. J.* (John Goff), *Mrs. Santiago* (Gloria Irizarry), *Engineer Sam* (Joe Berry), *Preacher* (Richard Kennedy), *Wilson* (Jim Beach), *The Big Bopper* (Gailard Sartain), *Richie Valens* (Gilbert Melgar), *Eddie Foster* (Albert Popwell), *Sam* (Paul Mooney), *Luther* (Stymie Beard), *Eddie Cochran* (Jerry Zaremba)

Lubbock, Texas, 1956. Three young musician friends, Buddy Holly (Gary Busey), Jesse Clarence (Don Stroud), and Ray Bob Simmons (Charles Martin Smith), perform one of Buddy's songs, "That'll Be the Day," in a live broadcast over local radio station KDAV. Struck by the song's originality and style, the station manager, Riley Randolph (William Jordan), sends a tape of it to Coral Records in New York. As a result of the broadcast, however, Buddy receives considerable flak from the staunch, conservative Lubbock community, who thinks his "rock and roll" music is disgraceful. Undaunted by the disapproval of their parents and neighbors, the boys travel to Nashville in the hope of being discovered, but they are rejected after auditioning for a record producer, who explains that their uninhibited music sounds too "Negro" for mass consumption.

Disheartened, they return home to Lubbock and are amazed to learn that while they were away Coral released "That'll Be the Day" and it became a sizable hit. During a rehearsal some time later, Buddy's train of thought is interrupted by the chirping of a cricket, which inspires him to call his trio "Buddy Holly and the Crickets." Summoned to New York to sign a recording contract with Coral, Buddy breaks with his girlfriend Cindy Lou (Amy Johnston), and this inspires him to write a song about the fiery passions of young love called "Peggy Sue."

In New York, Buddy persuades Coral executive Ross Turner (Conrad Janis) to allow him to act as his own producer. Later, Buddy falls in love with Turner's beautiful secretary, Maria Elena Santiago (Maria Richwine), who repeatedly refuses to go out with him because her strict Catholic aunt (Gloria Irizarry) has forbidden her to see musicians socially. Visiting Mrs. Santiago at her home, however, Buddy wins her over with his warmth and honesty, and secures her permission to date Maria. With the release of several giant record hits, Buddy and the Crickets skyrocket to stardom, and Buddy marries Maria Elena. Soon growing tired of the hectic pace of performing and desperately homesick for Lubbock, Jesse and Ray Bob desert Buddy and return to Texas.

Remaining in New York, Buddy reluctantly agrees to go on an extensive promotional tour. At one point in his travels, he gives a smash, sellout concert in Clear Lake, after which he learns that the Crickets have decided to join him at his next appearance in Minnesota. When the bus that was to have taken him there breaks down, Buddy and fellow artists The Big Bopper (Gailard Sartain) and Richie Valens (Gilbert Melgar) charter a small plane, which crashes on the morning of February 3, 1959.

Buddy Holly is a legend in American music, and he is regarded by many as the "father" of rock and roll. His many "classic" songs, written and recorded in the late fifties, were among the most distinctive and innovative of their time. Like the songs of Elvis Presley, they departed drastically from the traditional forms of popular music, and their obvious celebration of sexuality made them exciting and refreshing to young people of the period. Holly became something of a cult figure during the seventies, and throughout the decade his music was recorded by contemporary artists such as Linda Ronstadt.

This film, produced on a medium budget and lacking a "name cast," is nonetheless one of the small gems of seventies cinema. It traces Holly's life from his beginnings as a talented, hip, rebellious nineteen-year-old singer-composer in small-town Texas, through his meteoric rise to stardom, and finally to his tragic death in a plane crash at age twenty-two.

Released in 1978, The Buddy Holly Story became the surprise hit of the year, and it is a splendid film in every respect. It perfectly recreated the world of fifties rock and roll, and it contained a stunning performance by Gary Busey as Holly. Holly's many songs—"That'll Be the Day," "Peggy Sue," "It's So Easy," "Maybe Baby," and the beautiful "True Love Ways"—are brilliantly performed in the film by Busey, Don Stroud, and Charlie Martin Smith, who capture the look and sound of Holly and the Crickets with uncanny accuracy.

ANIMAL HOUSE

A Universal Picture; Directed by John Landis; Produced by Matty Simmons and Ivan Reitman; Screenplay by Harold Ramis, Douglas Kenney, and Chris Miller; Photography by Charles Correll; Film editor: George Folsey, Jr.; Art direction: John J. Lloyd; Set decorations: Hal Gausman; Special effects: Henry Millar; Assistant director: Cliff Coleman; Costumes by Deborah Nadoolman; Makeup by Lynn Brooks and Gerald Soucie; Filmed in Technicolor; Running time: 109 minutes

CAST:
Dave Jennings (DONALD SUTHERLAND), John "Bluto" Blutarsky (JOHN BELUSHI), Eric "Otter" Stratton (Tim Matheson), Dean Wormer (John Vernon), Marion Wormer (Verna Bloom), Gregg Marmalard (James Daughton), Doug Niedermeyer (Mark Metcalf), Mandy Pepperidge (Mary Louise Weller), Larry "Pinto" Kroger (Thomas Hulce), Kent "Flounder" Dorfman (Stephen Furst), Donald "Boon" Schoenstein (Peter Riegert), Mayor Carmine De Pasto (Cesare Danova), Robert Hoover (James Widdoes), Babs Jansen (Martha Smith), Clorette De Pasto (Sarah Holcombe), Shelly Dubinsky (Lisa Baur), Chip Diller (Kevin Bacon)

Faber College, 1962. After being rejected by all the other fraternities on campus, freshmen Larry Kroger (Thomas Hulce) and Kent Dorfman (Stephen Furst) become members of the infamous Delta House. Following their initiation, the two are rechristened "Pinto" and "Flounder" by the Delta chairman, Eric "Otter" Stratton (Tim Matheson).

A group of fun-loving degenerates known for their irreverence, poor grades, and all-night beer busts, the Delta brothers are under the constant scrutiny of Dean Wormer (John Vernon), a stuffy conservative looking for an excuse to expel them. To help his cause along, Wormer forms an alliance with Gregg Marmalard (James Daughton), the chairman of Omega House, Delta's conservative rival.

Obsessed with bringing about Delta's downfall, Wormer orders Marmalard to begin an all-out war against Delta in an effort to break their spirit. Eagerly complying with Wormer's request, Marmalard instructs his comrade Doug Niedermeyer (Mark Metcalf), a gung-ho martinet in officer's training, to "put the screws" to Flounder during ROTC drills. In retaliation, Flounder leads Niedermeyer's prize horse to the Dean's office after hours, and there dispatches it "accidentally" with a starting pistol.

Martha Smith (center)

Meanwhile, the slobbish John "Bluto" Blutarsky (John Belushi), Delta's most notorious member, falls in love with Marmalard's girlfriend, Mandy Pepperidge (Mary Louise Weller). After class one night, he sneaks over to the sorority house, climbs a ladder outside Mandy's window and watches as she slowly

Stephen Furst, John Belushi, Bruce McGill

226

James Widdoes, Tim Matheson

undresses after coming back from a sterile date with the sexless Marmalard. The next day, Bluto initiates a "food fight" in the cafeteria, during which the upper classmen of Omega are pelted with leftovers from the day's lunch.

To make certain the Dean has no "academic" grounds for Delta's expulsion, Bluto steals copies of an upcoming mid-term, then passes them out to his brothers. As it turns out, however, Bluto swiped the wrong exam, and as a result Delta's grade average

subsequently plummets. To cheer themselves up, they throw a mad "toga party," during which handsome ladies' man Otter seduces the Dean's lascivious wife Marion (Verna Bloom).

After learning that hard liquor was served at the party, Wormer orders the Deltas to stand trial before a disciplinary committee. Found guilty of breaking one of Faber's cardinal rules, the Deltas are expelled. As an added penalty, they are banned from the college's annual year-end parade. To get even, the

Deltas decide to "crash" the parade, and they convert several automobiles into "armored attack" floats. During the festivities, the Deltas stage an uproarious "commando raid," during which Wormer almost faints in disbelief. Rather than endure their wrath any further, Wormer reinstates the Deltas with academic honors.

Martha Smith

Seventies screen comedy was almost completely dominated by Woody Allen, Mel Brooks, and Neil Simon, and the work of these three artists provided audiences with a much-needed escape from the somber drama of most of the decade's films. Allen, Brooks, and Simon were almost singularly responsible for the "classic" comedies of the seventies—*Play It Again, Sam; Annie Hall; Blazing Saddles; Young Frankenstein; The Sunshine Boys;* and *The Goodbye Girl*, to name but a few—and nearly all their efforts were major box-office triumphs. There was, however, one genuine comedy "classic" that was not the work of Allen, Brooks, or Simon: Universal's marvelous, insane farce, *Animal House*, a unique combination of college nostalgia, slapstick, and no-holds-barred craziness.

James Daughton, Mary Louise Weller, Tim Matheson, John Belushi

The picture was the joint creation of Universal and Matty Simmons, publisher of the monthly *National Lampoon* magazine, and the screenplay was the work of Harold Ramis, Douglas Kenney, and Chris Miller, who based the wacky adventures of the Delta gang on some of their own college experiences. The film was directed by John Landis, a gifted young craftsman with a penchant for crazy comedy. His first two films—*Schlock* (1971) and *The Kentucky Fried Movie* (1976)—were not especially successful, but they did reveal Landis's uncanny ability to make exceedingly goofy material work, and their ingenuity is what eventually won Landis the *Animal House* assignment.

Released in 1978, *Animal House* was an instant hit, and it had a long and successful run. It featured a brilliant comic performance by John Belushi, already known to millions as a regular on television's "Saturday Night Live," and it eventually grossed upwards of $80 million, making it one of the year's most profitable films.

John Belushi

THE BOYS FROM BRAZIL

A Producer Circle Picture; Directed by Franklin J. Schaffner; Produced by Martin Richards and Stanley O'Toole; Screenplay by Heywood Gould; From the novel by Ira Levin; Photography by Henri Decae; Film editor: Robert Swink; Production designer: Gil Parrondo; Set decorations: Vernon Dixon; Music by Jerry Goldsmith; Costumes by Anthony Mendleson; Makeup by Bill Lodge and Christopher Tucker; Sound recording by Derek Ball; Filmed in Panavision and DeLuxe Color; Running time: 125 minutes

CAST:

Dr. Josef Mengele (GREGORY PECK), *Ezra Lieberman* (LAURENCE OLIVIER), *Edward Seibert* (JAMES MASON), *Esther Lieberman* (Lilli Palmer), *Frieda Maloney* (Uta Hagen), *Barry Kohler* (Steven Guttenberg), *Sidney Beynon* (Denholm Elliott), *Mrs. Doring* (Rosemary Harris), *Henry Wheelock* (John Dehner), *David Bennett* (John Rubinstein), *Mrs. Curry* (Anne Meara), *"The Boys"* (Jeremy Black), *Professor Bruckner* (Bruno Ganz), *Mundt* (Walter Gotell), *Mr. Harrington* (Michael Gough), *Nancy* (Linda Hayden)

Barry Kohler (Steven Guttenberg), a member of the Young Jewish Defenders Organization, is monitoring the activities of a group of neo-Nazis

Laurence Olivier

Laurence Olivier, Anne Meara
Jeremy Black, Laurence Olivier

operating in Paraguay. After planting an electronic "bug" in their headquarters, he is astonished to learn that the head of the organization is Dr. Josef Mengele (Gregory Peck), one of the most infamous members of the Third Reich, well known for his gruesome biological experiments on the inmates at Auschwitz. Kohler learns that Mengele and his associates are planning the assassinations of ninety-four civil servants throughout Europe and North America, and that the victims are to be killed on or before their sixty-fifth birthdays.

Realizing Kohler's story was accurate, Lieberman, along with Kohler's friend and comrade David Bennett (John Rubinstein), visits several men on the list, hoping to discover what they have in common and why the Nazis want them dead. They find that the civil servants and their families all have similar social and economic backgrounds, and that each of them has one adopted son. The sons of the various families are identical in every respect—short, dark, arrogant children with piercing blue eyes. When Lieberman learns that the families adopted the boys simultane-

Gregory Peck

Kohler relays this information to Ezra Lieberman (Laurence Olivier), a hunter of Nazi war criminals who lives in Vienna, and sends the old man the names and addresses of the doomed men. Later, Kohler is murdered by Mengele's hulking bodyguards, and Lieberman visits his friend, newspaperman Sidney Beynon (Denholm Elliott), telling him the young man's story and showing him the list of names. After checking with various news sources throughout the world, Beynon informs Lieberman that several men on the list have, indeed, met with violent deaths recently.

ously from Frieda Maloney (Uta Hagen), a convicted war criminal, he visits her in prison, where he discovers the incredible truth. The boys are actually genetic clones of Adolph Hitler, manufactured by Mengele and adopted by carefully chosen families similar to Hitler's.

Mengele's plan becomes obvious to Lieberman—to have each of the youngsters grow up in an environment similar to Hitler's, and to have the father's killed at the age Hitler's own father died. Realizing that Mengele is hoping to use the children to institute a "Fourth Reich," Lieberman races to

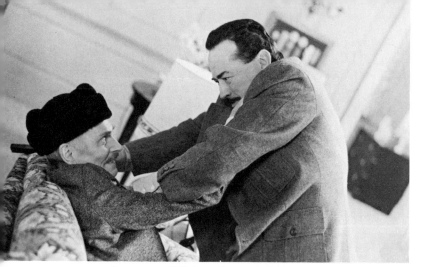

Laurence Olivier, Gregory Peck

the New England home of Henry Wheelock (John Dehner), the next man on the list. When he arrives at the Wheelock ranch, however, he is confronted by Mengele, who informs Lieberman that he has just disposed of Mr. Wheelock. Lieberman tangles with Mengele, but the old man is no match for the Nazi, and he is seriously hurt in the scuffle.

The young Hitler clone, Bobby Wheelock (Jeremy Black), suddenly returns from fishing and is told by Lieberman that Mengele has just murdered his father. Hearing this, the younster unleashes several large watchdogs, who tear Mengele to shreds, ending the Nazi's reign of terror.

Later on, Lieberman recovers in the hospital, where he is visited by young Bennett, who insists that he be given the names of the Hitler clones so that they may be wiped out as a precaution. Rather than contribute to any further bloodshed, however, Lieberman burns the list, leaving the fate of the clones a mystery.

Published in 1976, Ira Levin's *The Boys From Brazil* was an exceptional thriller. The story of an aged Nazi hunter who tracks down a group of Hitler clones created by one of the Führer's right-hand men, it was a skillful combination of science fiction and contemporary drama, and it became a major best-seller.

The film version, directed by Franklin J. Schaffner (*Patton*) and starring Gregory Peck and Laurence Olivier, appeared in 1978, and, while far from perfect, it emerged as an extremely entertaining motion picture. This was a big, sumptuous, "tongue-in-cheek" film that, like *The Omen*, never took itself too seriously but nonetheless managed to provide its audience with two hours of splendid fun.

Audiences found the rather far-fetched plot both clever and intriguing, and they thoroughly enjoyed the acting of Peck and Olivier. The film also contained a solid supporting performance from James

Mason as Peck's strong-willed aide, and Jeremy Black—the young actor who played the "Hitler" children—acted with chilling believability.

However, *The Boys From Brazil* clearly belonged to Peck and Olivier, and the film was an acting tour de force for the two veterans. Peck obviously relished the opportunity to play a completely villainous character for a change, and his all-out portrayal of the monstrous Nazi sadist Josef Mengele is one of his best in recent years. Laurence Olivier is equally superb as the doting, fragile, and scholarly Nazi hunter, Ezra Lieberman. Olivier plays Lieberman to such perfection that it is difficult to believe that, only two years earlier, Olivier turned in perhaps the screen's finest portrait of an evil Nazi, the unforgettable Szell in *Marathon Man*. The vast difference between the two characters makes it clear that Olivier's versatility has definitely sharpened with time.

SUPERMAN

A Warner Bros. Picture; Directed by Richard Donner; Produced by Pierre Spengler; Executive producer: Ilya Salkind; Associate producer: Charles F. Greenlaw; Creative consultant: Tom Mankiewicz; Screenplay by Mario Puzo, David Newman, Leslie Newman, and Robert Benton; Story by Mario Puzo;

Marlon Brando, Terence Stamp, Jack O'Halloran, Sarah Douglas

Superman created by Jerry Siegel and Joe Shuster; Photography by Geoffrey Unsworth; Music by John Williams; Film editor: Stuart Baird; Production designer: John Barry; An Alexander and Ilya Salkind Production; Running time: 143 minutes

Jor-El (MARLON BRANDO), *Lex Luthor* (GENE HACKMAN), *Superman/Clark Kent* (CHRISTOPHER REEVE), *Lois Lane* (MARGOT KIDDER), *Otis* (Ned Beatty), *Perry White* (Jackie Cooper), *Pa Kent* (Glenn Ford), *Eve Teschmacher* (Valerie Perrine), *1st elder* (Trevor Howard), *Gen. Zod* (Terence Stamp), *Vond-Ah* (Maria Schell), *Ma Kent* (Phyllis Thaxter), *Lara* (Susannah York), *Young Clark Kent* (Jeff East), *2nd elder* (Harry Andrews), *Ursa* (Sarah Douglas), *Jimmy Olsen* (Marc McClure), *Non* (Jack O'Halloran)

1948. On the distant planet Krypton, Jor-El (Marlon Brando), a beneficent, high-ranking official, prosecutes three political subversives—Zod

Phyllis Thaxter, Glenn Ford

(Terence Stamp), Ursa (Sarah Douglas), and Non (Jack O'Halloran)—for attempting to overthrow the government. Shortly after the trial, it is learned that Krypton is on a deadly collision course with its own sun, and that it's only a matter of time before the planet is destroyed. Learning of this, Jor-El and his wife Lara (Susannah York) place their infant son in a small, crystalline rocket, then launch him on a course for the planet Earth, located in a galaxy millions of miles away.

After a long journey through space, the small craft makes a spectacular landing in the American Midwest, where it is discovered by a childless middleaged couple, Jonathan and Martha Kent (Glenn Ford and Phyllis Thaxter). Smitten with the rocket's small inhabitant, John and Martha decide to adopt him. As the child grows into young manhood, he becomes aware that he is not like other people. It seems that his alien molecular structure, coupled with the

Earth's atmosphere, has given him superhuman powers, including great strength and speed, X-ray vision, and the ability to fly.

When, some years later, John Kent succumbs to a heart attack, young Clark bids his stepmother farewell and obeys a strange impulse to travel to the Arctic. There, Jor-El's spirit materializes, telling Clark that his destiny is to use his superhuman

Marlon Brando, Susannah York

abilities to help right the wrongs on the troubled planet Earth. Jor-El's spirit then takes Clark on a twelve-year spiritual retreat, during which it teaches him great wisdom to go along with his great strength.

At the end of this time, Clark, now thirty, assumes the pose of a bumbling but eager young news reporter looking for work in the city of Metropolis. He is hired by Perry White (Jackie Cooper), of the *Daily Planet*, and soon falls in love with co-worker Lois Lane (Margot Kidder), a brash lady reporter. Not long after, Lois is involved in a helicopter

Christopher Reeve

mishap, and seeing that her life is in danger, Clark for the first time assumes the role of Superman, an invincible crusader dedicated to fighting for "truth, justice, and the American way."

Shortly after this initial exposure, Superman begins a crime-fighting wave unparalleled in history, and his exploits become known throughout the world. He grants Lois Lane an exclusive interview, after which he takes her on a romantic mid-night flight high above the city.

Meanwhile, master criminal Lex Luthor (Gene Hackman) is plotting a particularly diabolical

Christopher Reeve

scheme—to destroy the entire West Coast so as to increase the value of the property he owns east of it! Determined to have no interference from Superman, Luthor secures a sample of kryptonite, a glowing, radioactive substance known to be fatal to anyone from the planet Krypton. Enticing the unsuspecting Superman into his underground lair, Luthor pushes him into a swimming pool containing a small chunk of the deadly mineral. Rendered powerless, the "man of steel" almost drowns, but at the last instant he is rescued by Luthor's soft-hearted mistress, Eve Teschmacher (Valerie Perrine).

Valerie Perrine

When Alexander and Ilya Salkind announced that they were producing a $50-million motion picture based on the exploits of a comic-book character, many people in the industry reacted with great skepticism. The idea of bringing Superman to the screen in 1978 with any credibility seemed an impossible task to some, even though he still ranked as one of the great fantasy heroes of all time. The character had, of course, been a considerable hit in the Kirk Alyn serials of the late forties, and again in the famous television series of the fifties, the effectiveness of which had been enhanced by the plummy, tongue-in-cheek playing of the late George Reeves as the title character.

Though Superman continued to be a popular comic-book hero throughout the seventies, producing a multimillion-dollar epic based on his adventures seemed risky for a number of reasons. For one thing, the film would be released on the heels of *Star Wars* and *Close Encounters of the Third Kind,* and as such, comparisons with these two blockbusters would be inevitable. For another, unless the Salkinds could find the "ideal" actor for the title role, the picture could very easily backfire, with Superman's

Gene Hackman

Afterward, Superman manages to stop one of the nuclear missiles Luthor has launched to carry out his plan. The other strikes the San Andreas fault, causing a massive earthquake, during which Superman is forced to perform incredible feats to save California from destruction. Lois, who has flown to California to get an exclusive on the story, is killed in an avalanche caused by the quake. Unable to accept her death, Superman circles the Earth at tremendous speed, reversing its orbit and turning back time so that Lois is restored to life. Not long afterward, Superman brings Luthor and his dimwitted aide Otis (Ned Beatty) to justice.

236

amazing feats and garish costume leaving audiences laughing their heads off—which was something to ponder, considering how much was being invested.

To helm their film, the Salkinds secured the services of Richard Donner, a fine craftsman known primarily for the highly successful *The Omen* (1976). In addition, they assembled a truly impressive supporting cast, including Marlon Brando, Gene Hackman, Glenn Ford, Trevor Howard, Jackie Cooper, Margot Kidder, Terence Stamp, Susannah York, Valerie Perrine, and Ned Beatty. However, the task of finding the "ideal" Superman proved exceedingly difficult, and, interestingly, virtually every

Fortunately for all, the actor they eventually found fit the part beyond the wildest imaginings of anyone. At one point in his search for the ideal Superman, Ilya Salkind had glanced through a New York casting directory and had been impressed by the looks of a twenty-four-year-old actor named Christopher Reeve. Tall, handsome, intelligent, and ambitious, Reeve's prior credits had included a stage appearance opposite Katharine Hepburn in 1976's *A Matter of Gravity* and a part on the long-running television soap opera "Love of Life."

Remembering Reeve's photograph, Salkind arranged for the young actor to meet with director

Christopher Reeve, Margot Kidder, Jackie Cooper

major actor in Hollywood was considered for the role. James Caan, Robert Redford, Clint Eastwood, Charles Bronson, Sylvester Stallone, Steve McQueen, and even Olympic champion Bruce Jenner were mentioned in the early stages, but for a variety of reasons none of them worked out. Perhaps after realizing that a major star in the title role might well increase the potential for unintentional laughs, Donner and the Salkinds concluded that a little-known actor who suited the role physically might be more to the mark.

Donner in New York. Though equally impressed with Reeve's manner and presence, Donner thought him a bit too youthful and lanky for the "man of steel," but Salkind insisted that Reeve be given a screen test in England, where much of the film would be shot. Reeve's subsequent test was a knockout, and with proper lighting, full makeup, and costumes that included a little padding to bulk up his frame, Reeve bore an uncanny resemblance to the comic book character, and several days later the decision was made—Reeve had won the role hands down.

After he was signed, Reeve was ordered by Donner to undergo physical training to buildup his lanky physique, since the idea of using padding in the actual film appealed to no one, least of all Reeve. He began a series of workouts at London's Grosvenor House Gym, somewhat ironically, under the guidance of the hulking David Prowse, fresh from his triumph as supervillain Darth Vader in *Star Wars*. Within ten weeks, Reeve had gained thirty pounds of muscle and added two inches to his chest and shoulders.

The finished film featured superb special effects, an excellent score by John Williams, and fine supporting performances; but *Superman's* success was mostly due to the fine acting of Reeve in the lead role. Unlike the invincible Superman of old, Reeve portrayed him as both sensitive and vulnerable. This Superman was quite obviously in love with Lois Lane, and he approached his incredible feats with a crisp, casual, off-hand modesty that made him charming and believable to audiences of the seventies.

Christopher Reeve

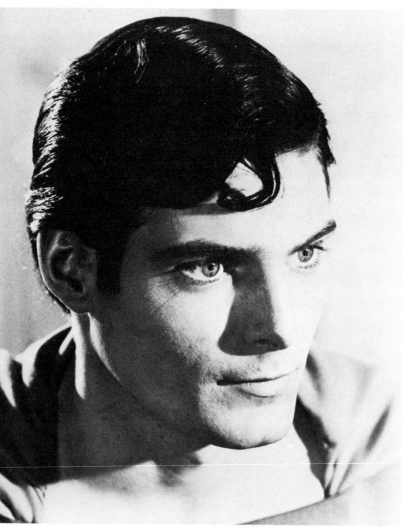

THE DEER HUNTER

Robert De Niro, John Savage

A Columbia-EMI-Warner Release; Directed by Michael Cimino; Produced by Barry Spikings, Michael Deeley, Michael Cimino, and John Peverall; Screenplay by Deric Washburn; Story by Michael Cimino, Deric Washburn, Louis Garfinkle, and Quinn K. Redeker; Photography by Vilmos Zsigmond; Film editor: Peter Zinner; Set decorations: Dick Goddard (USA) and Alan Hicks (Thailand); Special effects by Fred Cramer; Music by Stanley Myers; Main title theme performed by John Williams; Costumes by Eric Seelig; Makeup by Del Acevedo and Ed Butterworth; Sound recording by Darin Knight; Dolby consultant: Steve Katz; Filmed in Technicolor and Panavision; Running time: 182 minutes

CAST:
Mike (ROBERT DE NIRO), *Stan* (John Cazale), *Steven* (John Savage), *Nick* (Christopher Walken), *Linda* (Meryl Streep), *Axel* (Chuck Aspegren), *John* (George Dzundza), *Angela* (Rutanya Alda), *Steven's*

mother (Shirley Stoler), *Julien* (Pierre Segui), *Axel's girl* (Mady Kaplan), *Bridesmaid* (Amy Wright), *Stan's girl* (Mary Ann Haenel), *Linda's father* (Richard Kuss), *Bandleader* (Joe Grifasi), *Sergeant* (Paul D'Amato), *Cab driver* (Dennis Watlington), *Redhead* (Charlene Darrow), *Stock boy* (Michael Wollett), *Barman* (Frank Devore), *Doctor* (Tom Becker)

Clairton, Pennsylvania. Three young steel workers, Mike (Robert De Niro), Steven (John Savage), and Nick (Christopher Walken), have been close friends for most of their lives and are excited by the prospect of shortly leaving for Vietnam on a tour of duty.

Several days before their departure, they celebrate Steven's marriage to Angela (Rutanya Alda) and later go on a hunting trip with their friends Stan (John Cazale), Axel (Chuck Aspegren), and John (George Dzundza), owner of the local bar. While the others simply go along for the excitement, Mike is a dedicated, expert hunter who relishes the sport, and on the last day of the trip he bags a prize buck with one shot. After saying goodbye to their friends and families, Mike, Nick, and Steven leave for Vietnam, where their illusions of glory are quickly shattered by the horrors of war.

Following a brief skirmish with Vietcong soldiers raiding a Chinese village, the three are taken prisoner by the enemy. They are brought to a small Vietcong outpost where they, along with several other captives, are ordered to engage in a rather gruesome "parlor game," in which two prisoners are seated at opposite ends of a table and are forced at gunpoint to play Russian Roulette with a small revolver, while the Vietcong place bets on the outcome. Several Americans and Chinese are killed in the game, and when it comes to Steven's turn he nearly goes mad with fear.

Mike, however, engineers a daring escape plan with Nick. He defiantly invites the enemy to load the revolver with three bullets to make the game more interesting. When they do this, however, Mike turns

Meryl Streep

the gun on them, and, managing to kill several of the Vietcong, he and Nick escape downriver with Steven—who is seriously injured along the way.

Later, the three are separated, and Nick, who collapses from exhaustion, awakens to find himself in a Saigon hospital where, despite the sympathetic treatment of the doctors, his mind begins to disintegrate from his experience. When he leaves the hospital several weeks later, Nick is compulsively drawn to the city's sleazy underground gambling dens, where young Chinese play the Russian Roulette game for visiting businessmen seeking "unique" entertainment.

Mike subsequently returns home uninjured, but finds himself unable to face anyone except Nick's

Robert De Niro, John Savage

239

John Cazale, Chuck Aspegren, Robert De Niro,
John Savage, Rutanya Alda, Christopher Walken,
Meryl Streep, George Dzundza

George Dzundza, Robert De Niro

Christopher Walken

Robert De Niro

Robert De Niro

girlfriend Linda (Meryl Streep). Not knowing what has become of Nick and seeking comfort from each other, Mike and Linda become lovers. Mike later learns from Angela that Steven is now a patient at the local veterans' hospital. Mike visits Steven, now a legless cripple, and asks him if he knows anything about Nick. Steven says he doesn't but informs Mike that he has lately been receiving money from a mysterious source in Saigon. Realizing it is Nick who is sending the money, Mike returns to Saigon during the American withdrawal, and hires a guide to help him locate Nick.

Mike is led to one of the underground gambling dens, where Nick is the champion of the Russian Roulette games. Mike confronts Nick, now a mindless, drug-addicted zombie, and begs him to return home to Clairton. Nick, however, doesn't even recognize Mike, who in an effort to jar Nick's memory insists that he be allowed to play in the next game. The two once again face each other at opposite ends of a table, and bets are placed by the surrounding crowd. Before Nick's memory returns, however, he blows his brains out, which emotionally devastates Mike. Later, he takes Nick's body back to Clairton where, after the funeral, Nick's friends gather at John's bar to toast him by singing ''God Bless America.''

Almost immediately upon its completion, Michael Cimino's long-awaited Vietnam epic *The Deer Hunter* was rushed into theaters in December of 1978, so that it would be eligible to compete in the year's Academy Awards race. The producers were confident that the picture would win several Oscars, and they also realized that this would increase its box-office potential enormously. At the Awards ceremonies in April, *The Deer Hunter* emerged as the biggest winner of the evening, and it garnered Academy Awards for Best Picture, Best Director, and Best Supporting Actor in addition to several in technical categories.

The film, a mammoth entertainment running 182 minutes, was brilliantly executed by director Cimino and his cast, and it took the nation's audiences and critics completely by storm. Many reviewers went so far as to hail it as the *Godfather* of war movies,

John Cazale, Chuck Aspegren, Christopher Walken, Robert De Niro, John Savage

John Savage, Robert De Niro

which was a splendid compliment indeed, and the box-office returns during the first week of its release indicated that the film was going to be yet another of the decade's financial blockbusters.

There was, in fact, only one major criticism leveled against *The Deer Hunter,* and that was that the film tended to alter the truth drastically in the way it depicted certain aspects of the Vietnam War. The Russian Roulette games, for example, which figure so prominently in the drama were, according to some authorities, never actually used as a mode of torture by the Vietcong, and therefore their inclusion in *The Deer Hunter* was labelled a complete fabrication. From a dramatic standpoint, however, the games are so essential to the story's effectiveness that one can easily forgive the fact that they may not be historically accurate.

Sometime after the film's release, Michael Cimino stated that his primary intention in making *The Deer Hunter* was not to mirror what actually happened in Vietnam, but rather to fashion a story in which, above all, the audience would come to truly love and care about the characters. Cimino's intent is clearly obvious throughout the film, and in his opening scenes of the boys at home in Clairton, Cimino takes a great deal of time to establish the deep friendship and comradery of Mike, Nick, and Steven and to present the characters as three sensitive, vibrant, and life-loving young men. These early scenes explore the characters in such depth that, by the time the boys

land in Vietnam, the audience has become such a part of their lives that it can't help but care what happens to them. At this point, Cimino injects the Russian Roulette sequences to intensify the horror of the war experience. The fact that Mike, Nick, and Steven are forced to gamble with their own lives to provide hideous diversion for the enemy has far more effect on the audience that would simply having the characters killed or wounded in battle.

Chuck Aspegren, Robert De Niro

1979

THE CHINA SYNDROME

A Columbia-EMI-Warner Release; Directed by James Bridges; Produced by Michael Douglas; Screenplay by Mike Gray, T. S. Cook, and James Bridges; Photography by James Crabe; Film editor: David Rawlings; Production designer: George Jenkins; Set design: Richard McKenzie; Set decorations: Arthur Parker; Special effects: Henry Millar, Jr.; Costumes by Donfeld; Makeup by Don Schoenfeld and Bernadine Anderson; Sound recording by Willie Burton; Filmed in Metrocolor; Running time: 122 minutes

Jane Fonda, Michael Douglas

Jane Fonda

Jack Lemmon

CAST:
Kimberly Wells (JANE FONDA), *Jack Godell* (JACK LEMMON), *Richard Adams* (MICHAEL DOUGLAS), *Herman De Young* (Scott Brady), *Bill Gibson* (James Hampton), *Don Jacovich* (Peter Donat), *Ted Spindler* (Wilfred Brimley), *Evan McCormack* (Richard Herd), *Hector Salas* (Daniel Valdez), *Peter Martin* (Stan Bohrman), *Mac Churchill* (James Karen), *Greg Minor* (Michael Alaimo), *Dr. Lowell* (Donald Hotton), *D. B. Royce* (Paul Larson), *Barney* (Ron Lombard), *Tommy* (Tom Eure), *Bordon* (Nick Pellegrino), *Donny* (Daniel Lewk)

Kimberly Wells (Jane Fonda) is the star reporter of "human interest" stories at television station KXLA. Though one of the most popular newswomen in the business, Kimberly has never been given as assignment of any real importance, and for the past few years has remained merely an attractive decoration reporting trivial events on the evening news show. Though seemingly content with her position, her cameraman Richard Adams (Michael Douglas) thinks she's wasting her talents and should be covering "hard news."

During a routine interview with employees at the Ventana Nuclear Power Plant, Kimberly and Richard witness a serious mishap in the control room, and a "meltdown" is just barely avoided by the quick-thinking Jack Godell (Jack Lemmon), chief engineer of the plant. Unbeknownst to the Ventana employees, Richard secretly filmed the chaos in the control room during the accident, but when he tries to get it shown on KXLA, the station management objects on the grounds that it might "panic the

Director James Bridges, Michael Douglas

Jack Lemmon, Michael Douglas, Jane Fonda

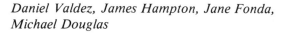

Daniel Valdez, James Hampton, Jane Fonda, Michael Douglas

citizenry." Sneaking into the station after hours, Richard steals the film and arranges to show it to the nuclear experts currently determining whether or not they will allow the Ventana consortium to build an even larger plant to be called Point Conception.

Meanwhile, Godell is disturbed when he learns the authorities plan to do nothing about the accident, and on his own time he begins examining the inner workings of Ventana, hoping to locate the potentially deadly defect. During his investigation he discovers the source of the trouble—a faulty valve, installed by the company to cut costs. Realizing that the mishap could easily happen again, Godell befriends Kimberly and Richard and gives them incriminating X-rays of the defective equipment.

Afterward, Richard turns them over to his soundman Hector Salas (Daniel Valdez) to transport to a hearing on the Point Conception project. On the way, however, Salas is ambushed by two mysterious men, who force him into a fatal highway accident. The same two men later pursue Godell on his way to testify at the hearing, but he manages to elude them.

Deciding to expose Ventana's defects in the most dramatic way possible, Jack commandeers the control room, holding his fellow employees at gunpoint. He then demands to be interviewed on the air by Kimberly so that he can tell the story to her viewers. Meanwhile, the Ventana corporate heads circulate the story that a madman has taken over the plant's control room, and that all efforts are being made to stop him before he does any serious damage. When

Kimberly arrives at the plant, Godell, on the brink of nervous collapse, is unable to contain his thoughts, and during the interview he ends up looking like a crackpot. Before he has the chance to tell the real story, the plant's security force bursts into the control room and shoots Godell dead.

One of the most controversial and oft-debated issues of the decade was whether or not the convenience and efficiency of the nation's nuclear power plants were worth the obvious risks they entailed. Curiously, however, the seventies managed to produce only one feature film dealing with the subject—James Bridges's *The China Syndrome*—an excellent, thought-provoking "doomsday" thriller that became the first major screen success of 1979. The film, a big-budget, major-studio production that featured Jane Fonda, Jack Lemmon, and Michael Douglas in perhaps their finest roles in the decade, involved a full three years of preparation before it was finally released to theaters.

Michael Douglas, who produced as well as starred in the film, had for many years been fascinated by the idea of making a picture about a nuclear accident, but in the project's early stages he had a great deal of trouble finding someone willing to finance such an enterprise. Most of the companies and individuals Douglas approached felt that a film dealing with a nuclear mishap would be too disturbing to attract a large audience. Of course, when the picture was eventually made and released, it became an immediate hit, and somewhat ironically an accident nearly identical to that in the movie occurred at the Three Mile Island nuclear plant near Harrisburg,

Director James Bridges and Jane Fonda

Michael Douglas

Pennsylvania, two weeks after *The China Syndrome* had its premiere. As a result, the film became more significant and hard-hitting than Douglas ever dreamed possible.

Interestingly, in the picture's planning stages, Mike Gray, author of the original screenplay, was assigned to direct, but after Douglas persuaded Columbia to back the project, the studio insisted on a more experienced director, and James Bridges was subsequently hired. Also, Douglas had at first planned not to appear in *The China Syndrome,* and he wanted the popular Richard Dreyfuss to play Richard Adams. However, the young actor's price skyrocketed to such an extent after *Close Encounters of the Third Kind* and *The Goodbye Girl* (both 1977) that Douglas ended up playing the part himself.

Jack Lemmon

The China Syndrome's intense aura of realism is enhanced by the fact that, unlike most of the decade's films, it contains no background music of any kind. Douglas had originally hired a composer for the picture, but later discovered that a music score was giving *The China Syndrome* a certain melodramatic quality—the one thing Douglas wanted to avoid at all costs.

Jack Lemmon and crew between scenes

MANHATTAN

A United Artists Picture; Directed by Woody Allen; Produced by Charles H. Joffe; Screenplay by Woody Allen and Marshall Brickman; Photography by Gordon Willis; Film editor: Susan E. Morse; Production designer: Mel Bourne; Set decorations: Robert Drumheller; Set dressers: Justin Scoppa, Jr. and Morris Weinman; Scenic artists: Cosmo Sorice and James Sorice; Music adapter and arranger: Tom Pierson; Costumes by Albert Wolsky and Ralph Lauren; Makeup by Fern Buchner; Sound recording by James Sabat; Production assistants: Robert E. Warren, Charles Zalben, and Cheryl Hill; Filmed in Panavision; Running time: 96 minutes

CAST:
Isaac Davis (WOODY ALLEN), *Mary Wilke* (DIANE KEATON), *Yale* (Michael Murphy), *Tracy* (Mariel Hemingway), *Jill* (Meryl Streep), *Emily* (Anne Byrne), *Connie* (Karen Ludwig), *Dennis* (Michael O'Donoghue), *Guest of honor* (Bella Abzug), *TV director* (Gary Weis), *TV producer* (Kenny Vance), *Willie Davis* (Damion Sheller), *Jeremiah* (Wallace Shawn), *Pizzeria waiter* (Ray Serra)

New York City. Successful television writer Isaac Davis (Woody Allen) is frustrated with his job and yearns to turn his talents toward more serious writing. Enormously neurotic and insecure despite his success, Isaac shares a fashionable apartment with Tracy (Mariel Hemingway), a seventeen-year-old drama student. Though the young girl continually assures Isaac that she loves him, the validity of the relationship weighs heavily on his mind, due to the fact that Tracy is less than half his age.

He discusses the relationship and his plans to quit television with his writer friend Yale (Michael Murphy) who, as it turns out, has many problems of his own. The married Yale has lately been suffering pangs of guilt over his affair with an intelligent but directionless girl named Mary Wilke (Diane Keaton), and is perplexed by his own inability to switch from "hack" work to serious writing.

One afternoon, Yale introduces Isaac to Mary, and Isaac is immediately put off by her pretentious, overbearing nature. However, when Isaac eventually discovers that this behavior is merely a defense and that beneath it all Mary is a warm and loving girl, he becomes her friend. Later, he visits his ex-wife Jill (Meryl Streep), currently involved in a lesbian relationship and writing an expose of her difficult life with the unstable Isaac. Despite Isaac's protests, Jill later publishes her book, which becomes an enormous best-seller. Back at his apartment, Isaac tries to dissuade Tracy from becoming too attached to him, and explains that the relationship will never work out due to the difference in their ages.

Meanwhile, Yale ends his affair with Mary, and, realizing that she and Isaac have become good friends, he advises Isaac to take up with her himself. Isaac and Mary become lovers, and he later tells Tracy to forget him and to go ahead with her plan to enroll in a London drama school. During the course of their affair, however, Mary confesses to Isaac that she still loves Yale and wants to marry him. Realizing that Yale also loves Mary, Isaac chastises his friend for not having the courage to make a commitment to the girl for whom he really cares.

Shortly afterward, Isaac quits his television job and, in an effort to establish himself as a serious writer, starts work on an epic tome about his beloved Manhattan. Realizing he has reached a major turning point in his life, Isaac takes stock of the things that matter most to him, and is surprised to find that Tracy is high on the list.

Woody Allen

Diane Keaton, Michael Murphy

Discovering that he's been deeply in love with her all along, he frantically begs her not to leave for London. However, for her own personal growth, she decides to attend the drama school, but assures Isaac that when she returns in six months she will still care for him. His insecurities surface once again, and he tells her that in six months she will have changed so

1979, the nation's critics immediately fell head-over-heels in love with it, and began an outpouring of praise virtually unparalleled in the history of cinema. Many referred to it as a "masterpiece," a term that is rarely used in reference to a popular, commercial screen comedy, while others actually called it the finest and most important film of the decade.

Mariel Hemingway, Woody Allen

much that she won't even remember his name. However, she assures Isaac this won't happen, and before departing encourages him to "have a little faith in people."

Woody Allen's *Manhattan* has the distinction of being the most widely acclaimed motion picture of the seventies. When the film made its debut in early

Admittedly, *Manhattan* is an enjoyable, offbeat comedy-drama that explores the tangled relationships of a group of neurotic artists and intellectuals in New York City, but the film as a whole hardly seems worthy of such extensive, high-blown plaudits. Though entertaining and well-made, *Manhattan* doesn't come close to the quality of Allen's earlier hit, *Annie Hall*—the film that deservedly won the

Diane Keaton, Woody Allen

Academy Award as Best Picture of 1977. The characters in *Manhattan* aren't nearly as well drawn as those in the earlier film, and with the exception of Allen's Isaac and Mariel Hemingway's Tracy, they aren't a particularly likable group of people either, which makes their problems much less important to the audience.

Still, the film has its qualities, and the beautiful black-and-white photography of Gordon Willis lends itself especially well to the opening scene of the film—a fantastic, breathtaking visual symphony exploring New York City by night, climaxing with a dazzling display of fireworks above the Manhattan skyline. The film also achieves a certain romantic poignancy toward the conclusion, when Isaac suddenly realizes how much Tracy means to him and begs her not to depart for London. Though the final scene between Allen and Mariel Hemingway is extremely well played and touching, fine talents such as Diane Keaton, Michael Murphy, and Meryl Streep are saddled with rather one-dimensional roles that give them little opportunity to develop full-blooded characterizations.

ALIEN

A 20th Century-Fox Picture; Directed by Ridley Scott; Produced by Gordon Carroll, David Giler, and Walter Hill; Screenplay by Dan O'Bannon; Story by Dan O'Bannon and Ronald Shusett; Photography by Derek Vanlint; Film editors: Jerry Rawlings and Peter Weatherley; Production designer: Michael Seymour; Visual design consultant: Dan O'Bannon; Set decorations: Ian Whittaker; Alien design: H. R. Giger and Roger Dicken; Alien head effects: Carlo Rambaldi; Special graphic effects: Bernard Lodge; Music by Jerry Goldsmith; Costumes by John Mollo; Makeup by Pat Hay; Sound recording by Derrick Leather; Filmed in Panavision and Eastmancolor; Running time: 117 minutes

CAST:
Dallas (Tom Skerritt), *Ripley* (Sigourney Weaver), *Lambert* (Veronica Cartwright), *Kane* (John Hurt), *Brett* (Harry Dean Stanton), *Ash* (Ian Holm), *Parker* (Yaphet Kotto), *Voice of "Mother"* (Helen Horton), *"Alien"* (Bolaji Badego)

The spacecraft *Nostromo,* a huge mineral tanker, is returning to Earth after a routine voyage. Having successfully completed their mission, the seven crewmen slumber in isolation chambers where their life functions are mechanically maintained.

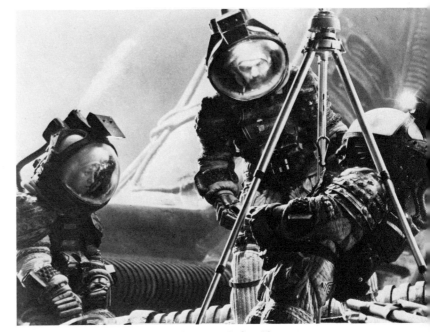

Veronica Cartwright, Tom Skerritt, John Hurt

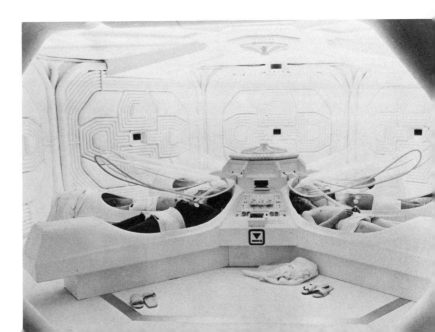

Soon, however, they are awakened prematurely by "Mother," the ship's computer, who relays an S.O.S. signal from a nearby planet. Since the company they work for requires them to respond to all such signals, Captain Dallas (Tom Skerritt) and crew members Kane (John Hurt) and Lambert (Veronica Cartwright) visit the planet via a small shuttle craft. Once there, they discover the bizarre remnants of an alien civilization, and Kane investigates an underground cavern containing several gigantic eggs. Suddenly, one of the eggs cracks open and a grotesque, crab-like creature leaps out and fastens itself to Kane's helmet.

Rendered unconcious by this, Kane is taken back to the *Nostromo*, where science officer Ash (Ian Holm) places him in quarantine, refusing to let the other crew members near him. Removing Kane's helmet, Ash sees that the creature has attached itself to the crewman's face, and an X-ray reveals that it is depositing fluid into Kane's stomach. Later, the

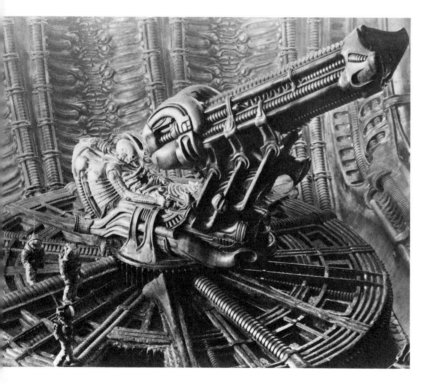

creature disappears and is subsequently found dead, and Kane revives with no recollection of the experience.

Not long afterward, however, Kane dies horribly when a tiny alien monster, apparently planted in Kane's body by the other creature, suddenly bursts through his chest. The small invader quickly scurries off, and the crew band together to find it. During the search, crew member Brett (Harry Dean Stanton) is killed by the now greatly enlarged alien, and Dallas meets a similar fate some time later.

Now in command of the ship, Ripley (Sigourney Weaver) interrogates "Mother" and learns that the real reason for their mission was to secure one of the deadly aliens for the company, anxious to exploit the commercial possibilities of an indestructible, totally evil life form. Suspecting that Ash was a part of the

scheme all along, Ripley confronts him with what she has learned and he attacks her. Maintenance Officer Parker (Yaphet Kotto) comes to her rescue, however, and when he bludgeons Ash with a large club, Ash—really a robot manufactured by the company to protect the alien from harm—"breaks apart."

The three surviving crew members, Ripley, Lambert, and Parker, elect to explode the *Nostromo* and escape in the shuttle craft. When Lambert and Parker are killed by the alien, Ripley zooms off in the shuttle, but soon discovers that the alien is also on board. Using one of the shuttle's small jets, however, she blasts the creature into space.

The decade's horror films were often accused of engaging in a kind of gruesome "one-upmanship," whereby each successive shocker attempted to outdo the earlier ones in terms of sensational, bloodcurdling effects. *The Exorcist* (1973) was the first major horror film of the seventies to become hugely successful, and its incredible special-effects scenes showing the grotesque, supernatural behavior of the possessed Regan both terrified and fascinated audiences, and the technical ingenuity with which they were executed inspired other filmmakers to try and

Yaphet Kotto, Veronica Cartwright

Ian Holm, Sigourney Weaver

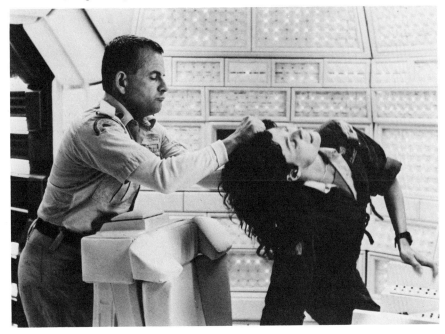

top them. Not surprisingly, such later films as *Carrie* (1976), *The Sentinel* (1977), *The Fury* (1978), and *Dawn of the Dead* (1979) contained scenes of horror exceeding the intensity of those in *The Exorcist,* and with the exception of *The Sentinel* all of them became enormous box-office hits as a result. Since Brian De Palma's *The Fury* featured what seemed to be the ultimate horror (a character literally exploding into a billion bits on screen), audiences and critics wondered how much farther horror pictures could go without becoming completely offensive. This question was answered in no uncertain terms when Ridley Scott's *Alien* made its debut in the summer of 1979.

A gripping, expertly made chiller about the crew of a commercial spacecraft that finds itself in a life-and-death struggle with a hideous monster from an uncharted planet, the film featured horrific interludes virtually unmatched by any of the decade's earlier entries. John Hurt's diaphragm suddenly erupting as the tiny monster viciously fights its way out of his chest is one of the goriest and most effective fright scenes in history, and the film's monster is a *totally* evil, nightmarish entity that apparently exists only to kill (even the "blood" of the first creature, spilled during an attempt to surgically remove the thing from Kane's face, is a deadly, acidlike substance that burns through several levels of the *Nostromo*'s hull).

Alien could hardly miss success, since it was a skillful combination of elements from several of the seventies' most popular films. It featured a relentless monster similar in temperament to the Great White shark in *Jaws,* a setting that was strongly reminiscent of *Star Wars,* and grisly goings-on harking back to *The Exorcist.* In addition to this, director Scott managed to maintain an atmosphere of total suspense throughout *Alien,* and the audience is kept constantly on the edge of its seat, never knowing where or when the monster is going to strike next. To heighten the tension, Scott never gives the audience a clear look at the monster, making the brief glimpses of it all the more frightening. Also, *Alien* does not kill off the creature at the conclusion, and since it is implied during the story that the alien is indestructible, perhaps a sequel or two will be in the offing.

ROCKY II

A United Artists Picture; Written and directed by Sylvester Stallone; Produced by Irwin Winkler and Robert Chartoff; Director of photography: Bill Butler; Music by Bill Conti; Art direction: Richard Berger; Supervising film editor: Danford B. Greene; Film editors: Stanford C. Allen, Janice Hampton, and James Symons; Makeup by Michael Westmore;

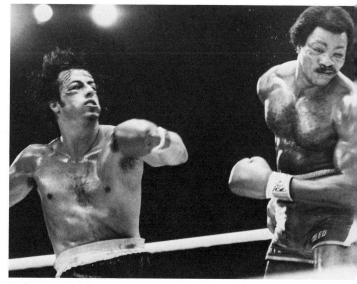

Sylvester Stallone, Carl Weathers

Set decorations by Ed Baer; Men's costumes: Thomas Bronson; Women's costumes: Sandra Berke; Boxing choreography: Sylvester Stallone; Boxing technical adviser: Al Silvani; Filmed in Technicolor; Running time: 119 minutes

CAST:
Rocky Balboa (SYLVESTER STALLONE), *Adrian* (Talia Shire), *Paulie* (Burt Young), *Apollo Creed* (Carl Weathers), *Mickey* (Burgess Meredith), *Apollo's trainer* (Tony Burton), *Gazzo* (Joe Spinell), *Agent* (Leonard Gaines), *Mary Anne Creed* (Sylvia Meals), *Meat foreman* (Frank McRae), *Cutman* (Al Silvani), *Director* (John Pleshette), *Announcer* (Stu Nahan), *Commentator* (Bill Baldwin), *Salesman* (Jerry Ziesmer)

Embarrassed by his poor showing against Rocky Balboa (Sylvester Stallone) in their heavyweight title fight, Apollo Creed (Carl Weathers) demands a rematch. Rocky, however, wants only to take his share of the purse and settle down with Adrian (Talia Shire), who has since become his wife.

Receiving a sizable check for the fight sometime later, Rocky buys a beautiful condominium and a custom sports car. Now something of a celebrity, he is besieged by offers from cosmetics companies that want him to endorse their products. Feeling this might be an easy way to make a living, Rocky agrees to appear in several television commercials. During the taping sessions, however, he finds the inane costumes and silly dialogue beneath his dignity, and he subsequently quits.

Now a man with responsibilities, Rocky's finances quickly deplete, and he is forced to sell his car to Paulie (Burt Young). Unable to find ordinary work because of his fame, Rocky begins to consider

Sylvester Stallone, Burgess Meredith, Stuart K. Robinson

Sylvester Stallone, Talia Shire

accepting Apollo's challenge, but Adrian is adamantly against it. However, when she becomes pregnant, Rocky decides to override her wishes and fight the champ. After signing for the rematch, he rehires his old coach Mickey (Burgess Meredith) to get him back into shape.

Angered by Rocky's decision to fight, Adrian refuses to speak to him during training, and without her blessing Rocky's approach to his workouts becomes lacklustre. Later, Adrian collapses in her pet store from overwork and emotional strain, and she is hospitalized. Though she gives birth to a healthy boy, she remains in a deep coma for several weeks. Rocky postpones training so he can stay at her bedside, and when she finally regains consciousness he offers to forget about the fight if it will make her happy. Adrian, however, has a change of heart, and tells Rocky that she now wants him to "fight and win."

His spirit renewed, Rocky embarks on the most rigorous training of his life. The rematch turns out to be even more violent and bloody than the first fight, only this time Rocky wins, becoming the new heavyweight champion of the world.

Rocky, one of 1976's biggest hits, was a major triumph for Sylvester Stallone. The film made him a millionaire and a front-ranking star, and after years of struggling the young actor suddenly found himself one of the most bankable properties in the industry. Surprisingly, however, the three-year period between *Rocky* and *Rocky II* turned out to be somewhat less than gratifying for Stallone.

Following *Rocky*, he was immediately hired to play a Hoffa-like labor leader in Norman Jewison's *F.I.S.T.*, a powerful but uneven and confused film in the *On the Waterfront* vein. The role, which called for the actor to age some twenty years over the course of the drama, was a tour de force for Stallone, but, while his performance was certainly adequate, the filmgoing public did not respond to the picture, and *F.I.S.T.* was not successful. While Stallone was disturbed by the lukewarm reception of *F.I.S.T.*, his next effort was even less satisfying. He wrote, directed, and starred in the film version of his own novel, *Paradise Alley*, a sentimental tale about three enterprising young brothers in New York's Hell's Kitchen. Though it was an honest attempt by Stallone to create a nostalgic entertainment that could be enjoyed by everyone, *Paradise Alley* was rather poorly made, and it did not succeed at the box office.

This led industry skeptics to conclude that Stallone's triumph in *Rocky* had been a fluke, and that the actor would never again equal its success. He, of course, proved them dead wrong with *Rocky II*, the spirited sequel. It was written and directed by

Stallone with a skill that made his work on *Paradise Alley* seem amateurish, and it became nearly as successful as the first film.

Though essentially just a replay of *Rocky*, the sequel was every bit as poignant and touching, and it contained, perhaps, the most spectacular fight ever staged for a motion picture. *Rocky II* easily matched the quality of the original, and its triumph at the box office gave Stallone's career a much-needed shot in the arm. Audiences were genuinely touched by the beautiful finale, in which a battered but victorious Rocky accepts the heavyweight champion's belt and tearfully declares to the world, "I did it!"

Talia Shire, Sylvester Stallone

APOCALYPSE NOW

A United Artists Picture; Produced and directed by Francis Ford Coppola; Written by John Milius and Francis Ford Coppola; Narration by Michael Herr; Photography by Vittorio Storaro; Production designer: Dean Tavoularis; Supervising editor: Richard Marks; Sound montage and design: Walter Murch; Music by Carmine Coppola and Francis Ford Coppola; Art direction: Angelo Graham; Set decoration: George R. Nelson; Costume supervisor: Charles E. James; Makeup by Jack Young and Fred C. Blau, Jr.; Documentary supervisor: Eleanor Coppola;

257

Dennis Hopper, Martin Sheen, Frederic Forrest

Filmed in Technicolor and Technovision; Running time: 139 minutes

CAST:
Col. Kurtz (MARLON BRANDO), Lt. Col. Kilgore (ROBERT DUVALL), Capt. Willard (MARTIN SHEEN), Chef (Frederic Forrest), Chief (Albert Hall), Lance (Sam Bottoms), Clean (Larry Fishburne), Photo journalist (Dennis Hopper), General (G. D. Spradlin), Colonel (Harrison Ford), Civilian (Jerry Ziesmer), Colby (Scott Glenn), Sgt. MP #1 (Bo Byers), Kilgore's gunner (James Keane), Mike from San Diego (Kerry Rossall), Injured soldier (Ron McQueen), Supply sergeant (Tom Mason), Playmate of the Year (Cynthia Wood), Playmates (Colleen Camp, Linda Carpenter), Soldier in trench (Jack Thibeau), Lt. Carlson (Glenn Walken), Machine gunner (Damien Leake), Johnny from Malibu (Jerry Ross)

Robert Duvall, Albert Hall, Martin Sheen

Saigon, the late sixties. Captain B. L. Willard (Martin Sheen) of U.S. Army Intelligence lies in a dingy hotel room, troubled by memories of the war and his present inactivity. He is in desperate need of another "mission," and gets his wish when he is hired to "terminate with extreme prejudice" a renegade American officer, Colonel Walter E. Kurtz (Marlon Brando) who, Willard is informed by superiors, has gone insane and established a bloody dictatorship on a native island somewhere in Cambodia. Willard is told by the General (G. D. Spradlin) who hires him that, for obvious reasons, his mission "does not exist, nor will it ever exist."

The following day, a gunboat is placed at Willard's disposal, and a four-man crew is commissioned to take him up the Mekong River to Cambodia. The crew (who, in Willard's words, are nothing more than "kids, rock and rollers with one foot in their graves") consists of Chief (Albert Hall), an efficient black NCO; Chef (Frederic Forrest), a hippie cook from New Orleans; Clean (Larry Fishburne), a seventeen-year-old ghetto youth; and Lance (Sam Bottoms), a young surfing champion from California.

The first stop on their journey is an American helicopter base, commanded by the slightly mad Lieutenant Colonel Kilgore (Robert Duvall), a flamboyant, fearless warrior who "loves the smell of napalm in the morning" and who plays Wagner's "Ride of the Valkyries" over loudspeakers during helicopter raids because it "scares hell out of the slopes." Willard and his crew accompany Kilgore

Marlon Brando, director Francis Coppola

and his boys on the raid on a Vietcong village, then resume their boat trip upriver.

At a supply depot, they witness a rather colorful USO show, during which three Playboy bunnies (Cynthia Wood, Colleen Camp, and Linda Carpenter) are flown in via helicopter to perform for several thousand GIs. However, their taunting, blatantly seductive dancing arouses the sex-starved soldiers to such an extent that several men charge the stage, forcing the USO crew to whisk the bunnies to safety. On the last mile of the journey, Chief and Clean are killed when enemy forces attack from the shoreline.

Finally reaching Kurtz's island some time later, Willard is "greeted" by native tribesmen and run-away American soldiers who have become the Colonel's followers, and is taken on a tour of the island by a flipped-out photojournalist (Dennis Hopper) who worships Kurtz as his personal god. Impressed by Kurtz's power over these people, Willard also sees examples of his tyranny—the severed heads and hanging corpses of those who have offended him.

anxious to see what the director of the *Godfather* films and *The Conversation* had done with a subject that had already been explored in two excellent pictures, *Coming Home* and *The Deer Hunter* (both 1978). With the exception of a few critics who, for some reason, felt compelled to dismiss *Apocalypse Now* as an "overblown, confusing bore," most people who saw the film were not disappointed, and Coppola's movie was heralded as both a technical masterpiece and a deeply affecting drama.

Though the film became a formidable success at the box office, its making had been a long, gruelling experience for Coppola, his actors, and his crew. Filmed on location in the Philippines because of its

Willard is granted an audience with Kurtz, and finds him to be a brilliant, spiritually troubled man, who reflects endlessly on the need for "horror" and "moral terror" in the world. Though secretly admiring and identifying with Kurtz, Willard performs his duty by killing him, then escapes from the island with Lance and the photojournalist.

Apocalypse Now, Francis Ford Coppola's brilliant, disturbing Vietnam drama, was released commercially in late 1979, following a heavily publicized premiere at the Cannes Film Festival. Initially, audiences went to the film out of curiosity, as they had been hearing about it for years, and were

geographic similarities to Vietnam, the project took nearly five years to complete, and throughout its shooting schedule rumors were constantly flying that Coppola's ambitious picture had fallen victim to insurmountable difficulties and would probably never be completed. While much of the gossip printed about *Apocalypse Now* was blatantly untrue (like the report stating that its budget had ballooned to $50 million), the filming had been one gigantic headache from the beginning, and there were, indeed, some serious setbacks along the way.

About midway through production, Martin Sheen suffered a severe heart attack, and Coppola was forced to do a great deal of shooting around him.

259

Marlon Brando

Martin Sheen

Dennis Hopper

Also, several major set pieces were destroyed by a typhoon, necessitating the crew to rebuild them from scratch. During its 238-day shooting schedule, the original $12 million budget inflated to around $31 million and during the final phases of production Coppola had to sink some personal assets into *Apocalypse Now* in order to get it finished.

In spite of everything, however, *Apocalypse Now* emerged as a superb motion picture, perhaps the best of the decade's Vietnam films. The tortured, stark imagery that marked most of its scenes was the work of Coppola and his director of photography, Vittorio Storaro, and their use of lighting and color to heighten the story's dramatic effect was exceptional filmmaking. Everything about the picture reflected Coppola's wish to, in his own words, "create a film that would give its audiences a sense of the horror, the madness, the sensuousness, and the moral dilemma of the Vietnam War."

The story of *Apocalypse Now* was inspired by Joseph Conrad's *Heart of Darkness*, and the screenplay was the collaborative effort of Coppola, John Milius, and former war correspondent Michael Herr, who wrote the narration for Captain Willard. Though the film's technical excellence is really what one remembers best, *Apocalypse Now* also contains truly memorable acting by its cast. Despite his third billing, Martin Sheen as the introspective, troubled Captain Willard is the central character, and Sheen's quietly intense performance is one of his finest. Also splendid is Robert Duvall as Lieutenant Colonel Kilgore, whose deranged state of mind seems to reflect the general insanity of the war. Though the role of Kurtz amounts to little more than a cameo, Marlon Brando makes the most of his limited screen time and turns in a performance of scope and substance. Brando manages to communicate all of Kurtz's fanaticism, madness, wisdom, and terror in very few scenes.

TIME AFTER TIME

A Warner Bros./Orion Picture; Written and directed by Nicholas Meyer; Produced by Herb Jaffe; Story by Karl Alexander and Steve Hayes; Photography by Paul Lohmann; Production designer: Edward C. Carfagno; Film editor: Donn Cambern; Assistant director: Michael Daves; Sound by Jerry Jost; Set decoration: Barbara Knieger; Men's costumes: Sal Anthony; Women's costumes: Yvonne Kubis; Make-up by Lynn Reynolds; Special effects by Larry Fuentes and Jim Blount; Filmed in Metrocolor and Panavision; Running time: 112 minutes

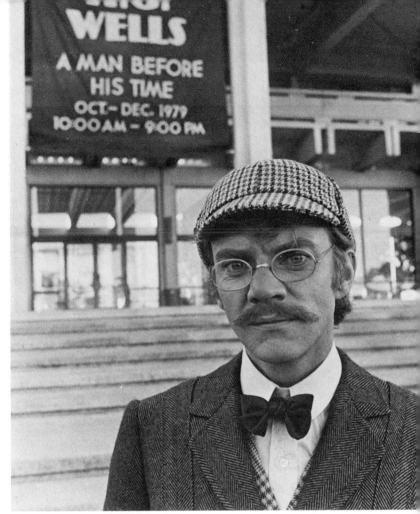

Malcolm McDowell

Malcolm McDowell, Mary Steenburgen

CAST:

H. G. Wells (MALCOLM McDOWELL), *Stevenson* (David Warner), *Amy* (Mary Steenburgen), *Lt. Mitchell* (Charles Cioffi), *Assistant* (Kent Williams), *Mrs. Turner* (Andonia Katsaros), *Shirley* (Patti D'Arbanville), *Edwards* (James Garrett), *Harding* (Keith McConnell), *Richardson* (Leo Lewis), *McKay* (Byron Webster), *Jenny* (Karin Mary Shea), *Carol* (Geraldine Baron), *Insp. Gregson* (Laurie Main), *Adams* (Joseph Maher), *Sergeant* (Michael Evans), *Jeweler* (Ray Reinhardt), *Bank officer* (Bob Shaw), *Diner* (Nicholas Shields)

London, 1893. Jack the Ripper, the mysterious slayer of prostitutes, gruesomely murders his sixth victim on a dimly lit street corner. Several blocks away, H. G. Wells (Malcolm McDowell), the young

Malcolm McDowell

writer, inventor, and philosopher, entertains a group of colleagues in his Victorian flat. He has gathered his associates this evening to show them his latest invention, and promises to do so the moment his closest friend, Dr. Stevenson (David Warner), arrives. When the doctor makes his appearance, Wells leads his guests to the basement, where he unveils his extraordinary creation—a time machine, capable of transporting a man to any era of the past or future.

Malcolm McDowell, Mary Steenburgen

Returning to the dining room for aperitifs, Wells and his guests are shocked when the police suddenly arrive and inform them that Stevenson is Jack the Ripper. The police search the premises from top to bottom, but are unable to find the killer anywhere. Suddenly, Wells realizes that Stevenson has used the machine to escape to some future time.

An optimistic believer that future society will be a "utopian" paradise, Wells is sickened by the thought of such a monster at large in the world of tomorrow, and he determines to bring the Ripper to justice. Examining the machine, Wells observes that the date and location on the time indicator is November 5, 1979—San Francisco, California. Venturing to this time and place, Wells abruptly materializes in a twentieth-century museum exhibiting a collection of "H. G. Wells memorabilia," and he is surprised to learn of his fame. Instead of the utopian world of his dreams, however, Wells soon discovers the society of the future to be cold, materialistic, and violent. Realizing he must convert his gold sovereigns to modern dollars, Wells visits the foreign currency exchange, where he meets and falls in love with Amy (Mary Steenburgen). Wells asks her about Stevenson, and she tells him that a man fitting his description exchanged several thousand gold sovereigns earlier in the day.

Tracing Stevenson to a local hotel, Wells confronts his former friend, pleading with the Ripper to return

David Warner

to Victorian London. The killer refuses, however, declaring to Wells that, at long last, he is "home," and proving it by showing Wells a montage of violent images on television. Later, Wells tries to convince local police about the Ripper, but his pleas are met with disbelief.

Later, the Ripper begins to terrorize San Francisco, and, determined to stop him, Wells begins trailing him everywhere. He has a final showdown with Stevenson at the "Wells" exhibit, and manages to coerce the killer into the time machine. After blasting Stevenson to infinity, Wells persuades Amy to return to nineteenth-century England with him.

Nicholas Meyer, who wrote and directed *Time After Time*, spent several years as a fledgling screen-

Mary Steenburgen, Malcolm McDowell

writer in Hollywood before he shot to national prominence with his best-selling novel, *The Seven-Per-Cent Solution*. Published in 1975, the book united two legendary characters—Sherlock Holmes and Sigmund Freud—in a clever, suspenseful mystery, and it

Malcolm McDowell

succeeded in capturing the wonderful atmosphere of the original Conan Doyle stories. The success of *The Seven-Per-Cent Solution* prompted Meyer to write a follow-up Holmes adventure, *The West End Horror*, which did moderately well but never caught on to the extent of the first book. Meyer contributed an excellent screenplay for Herbert Ross's film version of *The Seven-Per-Cent Solution* (1976), filled with crisp dialogue and full-blooded characters, allowing stars Nicol Williamson, Alan Arkin, and Robert Duvall to shine as Holmes, Freud, and Dr. Watson.

Meyer's next script—*Time After Time*—was, once again, a unique, charming period adventure bringing two famous historical figures—in this case H. G. Wells and Jack the Ripper—together in the same vehicle. Due to his past success, Meyer had little trouble persuading Warner Bros. to back the project, and they even agreed to let him direct, since the story line of *Time After Time* was relatively simple. Meyer shot the film on location in San Francisco, and made it an enjoyable, atmospheric combination of thriller, science fiction drama, and romantic comedy. The skill with which Meyer blended these elements truly belied his inexperience as a director.

In addition to Meyer's direction, Malcolm McDowell and David Warner turned in excellent performances as the two lead characters; Warner's portrayal of Jack the Ripper was the best since Laird Cregar's in the memorable 1944 film *The Lodger*. As Cregar had done, Warner managed to make his Ripper a frightening yet tormented and pathetic individual, somehow arousing the audience's sympathy despite his actions. The production's many qualities made *Time After Time* one of 1979's most popular films.

"10"

A Orion Picture; Released through Warner Bros.; Directed by Blake Edwards; Produced by Blake Edwards and Tony Adams; Written by Blake Edwards; Music by Henry Mancini; Photography by Frank Stanley; Film editor: Ralph E. Winters; Production designer: Rodger Maus; Sound mixer: Bruce Bisenz; Production manager: Chuck Murray; Assistant director: Mickey McCardle; Set decorations: Reg Allen and Jack Stevens; Special effects: Fred Cramer; Costume designer: Pat Edwards; Makeup by Bron Roylance and Ben Nye II; Hairstylist: Mary Keats; Script supervisor: H. Bud Otto; Jewelry by Tiffany and Co.; Filmed in Metrocolor and Panavision; Running time: 126 minutes

CAST:

George (Dudley Moore), *Sam* (Julie Andrews), *Jenny* (Bo Derek), *Hugh* (Robert Webber), *Mary Lewis* (Dee Wallace), *David* (Sam Jones), *Bartender* (Brian Dennehy), *The Reverend* (Max Showalter), *Josh* (Rad Daly), *Mrs. Kissel* (Nedra Volz), *Fred Miles* (James Noble), *Ethel Miles* (Virginia Kiser), *Covington* (John Hawker), *Neighbor* (Don Calfa), *Dr. Croce* (John Hancock)

Beverly Hills. On the night of his forty-second birthday, George (Dudley Moore), a popular songwriter, begins showing symptoms of "midlife crises." Over the succeeding weeks, he finds himself continually staring at young girls on the street, and he begins envying his high-living neighbor, whose life is one endless orgy. George's behavior causes great

Julie Andrews, Dudley Moore, Bo Derek

concern to his lover, singing star Samantha (Julie Andrews), and to his partner Hugh (Robert Webber), who has seemingly avoided midlife crises by turning gay.

While driving home one afternoon, George spies Jenny (Bo Derek), a gorgeous young woman en route to her marriage ceremony. Regarding her as "the most beautiful girl I've ever seen" (on a scale from one to 10), George follows her to the church. He later learns her name, and discovers that she and her husband are honeymooning in Mexico.

Driven by the impulse to see her again, George flies to Mexico and checks into the hotel where Jenny is staying. Later, he sees the couple on the beach, and begins indulging in romantic fantasies about the lovely young girl. When he sees that her husband has fallen asleep on a surfboard and is drifting out to sea, George rents a small boat and rescues him. George's heroic act makes headlines, and while her husband recuperates in the hospital with a severe sunburn, Jenny invites George to her room.

He finds her extremely grateful for what he has done, and she confesses to finding him an "attractive older man." The two go out to dinner, then return to Jenny's room, where she seduces George. After getting into bed with her, however, George finds her a little *too* frank and candid in her approach to sex, and he is unable to identify with her offhanded, unromantic attitude. He returns home where, having presumably learned his lesson, he proposes marriage to Samantha.

During the sixties, writer-producer-director Blake Edwards established himself as one of the cinema's foremost creators of slick, romantic entertainment. Films such as *Breakfast at Tiffany's* (1961), *The Pink Panther* (1963), and *A Shot in the Dark* (1964) were all enormously popular, featuring attractive casts, lavish production values, and especially soft, dreamy musical scores by Henry Mancini.

"10" (1979), which turned out to be the surprise "sleeper" of the year, perfectly recaptured the marvelous aura of the director's earlier hits. A light romantic comedy concerning the obsession of a middle-aged songwriter for a statuesque young beauty, "10" was a thoroughly charming entertainment, and it emerged as one of the year's highest-grossing films.

Dudley Moore, the superb British actor-comedian, turned in one of the seventies' best comic performances as George, and the performer's timing and delivery were at their absolute best throughout. The early scenes, in which George goes to extraordinary (and sometimes hazardous) lengths to get another look at his dream girl are hilarious, and will no doubt one day be regarded as "classics" of their kind.

Julie Andrews, in one of her best roles in recent years, nicely complements Moore, and the beautiful Bo Derek became, as a result of her appearance in "10" and an elaborate layout in *Playboy* magazine, the hottest new star of the year.

KRAMER VS. KRAMER

A Columbia Picture; Written for the screen and directed by Robert Benton; Produced by Stanley R. Jaffe; From the novel by Avery Corman; Director of photography: Nestor Almendros; Production designer: Paul Sylbert; Costumes designed by Ruth Morley; Casting: Shirley Rich; Film editor: Jerry Greenberg; Associate producer: Richard C. Fischoff; Production manager: David Golden; Set decorator: Alan Hicks; Makeup by Alan Weisinger; Hairstylist: Joe Coscia; Unit publicist: Ann Guerin; Filmed in Technicolor and Panavision; Running time: 105 minutes

CAST:
Ted Kramer (DUSTIN HOFFMAN), *Joanna Kramer* (MERYL STREEP), *Margaret Phelps* (Jane Alexander), *Billy Kramer* (Justin Henry), *John Shaunessy* (Howard Duff), *Jim O'Connor* (George Coe), *Phyllis Bernard* (Jobeth Williams), *Gressen* (Bill Moor), *Judge Atkins* (Howard Chamberlain), *Spencer* (Jack Ramage), *Ackerman* (Jess Osuna), *Interviewer* (Nicholas Hormann), *Teacher* (Ellen Parker), *Ted's secretary* (Shelby Brammer), *Mrs. Kline* (Carol Nadell), *Surgeon* (Donald Gantry), *Receptionist* (Judith Calder), *Norman* (Peter Lownds), *Waitress* (Kathleen Keller)

Meryl Streep, Howard Duff

266

Dustin Hoffman

Dustin Hoffman, Robert Benton, Meryl Streep

New York City. After eight years of marriage, Joanna Kramer (Meryl Streep) suddenly leaves her husband Ted (Dustin Hoffman), a successful art director for a major ad agency. Her reasons for walking out are that she no longer loves him and desperately needs to find her own identity.

She disappears, leaving Ted to care for their eight-year-old son Billy (Justin Henry). Highly successful at his job and in line for an important promotion, Kramer's performance at work falters due to emo-

and its star, Dustin Hoffman, was named Best Actor. The film also won the Academy Award for Best Picture. The critical accolades afforded *Kramer vs. Kramer* have been extraordinary, and, unlike those heaped upon several other seventies pictures, they are completely justified.

An extremely thoughtful and intelligent film, *Kramer vs. Kramer* is primarily about a divorced couple battling for legal custody of their young son and the emotional changes they go through as a

Dustin Hoffman, Meryl Streep

Meryl Streep, Howard Duff

tional strain and the demands of caring for his son, and he costs the company a major account. As a result, Ted is fired; later he learns that Joanna is suing him for custody of Billy.

As it turns out, Joanna has secured a high-paying job during her absence and now wants Billy to move in with her. Wanting very much to keep Billy, Ted hires attorney John Shaunessy (Howard Duff), who tells him he has no chance of winning the case without a job. Desperate, Kramer makes a last-minute appointment with a small ad agency, and, luckily, is hired on the strength of his impressive portfolio.

After the subsequent custody hearings, however, the judge rules in Joanna's favor, and, heartbroken, Ted tearfully tells Billy that they won't be living together anymore. In a last-minute change of heart, Joanna allows the boy to remain with his father—an act that seems unmotivated but that nonetheless pleased audiences.

Kramer vs. Kramer, one of the most talked-about motion pictures of the decade, was chosen as the Best Film of 1979 by the New York Film Critics' Circle,

result. While this kind of theme is hardly new in films, it happened to be extremely pertinent and timely for audiences of 1979. Many people seeing the picture have no doubt lived through a similar drama in real life and are thus able to strongly identify with the couple in the film. As portrayed by Dustin Hoffman and Meryl Streep, Ted and Joanna Kramer are brilliantly true-to-life, often appearing not to be screen characters at all, but real human beings. Their believability makes *Kramer vs. Kramer* a moving experience, which no doubt accounts for its incredible success with audiences.

Written for the screen and directed by the talented Robert Benton, *Kramer vs. Kramer* is perhaps 1979's most nearly perfect film, a movie in which *everything* seems to work beautifully—from the performances to the photography to the poignant yet unsentimental tone of the story. It has obvious similarities to 1978's *An Unmarried Woman,* which also dealt with divorce and the painful readjustment to single life.

Dustin Hoffman's Ted Kramer is a major piece of screen acting—subtle yet powerful—and the actor superbly conveys the anguish of a man whose entire life has suddenly been disrupted. Meryl Streep's finely shaded portrait of Joanna is also excellent, and the stars are ably supported by Jane Alexander, Howard Duff, and young Justin Henry.

Interestingly, the one complaint leveled against the film was that the ending was a little inconclusive. Not long after *Kramer's* release, a sequel to the film was officially announced.

THE ELECTRIC HORSEMAN

A Columbia Pictures and Universal Pictures Release; Directed by Sydney Pollack; Produced by Ray Stark; Screenplay by Robert Garland; Story by Paul Gaer and Robert Garland; Based on a story by Shelly Burton; Photography by Owen Roizman; Music by Dave Grusin; Film editor: Sheldon Kahn; Production designer: Stephen Grimes; Associate producer: Ronald L. Schwary; Art direction: J. Dennis Washington; Set decorations: Mary Swanson; Costume designer: Bernie Pollack; Special effects by Augie Lohman; Makeup by Gary Liddiard; Lenses and Panaflex camera by Panavision; Filmed in Technicolor; Running time: 121 minutes

CAST:
Sonny Steele (ROBERT REDFORD), *Hallie Martin* (JANE FONDA), *Charlotta* (Valerie Perrine), *Wendell* (Willie Nelson), *Hunt Sears* (John Saxon), *Fitzgerald* (Nicholas Coster), *Danny* (Allan Arbus), *Farmer* (Wilford Brimley), *Gus* (Will Hare), *Toland* (Basil Hoffman), *Leroy* (Timothy Scott), *Dietrich* (James B. Sikking), *Tommy* (James Kline), *Bernie* (Frank Speiser), *Bud Broderick* (Quinn Redeker), *Joanna Camden* (Lois Areno), *Lucinda* (Sarah Harris), *Louise* (Tasha Zemrus), *Dennis* (James Novak)

Timothy Scott, Robert Redford

Robert Redford

After being voted the "All-Time Champion Cowboy" for five years in a row, rodeo star Sonny Steele (Robert Redford) is hired by the giant conglomerate Ampco to represent Ranch Breakfast Cereal, one of the company's major subsidiaries. As chief spokesman for the cereal, Sonny becomes something of a celebrity, appearing in magazine and television ads, and at wild west shows as a "special attraction." Soon, however, the free-spirited cowboy grows weary of all the supermarket and high school football game appearances, and starts resenting his involvement with Ampco.

When the company holds its annual convention in Las Vegas, Sonny is ordered to participate in a garish stage revue, in which he will appear in a flashy "electric" cowboy suit astride Rising Star, a prize $12 million race horse owned by Ampco. At a press conference the day before the show, Sonny is needled by television reporter Hallie Martin (Jane Fonda), who doubts that Sonny truly believes in the product he represents.

Later, Sonny confronts the head of Ampco, Hunt Sears (John Saxon), telling him of his growing contempt for his job. Sears, however, reminds Sonny that his work is both simple and high-paying, and that he should be grateful for it. During rehearsals for the revue, Sonny grows to love Rising Star, and when he learns that the horse is being pumped full of tranquilizers for the stage appearance, Sonny "kidnaps" the animal. When Sears learns of this, he calls the police, who issue an all-points bulletin and a warrant for Sonny's arrest.

Wanting an exclusive on the story, Hallie tracks Sonny to the Vegas desert, where he tells her he

Willie Nelson, Robert Redford

Jane Fonda, Robert Redford

Timothy Scott, Robert Redford, Willie Nelson

"stole" Rising Star in order to set the animal free in the wilds of Utah. Hallie persuades Sonny to let her tag along, and during the journey they fall in love. She relays the story to her New York office, and news of Sonny's "noble" plan quickly spreads through the media.

Later, Sears is astonished to learn that Ranch Cereal sales have suddenly skyrocketed, and that Sonny has become a national hero. Ampco drops the charges against Sonny, and publicly endorses his "humane" gesture. In a magnificent Utah valley, Sonny lets Rising Star loose, and all ends happily.

The Electric Horseman, directed by Sydney Pollack, who had worked with Robert Redford a number of times in the past, was a simple, upbeat comedy-drama that won audiences with the same romantic charm that made earlier films such as *The Goodbye Girl* and *Heaven Can Wait* successful. The film was directed by Pollack at a brisk, lively pace, and the screenplay by Robert Garland contained some crackling dialogue for Redford and Jane Fonda. The film also featured country singer Willie Nelson in a solid supporting role as Redford's best friend, and some truly breathtaking location photography of Nevada and Utah.

But both audiences and critics agreed that the best thing about *The Electric Horseman* was the wonderful screen chemistry of its two stars. Many critics remarked that their scenes together "bristled with an erotic tension reminiscent of Tracy and Hepburn," and it was obvious that Redford and Fonda enjoyed making the picture very much. The stars are good friends in private life, and they had worked together previously in 1966's *The Chase* and in 1967's *Barefoot in the Park,* both of which were highly successful.

In his portrayal of Sonny, Redford created one of the most popular screen heroes of 1979, a simple, honest man determined to do what's right regardless of consequences. Fonda's Hallie Martin is also welldrawn, and it is interesting to watch as she changes from a cold, calculating media person, bent on using Sonny for her own gain, to an honest, loving person who comes to admire what he is doing. Also excellent in major supporting roles were John Saxon as the iron-willed conglomerate head and Valerie Perrine as Redford's beautiful, good-natured ex-wife.

Jane Fonda, Robert Redford

Klaus Kinski

NOSFERATU

Distributed by 20th Century-Fox; Written, produced, and directed by Werner Herzog; Based on the novel *Dracula* by Bram Stoker and the film script *Nosferatu* by Henrik Galeen; Photography by Jorg Schmidt-Reitwein; Lighting by Martin Gerbl; Film editor: Beate Mainka-Jellinghaus; Production design: Henning Von Gierke and Ulrich Bergfelder; Special effects by Cornelius Siegel; Music by Popol Vuh and Florian Fricke; Sound by Harald Maury; Costumes by Gloria Storch; Makeup by Reiko Kruk and Dominique Colladant; Filmed in Eastmancolor; Running time: 107 minutes

CAST:
Count Dracula (KLAUS KINSKI), *Lucy* (ISABELLE ADJANI), *Jonathan Harker* (Bruno Ganz), *Renfield* (Roland Topor), *Dr. Van Helsing* (Walter Ladengast), *Warden* (Dan Van Husen), *Harbormaster* (Jan Groth), *Schrader* (Carsten Bodinus), *Mina* (Martje Grohmann), *Town official* (Ryk de Gooyer), *Coachman* (John Leddy), *Coffinbearer* (Tim Beekman), *Nun* (Beverly Walker)

Despite the forebodings of his wife Lucy (Isabelle Adjani), real estate broker Jonathan Harker (Bruno Ganz) travels to Transylvania to close a property deal with the mysterious Count Dracula (Klaus Kinski). When he arrives at the Carpathian province several weeks later, however, he is unable to secure coach transport to Dracula's hilltop castle because the superstitious villagers refuse to go near it. Harker is forced to make the journey on foot, and arrives at Dracula's estate shortly after sundown.

Understandably apprehensive due to the villagers' all-consuming dread of the place, Jonathan becomes even more unnerved when he meets Dracula, a rather pale, ghoulish-looking gentleman with a morbid fascination for death. The Count is immediately smitten when Harker shows him a picture of Lucy, and despite Dracula's bizarre behavior and appearance Harker completes the property deal—which calls for the Count to lease a large estate near the town of Wismar, Harker's home.

Forced to stay at the castle because of his failure to find lodging in the village, Harker begins having dreadful nightmares about his host, in which the Count drains his blood by biting into his jugular vein. This, coupled with the fact that Jonathan never sees the Count during the day, leads Harker to suspect that Dracula is a vampire. Later, his suspicions are confirmed when he sees Dracula sneaking away one evening aboard a coach laden with coffins. Realizing that Dracula will attempt to satisfy his lust for Lucy when he arrives in Wismar, Jonathan escapes from the castle and begins the long journey home.

Meanwhile, Dracula stows away on board a cargo ship bound for Wismar. When the ship reaches port several weeks later, the town officials are horrified to find the entire crew slain and the vessel infested by rats. Following Dracula's arrival, the city falls victim to a deadly plague, and Harker returns home in a hypnotic, incoherent state.

After reading Jonathan's diary relating his experiences at Castle Dracula, Lucy realizes what is happening. Consulting a book about vampires, Lucy discovers that the unholy creature may be destroyed only if a woman pure in heart makes him "linger with her beyond the cockcrow." She is later visited by Dracula, and after he confesses his love for her she sacrifices herself to him, keeping the monster at

Bruno Ganz, Klaus Kinski

Isabelle Adjani

Bruno Ganz, Klaus Kinski

Klaus Kinski

Dan Van Hensen, Roland Topor, Walter Ladengast

her bedside until the rays of the morning sun destroy him. However, Jonathan, now a vampire himself, later departs to continue Count Dracula's reign of terror.

Horror films almost completely dominated the motion picture screens of 1979. Following the premiere of Ridley Scott's phenomenally successful *Alien,* film companies proceeded to bombard the public with an incredible array of shockers, including such titles as *Prophecy, Dawn of the Dead, Halloween, Phantasm, The Legacy,* and *When a Stranger Calls.* Typical of the decade's fright pictures, these contained excellent special effects as well as some of the most bloodcurdling moments in horror film history.

Aside from *Alien,* which was the best and most creative of the lot, the year's most interesting entry also turned out to be the decade's last major horror film, Werner Herzog's *Nosferatu.* A German import featuring a pair of international stars, Klaus Kinski and Isabelle Adjani, in the leads, the film was a superb reworking of the *Dracula* story, and it had a moderately successful American run late in the year.

Virtually a scene-for-scene remake of the famous F. W. Murnau silent "classic" of 1922, Herzog's *Nosferatu* was unique among the horror films of the seventies. It proved that a horror picture could, even in these jaded times, still be effective without resorting to blatant shock effects. Its terror was cold and ethereal, and its Dracula had sympathetic qualities reminiscent of the "classic" monsters of old, making him the antithesis of the relentlessly evil creatures of *Alien* and *Prophecy.*

Dominated by Klaus Kinski's splendid portrayal of Dracula, the film was rather slow and confusing at times, but it was still far more effective than the year's other vampire films.

George Hamilton's hugely successful *Love at First Bite,* released earlier in the year, was more comedy than horror picture, and Universal's stylish but flat remake of their own *Dracula* was disappointing despite good performances from Frank Langella as the Count and Laurence Olivier as his nemesis, Professor Van Helsing.

Though Herzog's *Nosferatu* contained some exceptional camerawork (by Jorg Schmidt-Reitwein), the makeup for Klaus Kinski is probably what audiences remember best, and it was nearly identical to that used in the 1922 film. One of the most frightening guises ever designed for a screen monster, the makeup gave the character a loathesome quality, making him a far cry from the handsome, "sexy" Draculas of Bela Lugosi, Christopher Lee, George Hamilton, and Frank Langella.

Isabelle Adjani, Klaus Kinski

THE BLACK HOLE

A Walt Disney Production; Directed by Gary Nelson; Produced by Ron Miller; Screenplay by Jeb Rosebrook and Gerry Day; Story by Jeb Rosebrook, Bob Barabash, and Richard Landau; Photography by Frank Phillips; Music by John Barry; Production design by Peter Ellenshaw; Art directors: John B. Mansbridge, Al Roelofs, and Robert T. McCall; Film editor: Gregg McLaughlin; Robots designed by George McGinnis; Production manager: John Bloss; Costumes designed by Bill Thomas; Set decoration: Frank R. McKelvy and Roger M. Shook; Assistant director: Tom McCrory; Makeup by Nadia; Special

(JOSEPH BOTTOMS), *Dr. Kate McCrae* (YVETTE MIMIEUX), *Harry Booth* (ERNEST BORGNINE), *Capt. S.T.A.R.* (Tommy McLoughlin)

At some time in the distant future, the commercial spacecraft *Palomino* explores the galaxy in search of intelligent life forms. Its five-man crew consists of Captain Dan Holland (Robert Forster), Dr. Alex Durant (Anthony Perkins), Dr. Kate McCrae (Yvette Mimieux), Lieutenant Charles Pizer (Joseph Bottoms), and crewman Harry Booth (Ernest Borgnine). During a routine exploration, the *Palomino* encounters an enormous "black hole," a huge pocket of space that engulfs everything in its path.

Production rendering of the "Cygnus" by the production designer, Peter Ellenshaw

sound effects: Steven Katz; Miniature mechanical effects and chief model maker: Terence Saunders; Animation special effects designed by Joe Hale; Animation special effects executed by Dorse A. Lanpher and Ted C. Kierscey; Filmed in color; Running time: 97 minutes

CAST:
Dr. Hans Reinhardt (MAXIMILIAN SCHELL), *Dr. Alex Durant* (ANTHONY PERKINS), *Capt. Dan Holland* (ROBERT FORSTER), *Lt. Charles Pizer*

Captain Holland issues the order to pull away, but before they are able to do so, the crew notices another Earth ship—the *Cygnus*—hovering near the entrance of the black hole, somehow resisting the pull of its gravity. Deciding to investigate, Holland and his crew board the *Cygnus* and discover it to be manned by a crew of robots. The ship's only human occupant is Dr. Hans Reinhardt (Maximilian Schell), a brilliant but slightly mad scientist who, having lost his real crew years earlier under mysterious circumstances, has fashioned mechanical beings to take

Joseph Bottoms

their place. He tells the *Palomino* crew of his plan to sail straight into the black hole, where he believes the secrets of the universe might be learned.

Inspired by this, the idealistic Dr. Durant insists on going with Reinhardt, but the rest of the *Palomino* crew want only to escape. When, later on, it becomes apparent that Reinhardt intends keeping them aboard the *Cygnus* against their will, they try to escape by force, and in the chaos Dr. Durant is killed by Reinhardt's monstrous robot bodyguard, Maximilian.

Following this, the *Palomino* crew make their way to the *Cygnus*'s shuttle craft and manage to launch it successfully. Suddenly, the *Cygnus* is bombarded by a shower of meteors, and Reinhardt is killed. Unbeknown to the *Palomino* crew, the shuttle has been programmed to enter the black hole, which it does. Once inside, the crew experience strange, dreamlike visions of eternity, then are miraculously placed on a safe course for Earth.

Of the many films released during the final months of the decade, *The Black Hole, 1941,* and *Star Trek,* while far from being the best, were among the most intriguing motion pictures of the period.

Aside from being large-budget, major-studio productions, the three films had many other things in common as well. They were made by some of the most talented people in the industry, and expectations as to their quality were extremely high. They were all designed as "escapist" entertainment—films that were simply fun to watch, containing no "message" of any kind. Most important of all, however, they were all box-office hits despite the fact that they were not especially strong films—far below the usual standard of the people who made them.

Their success is something of a phenomenon, because it illustrates just how badly audiences of the seventies needed this kind of light, escapist fare as a change of pace from the horror, violence, and depressing social commentary that all but dominated the decade's cinema.

The Black Hole, the Disney studio's multimillion-dollar "answer" to *Star Wars* and *Close Encounters of the Third Kind,* is perhaps the best of the three, though it is not a memorable film in any but a technical sense. Its special effects *are* superb (particularly the shots of the black hole gyrating through space and the unforgettable scene in which a gigantic meteor tumbles down the main corridor of the *Cygnus* while the *Palomino* crew run for their lives). However, the script of *The Black Hole* was less than sensational featuring "stock" situations and clichéd dialogue. Despite this, audiences enjoyed all the colorful effects, and were more than willing to overlook the script's many flaws.

Yvette Mimieux, Maximilian Schell

John Belushi

1941

A Universal-Columbia Presentation; An A-Team Production; Directed by Steven Spielberg; Produced by Buzz Feitshans; Executive producer: John Milius; Screenplay by Robert Zemeckis and Bob Gale; Story by Robert Zemeckis, Bob Gale, and John Milius; Photography by William A. Fraker; Production designer: Dean Edward Mitzner; Film editor: Michael Kahn; Music by John Williams; Costumes by Deborah Nadoolman; Special effects by A. D. Flowers; Miniature supervisor: Greg Jein; Art direction: William F. O'Brien; Visual effects supervisor: Larry Robinson; Lighting design by Robin Leyden; Filmed in Panavision and Metrocolor; Running time: 118 minutes

CAST:
Sgt. Tree (DAN AYKROYD), Ward Douglas (NED BEATTY), *Wild Bill Kelso* (JOHN BELUSHI), *Joan Douglas* (LORRAINE GARY), *Claude* (MURRAY HAMILTON), *Von Kleinschmidt* (CHRISTOPHER LEE), *Lt. Birkhead* (TIM MATHESON), *Adm. Mitamura* (TOSHIRO MIFUNE), *Maddox* (WARREN OATES), *Maj. Gen. Stillwell* (ROBERT STACK), *Sitarski* (Treat Williams), *Donna* (Nancy Allen), *The snake farmer* (Lucille Benson), *Macey* (Jordan Brian), *Foley* (John Candy), *The patron* (Elisha Cook, Jr.), *Herb* (Eddie Deezen), *Betty* (Dianne Kay)

December 13, 1941. The Japanese sneak attack on Pearl Harbor has sent California into an uproar. Rumors begin spreading that the enemy plans to strike there next, and citizens start demanding the military take steps to prevent this.

To avoid a panic, the government appoints Major General Stillwell (Robert Stack) commander of a small garrison whose duty is to protect the state from enemy attack. Prepared for any offense which may occur, Stillwell stations M-3 tanks in downtown Los Angeles, and places a 40mm cannon outside the oceanfront home of private citizen Ward Douglas (Ned Beatty). Stillwell later visits a local Air Force

279

Dan Aykroyd, John Belushi

Eddie Deezen, Murray Hamilton

Dan Aykroyd, Ned Beatty, Lorraine Gary

Dan Aykroyd (standing)

shot down by Wild Bill Kelso (John Belushi), a hot-shot, trigger-happy P-40 pilot. Luckily, Birkhead and Donna escape injury. Also mistaken for the enemy by Stillwell's men, Kelso is shot down and makes a spectacular crash landing on Hollywood Boulevard.

Meanwhile, Douglas spies the enemy sub off the coast and takes matters into his own hands by manning the 40mm cannon. Not knowing how to aim or fire it properly, Douglas blows his home apart—much to the distress of his wife Joan (Lorraine Gary). The sub opens fire on the coastline, destroying a large, colorful ferris wheel at the local amusement park. Thinking they have wiped out an important American industrial structure, the enemy retreats, making further American action unnecessary.

Following *Jaws* and *Close Encounters of the Third Kind,* director Steven Spielberg decided to turn his talents to lighter subject matter. He had never made a purely comedic film (his *Sugarland Express* contained humorous interludes but was primarily a serious drama) and was anxious to try his hand at a medium in which he had never worked. He chose a

Bobby DiCicco, Dianne Kay atop an M-3 tank

base to check the readiness of U.S. fighters, and Lieutenant Birkhead (Tim Matheson), an amorous young officer, falls in love with Stillwell's secretary, Donna (Nancy Allen). However, she rebuffs his request for a date, and Birkhead later learns that she has a "thing" for airplanes, and is sexually responsive only when she's in one.

Meanwhile, an enemy sub commanded by Admiral Mitamura (Toshiro Mifune) stations itself off the coast of Los Angeles. Conferring on where they should attack first, Mitamura and his Nazi henchman, Von Kleinschmidt (Christopher Lee), agree to strike the area known as Hollywood.

Later that night, the city of Los Angeles is placed under martial law, and Stillwell's troops ready themselves for battle while the General attends a screening of Walt Disney's *Dumbo.* Determined to seduce Donna, Birkhead takes her up in a small transport plane. Mistaken for a Jap invader, he is

story property written by his friends Robert Zemeckis, Bob Gale, and John Milius—a crazy, no-holds-barred vehicle dealing with the chaotic aftermath of the Pearl Harbor invasion, when California prepared itself for an attack that never took place.

Working through Universal and Columbia, Spielberg fashioned the biggest, noisiest, most expensive screen comedy ever made, and gave it the title *1941,* which was appropriate considering the subject matter. Upon its release, the film received a critical lambast similar to that levelled against *The Black Hole* and *Star Trek*. Critics hated the film, calling it crude, overblown, and unfunny, but it managed to attract audiences nonetheless—and was actually listed among the industry's leading moneymakers for several weeks.

Admittedly, *1941* is not in the same league with Spielberg's other films, and it simply does not work a great deal of the time, but it does exude a certain madcap lunacy and total abandon that many seemed to enjoy. Also, it should be pointed out that, despite its weaknesses, *1941* is an extraordinarily beautiful film visually, and it captures the mood and feel of the forties perhaps better than any other seventies movie.

It is surprising that the picture emerged as less than superb, since it had some formidable talents working on it. Aside from Spielberg, its executive producer was John Milius, one of the seventies' most versatile screen talents, who over the decade made his mark as a writer (of *Jeremiah Johnson, Magnum Force,* and *Apocalypse Now*) and director (of *Dillinger* and *The Wind and the Lion*) as well as a producer. Its all-star cast included popular performers such as John Belushi and Dan Aykroyd as well as veteran stars such as Toshiro Mifune, Robert Stack, Christopher Lee, Slim Pickins, Lionel Stander, Ned Beatty, and Elisha Cook, Jr. Despite all that it had going for it, though, *1941* turned out to be a surprising disappointment.

STAR TREK

A Paramount Picture; Directed by Robert Wise; Produced by Gene Roddenberry; Screenplay by Harold Livingston and Gene Roddenberry; Photography by Richard Kline; Associate producer: Jon Povill; Film editor: Todd Ramsey; Music by Jerry Goldsmith; Art direction: Harold Michelson and Leon Harris; Set decorations: Linda De Scenna; Men's costumes: Jack Bear and Bill Mas; Women's costumes: Agnes Henry; Makeup supervisor: Fred Phillips; Make up artist: Janna Phillips; Filmed in color; Running time: 131 minutes

CAST:
Adm. James T. Kirk (WILLIAM SHATNER), *Mr. Spock* (LEONARD NIMOY), *Dr. Leonard "Bones" McCoy* (De Forest Kelley), *Cmdr. Willard Decker* (Stephen Collins), *Ilia* (Persis Khambatta), *Montgomery "Scotty" Scott* (James Doohan), *Sulu* (George Takei), *Uhura* (Nichelle Nichols), *Chekov* (Walter Koenig), *Christine Chapel* (Majel Barrett), *Janice Rand* (Grace Lee Whitney)

Space, the twenty-third century. While on a routine patrol, three Klingon attack cruisers are annihilated by a mysterious entity known as "the intruder." After destroying the Klingons, the "intruder" sets itself on a course for Earth, and increases its speed to warp seven, several hundred times the speed of light. As it enters the territory known as Federation Space, its path is picked up and monitored by Starfleet Command. Realizing that "the intruder" will collide with Earth unless it can be intercepted, the Command orders its strongest and most capable starship, the *U.S.S. Enterprise*, to investigate the strange invader.

Due to the seriousness of the mission, the command of the *Enterprise* is taken from young Captain Willard Decker (Stephen Collins) and assigned to the vessel's former captain, James T. Kirk (William Shatner), now an admiral. Kirk's former crew, including science officer Spock (Leonard Nimoy) and Dr. McCoy (De Forest Kelley), is pressed back into service, and a new member, the beautiful Ilia (Persis Khambatta), is commissioned to act as an adviser.

Venturing into space, the *Enterprise* later confronts "the intruder" at a distant end of the galaxy. The being turns out to be an enormous mechanical organism, continually communicating the need to relay a message to its "creator." Kirk, Spock, Ilia, and Decker enter "the intruder" and discover that its power source is the old NASA spacecraft *Voyager 6*, launched three centuries earlier to collect data and return its findings to Earth. Spock concludes that, during its three-hundred years of exploration,

Leonard Nimoy, William Shatner, DeForest Kelley,
George Takei

Persis Khambatta, Leonard Nimoy, William Shatner, Stephen Collins, DeForest Kelley

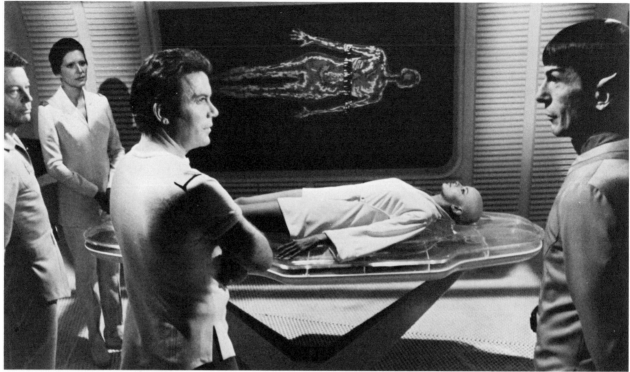

DeForest Kelley, William Shatner, Persis
Khambatta, Leonard Nimoy

Leonard Nimoy (l)

Voyager somehow evolved into an intelligent life form, which now seeks to relay the secrets of space to its "creator," the NASA scientist who designed it.

Through extraordinary means, Kirk enables *Voyager* to release its knowledge and in doing so terminate itself.

The 79 episodes of "Star Trek" produced for commercial television between 1966 and 1969 are among the most inventive programs devised for the small screen. Recounting the adventures of a government spacecraft—the *U.S.S. Enterprise*—on its five-year exploration of the universe, the series was exciting and imaginative science fiction, and its cast— William Shatner, Leonard Nimoy, De Forest Kelley, James Doohan, George Takei, Nichelle Nichols, Walter Koenig, and Grace Lee Whitney—was one of the sharpest ensemble acting units in television, never once disappointing their fans with a weak show.

It has been over ten years since the last episode of "Star Trek" aired on network television, yet despite this the popularity of the series continues to burgeon. Its reruns are played 308 times a week in 134 American cities, and it is seen in 131 international markets, for which it has been translated into 47 languages. It has inspired the formation of close to 400 fan clubs in the U.S. alone, and the "trekkies," as they are called, continue to hold annual "Star Trek" conventions in major American cities, which attract more people every year.

Because of the show's popularity, Paramount began in the mid-seventies, to toy with the idea of producing a full-length theatrical film based on the series. Following several false starts—during which

Persis Khambatta, Stephen Collins

Persis Khambatta, Stephen Collins, Leonard Nimoy, William Shatner

the project was planned, then cancelled, then planned, then cancelled again—Paramount made the official announcement on March 28, 1978—the studio was committing itself to produce a multimillion-dollar *Star Trek* movie, featuring the original cast under the direction of veteran director Robert Wise, with Gene Roddenberry serving as producer and co-writing the script. However, though this was an unbeatable combination of talent, the resulting film was curiously half-hearted and dull, emerging as a disappointment to all but the most devoted fans of the series.

Though *Star Trek—The Motion Picture* was lavishly produced on a budget of reportedly $45 million, its story line was hopelessly tangled and confusing. Moreover, the characters in the film were but poorly developed shadows of those on the television series, and many supposedly serious interludes gave way to unintentional comedy. The film featured dazzling photography by Richard Kline and superb art direction by Harold Michelson and Leon Harris, but these elements did little to compensate for the story's lack of excitement and the performers' lack of conviction.

288